This book belongs to...

....

Published in 2021 by Welbeck Editions
An Imprint of Welbeck Children's Limited, part of Welbeck Publishing Group.
20 Mortimer Street London W1T 3JW

Art Director: Margaret Hope
Designer: Ceri Hurst
Associate Publisher: Laura Knowles
Editor: Jenni Lazell
Additional contributions by Christina Webb

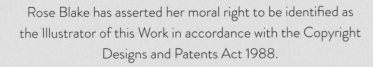

978-1-91351-947-6

Printed in Faridabad, India

9 8 7 6 5 4 3 2

MIX
Paper from
responsible sources
FSC® C010615

THE
WORLD
BOOK

Joe Fullman   Rose Blake

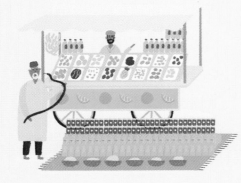

W
WELBECK
EDITIONS

CONTENTS

WHERE IN THE WORLD WOULD YOU LIKE TO GO TODAY?

INTRODUCTION

WELCOME TO THE WORLD WE CALL HOME!

In all of Space there's nothing quite like it. On the following pages, you'll be going on the ultimate globe-trotting tour. From Afghanistan to Zimbabwe, you can pay a visit to every country to discover its amazing history, geography, wildlife, culture, and cuisine, and find out what makes each one unique.

COUNTING COUNTRIES

There are 199 countries in this book, ranging from the biggest, Russia, which stretches halfway around the world, to the smallest (Vatican City), which is about the size of a village. But what exactly is a country? It's usually defined as an area of land controlled by a single government and that is recognized internationally as a country. However, it is not universally agreed what areas match this description, so you may find other sources that list a slightly different number. For instance, the international organization, the United Nations, recognizes 193 countries.

NON-COUNTRY TERRITORIES

The world isn't just made up of countries. Some areas of land that look like countries are actually disputed territories, which means that more than one country claims them. Others are not truly independent but belong to another country. These are known as dependencies or Overseas Territories. And there's a large area of land in Antarctica that doesn't belong to anyone.

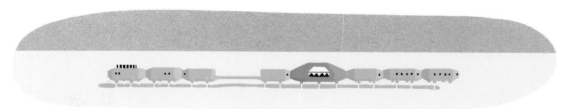

CONTINENT BY CONTINENT

Countries are not divided evenly among the world's seven continents.
Here's how many are found in each:

NORTH
AMERICA
23

EUROPE
49

ASIA
47

AFRICA
54

SOUTH
AMERICA
12

OCEANIA
14

ANTARCTICA
0

SNAPSHOT IN TIME

We tend to think of countries as fixed areas of land, but things change all the
time—borders get redrawn and new countries emerge, usually out of other
countries. If this book had been released in 1990, it would have been very
different. No fewer than 34 new countries have since come into being, many
following the break-up of the former communist states of the Soviet Union
and Yugoslavia. More new countries may emerge in the future, so this book
should be regarded as a snapshot in time of all the different places in the world
that people call home.

WORLD MAP

1. GUYANA
2. SURINAME
3. FRENCH GUIANA (FRANCE)
4. BELGIUM
5. LUXEMBOURG
6. NETHERLANDS
7. LIECHTENSTEIN
8. SWITZERLAND
9. SLOVENIA
10. CROATIA
11. BOSNIA AND HERZEGOVINA
12. SERBIA
13. MOLDOVA
14. ANDORRA
15. MONACO
16. SAN MARINO
17. VATICAN CITY
18. MONTENEGRO
19. ALBANIA
20. KOSOVO
21. NORTH MACEDONIA
22. ISRAEL & THE PALESTINIAN TERRITORIES
23. LEBANON
24. CYPRUS
25. ARMENIA
26. AZERBAIJAN

ARCTIC OCEAN

ICELAND

SWEDEN
FINLAND
NORWAY
DENMARK
ESTONIA
LATVIA
LITHUANIA
IRELAND
UNITED
KINGDOM
GERMANY
POLAND
BELARUS
CZECH
REPUBLIC
SLOVAKIA
UKRAINE
AUSTRIA
HUNGARY
FRANCE
ITALY
ROMANIA
BULGARIA
PORTUGAL
SPAIN
GREECE
GEORGIA
TURKEY
MALTA
TUNISIA
SYRIA
IRAQ
JORDAN
MOROCCO
ALGERIA
LIBYA
EGYPT
SAUDI
ARABIA
OMAN
UNITED ARAB
EMIRATES
QATAR
BAHRAIN
KUWAIT

RUSSIA

KAZAKHSTAN
MONGOLIA

UZBEKISTAN
KYRGYZSTAN
TURKMENISTAN
TAJIKISTAN
CHINA

NORTH
KOREA
SOUTH
KOREA
JAPAN

IRAN
AFGHANISTAN
PAKISTAN
NEPAL
INDIA
BHUTAN
MYANMAR
(BURMA)
BANGLADESH
VIETNAM
LAOS
THAILAND
CAMBODIA
TAIWAN

PACIFIC OCEAN

WESTERN
SAHARA
MAURITANIA
MALI
NIGER
CHAD
SUDAN
ERITREA
YEMEN
DJIBOUTI
SOMALIA

SENEGAL
THE GAMBIA
GUINEA-BISSAU
GUINEA
SIERRA LEONE
LIBERIA
BURKINA
FASO
CÔTE
D'IVOIRE
GHANA
TOGO
BENIN
NIGERIA
CENTRAL AFRICAN
REPUBLIC
SOUTH
SUDAN
ETHIOPIA

PHILIPPINES
BRUNEI
MARSHALL
ISLANDS
PALAU
FEDERATED STATES
OF MICRONESIA
NAURU

EQUATORIAL
GUINEA
CAMEROON
SÃO TOMÉ AND
PRÍNCIPE
GABON
REPUBLIC OF
THE CONGO
DEMOCRATIC
REPUBLIC OF
THE CONGO
UGANDA
KENYA
RWANDA
BURUNDI
TANZANIA
MALAWI
COMOROS
SEYCHELLES

SRI LANKA
MALDIVES
SINGAPORE
MALAYSIA
INDONESIA
TIMOR-LESTE
PAPUA NEW
GUINEA
SOLOMON
ISLANDS
TUVALU

ANGOLA
ZAMBIA
MOZAMBIQUE
MADAGASCAR
MAURITIUS
NAMIBIA
ZIMBABWE
BOTSWANA
ESWATINI
SOUTH AFRICA
LESOTHO

INDIAN OCEAN

VANUATU
FIJI
SAMO
TONGA

AUSTRALIA

NEW
ZEALAND

SOUTHERN OCEAN

ANTARCTICA

AME

NORTH
RICA

USA

Fittingly for the nation that brought us the Hollywood movie industry, the United States is a real superstar of a country. It's made up of 50 unique states that encompass a huge range of different landscapes, from snow-capped mountains and thick forests to deserts and tropical wetlands.

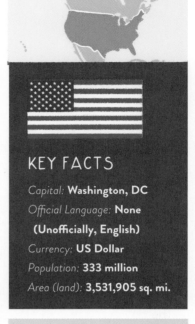

MUSIC AND MOVIES

The US entertainment industry is a global player that keeps turning out the hits. Many styles of music that are now listened to around the world have their origins in the US, including blues, jazz, rock 'n' roll, and rap. And the country's movie industry, centered in Hollywood, California, has long been the world's major provider of blockbuster movies.

KEY FACTS

Capital: **Washington, DC**
Official Language: **None (Unofficially, English)**
Currency: **US Dollar**
Population: **333 million**
Area (land): **3,531,905 sq. mi.**

The American flag has 13 stripes, representing the 13 original colonies that founded the country, and 50 stars, representing the states.

BIG BOX OFFICE

The top three highest-grossing movies of all time are American.

Movie	Year	Global Box Office
Avatar	2009	$2.84 billion
Avengers: Endgame	2019	$2.79 billion
Titanic	1997	$2.19 billion

MEGACITY SKYSCRAPERS

The US is home to some of the world's biggest and most multicultural cities, such as New York, Chicago, and Los Angeles, where you'll find some of the tallest buildings on Earth. The very first skyscraper was erected in Chicago in 1885 and was just 10 stories high. Today the country's tallest building is the 94-story, 1,776-foot One World Trade Center in New York.

REACHING FOR THE STARS

Since the mid-20th century, the US has sent various spacecraft blasting off across the solar system, orbiting planets, photographing comets, and even touching down on the surface of Mars. Perhaps the United States' greatest astronomical achievement came in 1969, when the Apollo 11 mission put the first people on the Moon.

The United States is the world's richest country. In fact, its economy accounts for around a fourth of the world's entire economy.

MANY TRIBES

There are over 500 American Indian tribal peoples. Some of the biggest include:
• Apache • Cherokee
• Chippewa • Iroquois
• Navajo • Sioux

MOUNTAINS, DESERTS, AND SWAMPS

In the US, the Rocky Mountains dominate the northwest, while the northeast is blanketed in deciduous forests. In the scorching deserts of the southwest, the Colorado River has carved out one of the world's largest gorges, the 277-mile-long, one-mile-deep Grand Canyon. In contrast, the southeast is home to the Everglades, a vast area of wetlands where alligators and snakes patrol the expanses of waterways.

AMERICAN INDIANS

The first inhabitants of the United States arrived around 20,000 years ago, spreading out and developing into many different tribes, including the Cherokee, Navajo, Choctaw, and Sioux peoples. After the arrival of Europeans from the 1500s onward, American Indians were forced from their lands. Today there are around 5.2 million American Indians, many of whom live on reservations—land within states that is managed directly by a tribe.

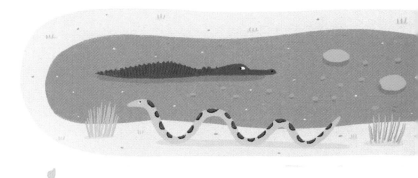

The US doesn't have an official language, although English is the one that's most widely spoken, with over 250 million native speakers. Spanish is the second most popular language, with over 40 million native speakers.

LADY LIBERTY

An icon of the United States, the 151-foot-tall Statue of Liberty, which stands in New York Harbor, was actually designed in France. It was given to the US in 1886 to commemorate the establishment of the country just over 100 years earlier.

THE WHITE HOUSE

The person in charge of the United States is the president, who is elected every four years. Each president can serve only two terms in office. There have been more than 45 presidents in total since the first, George Washington. Since 1801, all presidents have lived in the official residence known as the White House, which is located in the capital, Washington, DC.

FACE TO FACE TO FACE TO FACE

Between 1927 and 1941, Mount Rushmore in South Dakota had the giant 65-foot-high likenesses of four presidents carved into its side: George Washington, Thomas Jefferson, Abraham Lincoln, Theodore Roosevelt.

CANADA

Most people in this vast country—the world's second largest—live in a thin band of territory in the south where the climate is at its mildest. The nation's middle reaches are covered in great stretches of forest, while the north contains icy expanses of tundra where only the hardiest creatures (and people) survive.

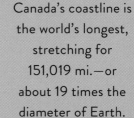

KEY FACTS

Capital: **Ottawa**
Official Languages:
English, French
Currency: **Canadian Dollar**
Population: **37.7 million**
Area (land): **3,511,023 sq. mi.**

WRAP UP WARM

It gets cold in Canada. Temperatures in its largest cities, Toronto and Montreal, can drop to below −4°F in the winter, although it's usually much warmer in the summer, averaging around 80°F in July. But that's nothing compared to Eureka, a small research settlement in Nunavut in the far north, where temperatures have been known to hit −67°F.

Canada's coastline is the world's longest, stretching for 151,019 mi.—or about 19 times the diameter of Earth.

FIVE CANADIAN WINTER SPORTS

- ice hockey (the official winter sport)
- dog sledding • snow mobile racing
- snow kiting • ice sailing

LAKES, LAKES, LAKES

Canada has 50 percent of all the world's natural lakes. In total, about 9 percent of Canada's territory is lakes—an appropriately high total for the country that invented the kayak.

MONSTER MYSTERIES

Some people think that Canada's lakes may be home to something a bit larger than fish. Over the years, many legends have sprung up about mysterious, dinosaur-like creatures lurking in their depths, including Ogopogo in Okanagan Lake, Caddy in Cadboro Bay, and Mussie of Muskrat Lake. Of course, there's no proof that any of them exist, although that doesn't mean they're not there (they could be just really good at hiding).

NIAGARA FALLS

Canada' southeast border is marked by the tumbling waters of Niagara Falls, one of the country's most popular tourist attractions. Around 845,350 gallons of water travel over the falls every second—along with the occasional person. Ever since a 63-year-old teacher named Annie Edson Taylor did it for the first time in 1901, several people have gone over the falls inside a wooden barrel. Ouch!

The land border between Canada and the US is the world's longest, stretching for 5,525 mi.

Maple trees are common throughout the country, and the production of maple syrup—made from the sap of maple trees —is an important industry.

INUIT INGENUITY

The Inuit people have lived in the far north of Canada for around 1,000 years. They adapted well to the frozen terrain: fishing and hunting marine mammals such as seals and whales, traveling in dog-pulled sleds, and making shelters called igloos out of snow. Today the Inuit people live in modern houses and drive modern vehicles, but they still maintain many other of their traditions.

ANIMALS TO SPOT IN CANADA
(from big to small):

• humpback whales • narwhals • polar bears • brown bears • black bears • moose • caribou • cougars • gray wolves • wolverine • beavers (the national animal) • puffins • pikas

MEXICO

With lava-spewing volcanoes, tropical forests, parched deserts, underground lakes, and long sandy beaches, Mexico's landscape is as diverse and intriguing as its history. Today the country is a mixture of many cultures and many people; its capital, Mexico City, is the largest urban center in all of North America.

KEY FACTS

Capital: **Mexico City**
Official Language: **None (Unofficially, Spanish)**
Currency: **Mexican Peso**
Population: **129 million**
Area (land): **750,561 sq. mi.**

DINOSAUR DEMISE

Sixty-six million years ago, a vast asteroid slammed into the country's eastern coast at a place now called Chicxulub. The impact created a crater 12 miles deep and 93 miles wide. It sent vast amounts of gas and dust up into the atmosphere, altering the climate and causing the extinction of the dinosaurs.

GREAT CIVILIZATIONS

Before the Spanish arrived in the 1500s, no fewer than six great civilizations had emerged in Mexico over a 3,000-year period. The country is dotted with the remains of their great cities, which were filled with pyramid-shaped temples and intricately carved statues.

CIVILIZATIONS

Olmecs • Teotihuacán • Maya • Zapotecs • Toltecs • Aztecs

NEW CITY ON OLD

The Aztecs controlled an empire of some six million people, centered on their capital city, Tenochtitlán. Following the Spanish conquest of the Aztecs in the 1520s, Tenochitlán was destroyed and rebuilt, eventually becoming Mexico City. Although their empire is gone, the Aztec language (Nahuatl) is still spoken by around 1.7 million people.

SINKING CITY

The Aztec capital, Tenochtitlán, was built on an island in the middle of a lake. When the Spanish took over, they began draining the lake to expand the city—not entirely successfully. Much of the land is still waterlogged, and many of Mexico City's buildings are now sinking—some by as much as 30 feet over the past 100 years.

DAY OF THE DEAD

Mexicans celebrate the Day of the Dead festival from November 1 to 2, and it's perhaps the ultimate family reunion. The celebration is best known for its elaborate, skeleton-themed costumes, but it's really about reuniting living family members with those who have passed away. Spirits of the deceased are enticed to the family home with flowers and some of their favorite foods, books, and music. Families also go to the graveyard to clean the graves and celebrate the former lives of those there.

MEXICAN TORTILLA DISHES

Each can be filled with a mixture of meat, beans, vegetables, rice, cheese, and sauces:
- Burrito—*Filled tortilla wrapped into a tube shape*
- Quesadilla—*Filled tortilla folded in half and fried*
- Taco—*Open tortilla*
- Enchilada—*Filled tortilla, covered in savory sauce and then baked.*

CRYSTAL CAVES

The ground underfoot can hold many surprises in Mexico. The country lies on three tectonic plates, which occasionally shift position, causing earthquakes and volcanic activity.

In 2000, miners drilling a tunnel beneath the town of Naica came upon a natural marvel: a 980-foot-long cave filled with giant crystals. Glistening like giant icicles, these are the largest crystals ever found, with the largest weighing 50 tons.

THE GREAT REGENERATOR

Native to the waterways around Mexico City, the axolotl is an amphibian with a special ability: if it loses a limb or its tail, it can regrow them. It can even regrow parts of its eyes and brain. Unfortunately, the animals are critically endangered because of habitat loss.

MONARCH MIGRATION

Every year, Mexico marks the final stage in one of the natural world's most epic journeys. In the autumn, hundreds of millions of monarch butterflies head south from the US and Canada in search of warmer winter weather. Some of these butterflies travel 3,000 miles. After months of flight, they arrive in Mexico's Monarch Butterfly Reserve, where their orange wings blanket the trees.

GUATEMALA

Guatemala is a small country with a lot packed into it, including mountains, more than 30 volcanoes (four of them still active), long stretches of beach, and thick bands of rainforest. The climate is tropical and hot, so much of the population lives in villages in the highlands where temperatures are cooler.

KEY FACTS

Capital: **Guatemala City**
Official Language: **Spanish**
Currency: **Quetzal**
Population: **17.2 million**
Area (land): **41,374 sq. mi.**

MAYAN MONUMENTS

Guatemala's past is everywhere. The ruins of more than 1,500 Mayan sites dot the landscape. The largest is Tikal, once the largest city in the entire Mayan world. Here, surrounded by forest, giant pyramids peer over the trees. The Mayan civilization dominated this part of the world from around CE 200 to 900 before mysteriously collapsing. Today some 40 percent of the population is of Mayan descent.

The country's name is believed to come from the Mayan for "Place of Many Trees."

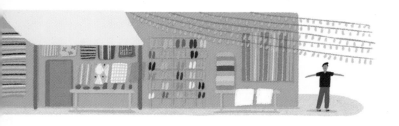

MAJOR MARKET

The country is famous for its large street markets, and none are larger than the one held twice a week in the town of Chichicastenango. It's as full of goods as its name is of letters. Known by locals as "Chichi," the market draws in people from all over with its vast range of items for sale, including colorful textiles, carvings, leather goods, and fresh fruits and vegetables.

¡Guatemala Feliz! ("Happy Guatemala!")
—First line of national anthem

BIRD MONEY

If you visit the misty cloud forests of Guatemala's mountains, you may be lucky enough to catch a glimpse of the national bird, the quetzal. This beautiful creature was important to the Maya, who used its shimmering green tail feathers as currency. The country's currency is still called the quetzal, although the feathers are no longer used!

NO WORRIES

The Maya practice of crafting "worry dolls" for children has survived into the modern age. Made of wire, wool, and colorful textiles, the 1-inch-long figures are given to children who tell the doll about any worries they might have, then put the doll under their pillow while they sleep. When the child awakes in the morning, the doll will have taken away their worries.

BELIZE

This is a country where the natural and historic wonders almost outnumber the people. The ruins of Maya settlements are scattered throughout the country. Today it's a wildlife-watcher's paradise, with jaguars and toucans patrolling the country's dense forests and a mass of marine life inhabiting the barrier reef off shore.

KEY FACTS

Capital: **Belmopan**
Official Language: **English**
Currency: **Belize Dollar**
Population: **399,600**
Area (land): **8,805 sq. mi.**

Home to just 16,500 people, Belmopan is one of the world's smallest capital cities.

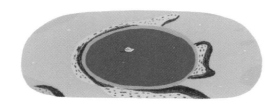

WATERY WONDERS

Belize boasts the world's second-largest reef system (after Australia's Great Barrier Reef), which provides a home to a rich assortment of tropical fish. The Great Blue Hole is a sinkhole, a sort of giant underwater cave, that's become one of the world's top diving destinations.

FOREST FRIENDS

Almost two-thirds of the country is covered in tropical forest. Here visitors may encounter parrots, howler monkeys, and tapirs. The very lucky may even catch a glimpse of an elusive jaguar.

EL SALVADOR

El Salvador is both Central America's smallest country and its most densely packed, with over six million people crammed into its narrow confines. Much of the economy is based on agriculture, particularly the growth and export of coffee and sugar, and the manufacture of clothing and textiles.

KEY FACTS

Capital: **San Salvador**
Official Language: **Spanish**
Currency: **US Dollar**
Population: **6.5 million**
Area (land): **8,000 sq. mi.**

LAND OF VOLCANOES

It may be small, but El Salvador boasts over 20 volcanoes, several of which are still active. The most recent major eruption took place in 2005, when the Santa Ana volcano unleashed a great torrent of ash, rocks, and mud. The country has also endured numerous severe earthquakes.

QUICK TOUR

The people of El Salvador like to view their country's small size in a positive light. In fact, the tourist board has marketed El Salvador as the "45-minute country," as it shouldn't take longer than that to drive to any of its main sights.

Surfers flock to Punta Roca beach, where the waves can reach 8 ft.

HONDURAS

Honduras means "depths" in Spanish. This is probably a reference to the deep waters of its Caribbean coastline, but it could apply to the country itself, which is made up of a great mixture of environments. There are big cities, towering mountains, tropical forests, and a dense network of coral reefs.

KEY FACTS

Capital: **Tegucigalpa**
Official Language: **Spanish**
Currency: **Lempira**
Population: **9.2 million**
Area (land): **43,201 sq. mi.**

September 15, 1821
—date Honduras declared independence from Spain.

COPAN

Honduras was inhabited for thousands of years before Europeans arrived. The Maya built the great city of Copán in the western part of the country. Today visitors can tour the site, which is filled with the remains of temples and carved stone statues of monkeys, jaguars, and other wildlife that played an important role in the Maya's religion.

SAWDUST CARPETS

Comayagua, a city in western Honduras, is famous for its "sawdust carpets" that appear every year in the week before Easter. These colorful pictures, depicting scenes from the life of Christ, are drawn on the city's streets using dyed sawdust. Hundreds of local families are involved in the creation of the carpets—which can take months to design—and they compete with each other to come up with the best patterns.

ANCIENT TIMES

The cathedral in Comayagua, around which the sawdust carpets are laid, has another claim to fame. It holds the oldest clock in the Americas—and the third-oldest in the world. It was built around 1100 in Spain by Muslim craftsmen—at that time, much of Spain was occupied by the Moors, an Islamic people from North Africa. In the mid-1700s, it was shipped to Honduras, then part of the Spanish Empire, where it has remained ever since.

NICARAGUA

Known as the "land of lakes and volcanoes," Nicaragua is the largest country in Central America and has coasts on both the Pacific and Atlantic oceans. Most of the people here identify as mestizo, tracing their heritage to both Spanish colonists and to the many indigenous tribes who first inhabited the land.

KEY FACTS

Capital: **Managua**
Official Language: **Spanish**
Currency: **Córdoba**
Population: **6.2 million**
Area (land): **46,328 sq. mi.**

Nicaragua's coast is known as the Mosquito Coast, not after the insects, but after the local Miskito people.

PROTECTED PLACES

Much of Nicaragua is covered in forests, which have been protected in a network of reserves and refuges to provide a haven for wildlife. The Bosawás Biosphere Reserve in the northern part of the country covers around 7 percent of Nicaragua's territory, making it the second-largest stretch of rainforest in the Americas (after the Amazon).

BIODIVERSITY CHECK

Mammal species: 180
Reptile & amphibian species: 240
Bird species: 700

NEW VOLCANO

Nicaragua has 19 volcanoes. The newest is Cerro Negro, which first appeared in 1850 and has erupted several times since. Despite the dangers of being so close to an active volcano, many people flock here to take part in the extreme sport of "volcano boarding"—hurtling down the fine, snow-like ash on the volcano's sides on a sled.

LAKE NICARAGUA

The southwest area of the country is dominated by Lake Nicaragua, the largest lake in Central America. Its waters are home to numerous fish, including bull sharks—the only sharks found in freshwater lakes anywhere in the world.

Nicaragua gained independence from the Spanish Empire on September 15, 1821.

COSTA RICA

Costa Ricans live in one of the region's most unspoiled environments, as summed up by the local phrase *pura vida* ("pure life"), which is often used as a greeting. With tourism a major part of its economy, the country strives to preserve its incredible landscapes and biodiversity.

KEY FACTS

Capital: **San José**
Official Language: **Spanish**
Currency: **Colón**
Population: **5.1 million**
Area (land): **19,714 sq. mi.**

NO MORE WARS

Costa Rica is one of the few countries not to have an army. It was abolished after the country's brief civil war in 1948. From that point on, it was decided that all conflicts would be solved without resorting to weapons. The country has been at peace—both with itself and with its neighbors—ever since.

Costa Rica is regularly voted one of the happiest nations on Earth.

MONKEY MADNESS

Costa Rica is home to five species of monkeys, listed here from smallest to biggest:

• squirrel monkey •
white-faced capuchin
• Geoffroy's spider
monkey • mantled
howler monkey.

QUARTER PROTECTION

Around a quarter of Costa Rica's territory is protected in a network of national parks and private refuges, helping preserve the country's incredible biodiversity. Though covering just 0.03 percent of the world's surface, the country boasts an astonishing 5 percent of the world's species—including 18 percent of the world's butterflies alone.

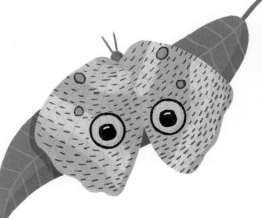

TAKING LIFE SLOW

While monkeys always seem to be on the go, Costa Rica's sloths take a very different approach to life. They spend most of their time motionless, and when they do move, they do so extremely slowly—in fact, they're one of the slowest-moving animals on Earth, with a top speed of about 300 yards per hour. The country is home to two species: the brown-throated three-toed sloth and Hoffmann's two-toed sloth.

Costa Rica's thickly forested Cocos Island was the inspiration for the Isla Nubar in the *Jurassic Park* and *Jurassic World* movies.

PANAMA

Panama is the meeting point of the Americas, where the northern continent joins its southern neighbor. It also provides a link between oceans via its most famous feature, the Panama Canal. Elsewhere are great swathes of jungle, long sandy coasts, and the vibrant capital city where almost one-fourth of the population lives.

KEY FACTS

Capital: **Panama City**
Official Language: **Spanish**
Currencies: **Balboa/US Dollar**
Population: **3.9 million**
Area (land): **28,703 sq. mi.**

Just 50 mi. long, the canal cuts most ship journeys by thousands of miles.

At its narrowest point, Panama is just 30 mi. wide.

A MAN, A PLAN, A CANAL—PANAMA

The Panama Canal lets ships pass between the Atlantic and Pacific oceans without having to go all the way around South America. It was constructed between 1904 and 1914 by the US. In fact, the US continued to control the canal until 1999, when it was finally taken over by the Panamanian government. Around 14,000 ships pass through it every year. Tolls from the canal still account for about one-third of the country's income.

IMPENETRABLE FOREST

The section of mountainous rainforest near the country's border with Colombia is so thick that it's considered basically impassable. Known as the Darian Gap, this is the only part of either continent without any roads. Even the Pan-American Highway, which otherwise runs all the way from the top of North America to the foot of South America, comes to a halt here.

CITY FOREST

The forest is everywhere in Panama, even in the capital city itself, where a small section of tropical jungle can be found in the Parque Metropolitano. Here you can walk alongside sloths, parrots, and other wildlife, just a short distance from the shops, restaurants, and hotels of downtown.

HUMMINGBIRD HAPPINESS

Panama is home to around 60 species of hummingbirds, including:
- snowy-bellied hummingbird
- purple-throated mountaingem
- long-billed starthroat
- volcano hummingbird
- violet sabrewing

THE BAHAMAS

This nation is made up of around 700 islands stretched out across the Atlantic Ocean, but only about 30 are inhabited. Boasting long, sandy beaches, a sunny climate, and waters filled with giant fish such as marlin and wahoo, the country is a popular tourist destination.

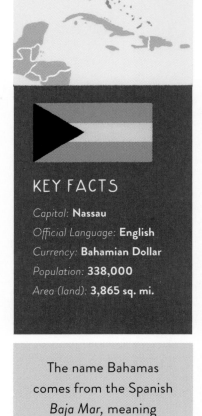

KEY FACTS

Capital: **Nassau**
Official Language: **English**
Currency: **Bahamian Dollar**
Population: **338,000**
Area (land): **3,865 sq. mi.**

PLUNDERING PIRATES

In the early 1700s, the Bahamas was a base for some of the most famous pirates of the age, including Calico Jack and Blackbeard. These fearsome buccaneers grew rich attacking and plundering the region's ships and towns. In 1718, the British government took control of the islands and began stamping out piracy.

The name Bahamas comes from the Spanish *Baja Mar*, meaning "shallow sea."

PINK IS THE COLOR

There's a famous beach on Harbour Island with bright pink sand—it gets its color from the red shells of microscopic marine animals living in the water. The country is also home to one of the world's largest colonies of pink flamingos. Around 80,000 of these long-legged birds form a huge flock on Inagua Island.

Bahamas National Dish:
Cracked conch
(pronounced "konk")
with rice and peas

Lucayan National Park on Grand Bahama, the northernmost island, is home to one of the world's largest underwater cave systems.

Christopher Columbus first visited here during his maiden voyage to the "New World" in 1492.

JUNKANOO

Every year on December 26 and New Year's Day, towns stage lively celebrations known as Junkanoo festivals. These involve parades where people dress in colorful costumes and dance through the streets to accompaniment of traditional music.

CUBA

Known the world over for its music, dancing, and unique style, Cuba is the largest nation in the Caribbean. It occupies a long, thin island with great mountain ranges in the west and east where the forests support several unique species of wildlife. Much of the middle is flat and set aside for farming.

KEY FACTS

Capital: **Havana**
Official Language: **Spanish**
Currencies:
Peso/Convertible Peso
Population: **11.1 million**
Area (land): **42,402 sq. mi.**

CUBA VS. UNITED STATES

Cuba has been a communist country since 1959. That was when revolutionaries overthrew the military dictatorship then in charge of Cuba and took control of the country's industries, many of which were American owned. This brought the country into conflict with the US, which has banned trade with the country ever since. Many people in Cuba still drive old American cars from the 1940s and '50s, from before the Revolution.

A TOUCH OF THE SON

Many styles of music that are popular around the world have originated in Cuba, including rumba and mambo. One of the best known is son cubano, which first emerged in the early 20th century. It's a highly rhythmic style that utilizes several percussion instruments, including claves (wooden sticks), shakers, maracas, and bongos, as well as the *tres*, a type of Cuban guitar.

It's a New Year's Eve tradition in Cuba to burn rag dolls to symbolize getting rid of your troubles and looking forward to the future.

TINY CREATURES

Cuba's forests are home to two of the world's smallest creatures. One is the bee hummingbird. The world's littlest bird, this tiny flutterer is just 2 inches long. But even that is a giant compared with the Monte Iberia frog which, at 0.4 inches long, is the world's second-smallest frog. It's so tiny that it's almost impossible to spot.

CUBAN CROCODILE

Seen from above, the island of Cuba is said to look like a crocodile. This seems fitting, as the island is home to a rare species of the reptile, the Cuban crocodile. It can grow up to 11.5 feet long and is known as the "leaping crocodile" for its ability to jump out of the water and snatch animals from overhanging branches.

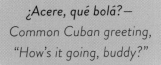

¿Acere, qué bolá?—
Common Cuban greeting,
"How's it going, buddy?"

JAMAICA

This mountainous island has many different environments—including rainforest, woods, swamps, mangroves, and coral reefs—but just two cities. There's lively crowded Kingston in the southeast, home to almost half the population, and Montego Bay in the northwest, which is popular with tourists.

NAMING THE HURRICANE

Jamaica and its neighbors lie in an area known as the Hurricane Belt, which means they are regularly battered by severe storms. The word "hurricane" was coined by the first people to first live here, the Taino —"Huricán" was their god of storms. The Taino also named the island itself, which they called "Xaymaca," meaning "land of wood and water."

REGGAE ROOTS

Jamaica is a very musical place that has given numerous new styles to the world. The most popular is undoubtedly reggae, which first became popular in the late 1960s, emerging out of other Jamaican styles, such as ska and rocksteady.

SUPER SPEEDS

Jamaican sprinters are among the most successful in history! Jamaica won gold at the women's 100 meters at the Olympic Games in 2008, 2012, and 2016. The male athlete Usain Bolt is the fastest human in history. In 2009, he set a world record for the 100 meters of 9.58 seconds.

RASTAFARIANS

Most of the people in Jamaica are Christian. In fact, the country has over 1,600 churches, more per square mile than any other country on Earth! Some people follow a different religion, however, called Rastafarianism. Rastas believe that Haile Selassie, the emperor of Ethiopia from 1930 to 1974, was the messiah. They also believe in living "naturally" and not cutting their hair, which they twist into dreadlocks.

KEY FACTS

Capital: **Kingston**
Official Language: **English**
Currency: **Jamaican Dollar**
Population: **2.8 million**
Area (land): **4,182 sq. mi.**

JAMAICAN MUSICAL MAESTROS

The country has produced numerous famous singers over the years:
• Bob Marley (1945–81)
• Jimmy Cliff (b. 1948)
• Desmond Dekker (1957–2006)
• Lee "Scratch" Perry (b. 1936) • Sean Paul (b. 1973) • Toots Hibbert (1942–2020)
• Shaggy (b. 1968).

Usain Bolt won gold medals in the 100 m and 200 m at three consecutive Olympics (2008–2016).

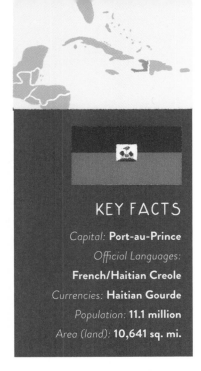

HAITI

Sharing the island of Hispaniola with the Dominican Republic, Haiti is the Caribbean's most mountainous country. Numerous festivals are held here throughout the year, most centered on the capital, Port-au-Prince. These include Rara, an exuberant mixture of music and parades held in the lead-up to Easter.

KEY FACTS

Capital: **Port-au-Prince**
Official Languages:
French/Haitian Creole
Currencies: **Haitian Gourde**
Population: **11.1 million**
Area (land): **10,641 sq. mi.**

The country's name is derived from *Hayti*, a word in the language of the indigenous Taino people meaning "Land of Mountains."

THE FIRST EUROPEANS

Christopher Columbus became the first European to visit Haiti in 1492 (which at the time he believed to be part of China). It was here that he attempted to establish a colony, although it was soon destroyed by the local people. Columbus is regarded with little fondness in the Caribbean today. He greatly exploited the local people, enslaving many of them to work on Spanish plantations.

VOODOO

Haiti's main religion is voodoo (or vodou) a mixture of Catholicism and the beliefs of people of West Africa. Followers try to communicate with deities, or spirits, known as lwa, who are worshipped in rituals involving drumming, singing, and dancing. It's believed that these spirits can possess people and control how they act.

EARTHQUAKES

Haiti has suffered more than its fair share of natural disasters over the years. It's been hit by numerous powerful hurricanes and tropical storms. In 2010, the country suffered its most severe earthquake in over 200 years, which is believed to have killed more than 200,000 people and left more than a million others homeless.

L'Union fait la force ("Unity Makes Strength") —*motto on Haiti's coat of arms*

DOMINICAN REPUBLIC

Haiti's neighbor, the Dominican Republic (or DR) is a hugely popular tourist destination, with giant hotels lining long stretches of its eastern and northern coasts. Inland are several natural wonders including the Caribbean's largest lake, Lake Enriquillo, and its highest mountain, Pico Duarte.

OLDEST NEW CITY

Founded by the Spanish in 1496, the DR's capital, Santo Domingo, is the oldest continuously occupied settlement in the Americas. It's also the site of the continents' oldest university and cathedral. Most of the country's most important industries have their headquarters here.

KEY FACTS

Capital: **Santo Domingo**
Official Language: **Spanish**
Currency: **Peso**
Population: **10.5 million**
Area (land): **18,656 sq. mi.**

La Bandera Dominica ("The Dominican Flag") —nickname given to the staple daily meal of rice, beans, and meat.

MUSICAL STYLES

The DR is particularly known for two styles of rhythm-heavy music: bachata and merengue. Fast paced and energetic, merengue is the official dance and music of the country. It's traditionally played by a small band using an accordion, a double-headed drum, and an instrument called a *güira*—a metal tube that's struck with a stiff brush to produce a sound somewhat like a maraca.

One of the country's top attractions, the Rio Damajagua Falls, is made up of 27 linked waterfalls.

AMBER

The Dominican Republic is one of the world's leading producers of amber—fossilized tree sap. The amber dates from around 25 million years ago, and some of it contains the preserved remains of tiny prehistoric creatures, such as insects and spiders, which became trapped in the sap all that time ago.

WHALES

The waters around the Dominican Republic are teeming with marine life. A large section is protected as the *Santuario de Mamíferos Marinos* (Marine Mammals Sanctuary). Here every year hundreds of humpback whales return to the warm waters of Samana Bay to give birth.

ST. KITTS & NEVIS

The smallest country in the Americas is made up of two islands: St. Kitts to the north and Nevis in the south. Both are mountainous and blanketed in thick forest. It was one of the first Caribbean islands to be colonized by Europeans and one of the last to gain independence, which finally happened in 1983.

KEY FACTS

Capital: **Basseterre**
Official Language: **English**
Currency: **East Caribbean Dollar**
Population: **54,800**
Area (land): **101 sq. mi.**

CARIBBEAN CULTURE

The islands stage a number of festivals throughout the year. The biggest is the carnival Sugar Mas, which takes place between Christmas and New Year's Day and involves a solid week of music, parades, food, and dancing. In the summer, Nevis stages Culturama, a 12-day festival dedicated to Nevisian arts. And on the first Monday in August, the entire country celebrates the freeing of the country's slaves in the 1830s.

The two islands are separated by a thin stretch of sea called the Narrows, which in parts is just 2 mi. wide. Every year, swimmers compete to race between the islands.

ANTIGUA &BARBUDA

This small nation consists of two main islands—the larger Antigua, which is formed of volcanic rock, and the smaller Barbuda, which is made of coral—plus a smattering of smaller islands. The country relies heavily on beach tourism for its income. It's also a popular yachting destination and stages an annual regatta, Antigua Sailing Week.

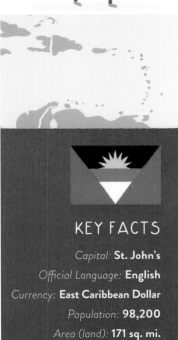

KEY FACTS

Capital: **St. John's**
Official Language: **English**
Currency: **East Caribbean Dollar**
Population: **98,200**
Area (land): **171 sq. mi.**

Antigua is nicknamed the "land of 365 beaches," as there's supposedly one for every day of the year.

REDONDA REVIVAL

Just a few years ago, the tiny island of Redonda was almost lifeless. Extensive mining of guano (bird poop) for fertilizer stripped much of surface bare. But thanks to conservation efforts, the island has staged a dramatic recovery. Seabirds, such as frigate birds and brown boobies, are nesting again, and other wildlife is on the rise.

ISLAND EVACUATION

In 2017, Barbuda was hit by a terrible tropical storm, Hurricane Irma. The devastation was so severe that the government evacuated the island's entire population to Antigua while Barbuda was cleaned up and repaired.

DOMINICA

Like many Caribbean islands, tiny Dominica is of volcanic origin. But, unlike most other islands, this volcanic activity is still going on, bubbling away beneath people's feet and resulting in a collection of hot springs, sulfurous pools, and geysers. More than half of the island is covered in lush rainforest.

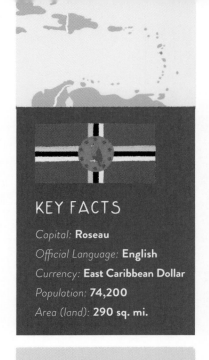

KEY FACTS

Capital: **Roseau**
Official Language: **English**
Currency: **East Caribbean Dollar**
Population: **74,200**
Area (land): **290 sq. mi.**

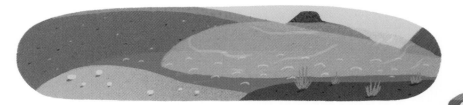

BOILING LAKE

In the middle of the island is one of the most unusual phenomena in the Caribbean—the Boiling Lake. Around 200 feet across, it looks like a giant bubbling cauldron. Volcanic activity beneath the water keeps the center at a constant rolling boil. And even at the edges, the temperature is still upwards of 176°F.

The dazzling sisserou parrot, found only on this island, is Dominica's national bird.

SAINT LUCIA

One of the most popular vacation destinations in the Caribbean, this lush island is a peaceful paradise. Sandy beaches ring a mountainous interior thick with forest and banana plantations.

GROS AND PETIT

On the southwestern coast of the island are Saint Lucia's most famous natural sights: two pointed volcanic "plugs"—giant lumps of rock that form inside the mouths of volcanoes. Known as Gros Piton and Petit Piton, the two peaks have become a symbol of the nation (they even feature on its flag).

KEY FACTS

Capital: **Castries**
Official Language: **English**
Currency: **East Caribbean Dollar**
Population: **166,500**
Area (land): **234 sq. mi.**

Dozens of countries are named after men, but Saint Lucia is the only one named after a woman.

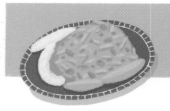

Saint Lucia's national dish: Green figs and saltfish

ST. VINCENT
AND THE GRENADINES

This Caribbean nation is made up of one big island (St. Vincent) plus 31 small ones (the Grenadines). Just eight of the Grenadines are inhabited. Boats are one of the main ways of getting around here and of seeing the region's plentiful coral reefs.

BOTANIC GARDENS

The capital boasts the second-oldest botanical garden in the Americas. Rare and exotic species have been grown at the Botanical Gardens St. Vincent and the Grenadines since 1765. Visitors can also see the rare St. Vincent parrot (the national bird) in the aviary here.

Parts of the Hollywood movie franchise *Pirates of the Caribbean* were filmed in the Grenadines.

GRENADA

There are nine islands in total in this country: the main island of Grenada plus eight smaller ones. Each has its own distinct character. Below the highest peak of Grenada—the dormant volcano Mount St. Catherine—are abundant, biodiverse forests and great plantations of cocoa and nutmeg.

UNDERWATER SCULPTURES

Grenada is home to one of the region's top museums, although you'll need to put on your swimming gear to visit it. The Molinere Underwater Sculpture Park consists of dozens of concrete sculptures of human figures standing on the sea floor. The aim is for them to gradually become covered in sealife and corals.

Grenada's main and most profitable crop is nutmeg. The spice was first introduced here in the mid-19th century, and now the country is one of the world's leading suppliers.

BARBADOS

The history of this small but perfectly formed tropical island stretches back 4,000 years. Today its culture is a vibrant mixture of West African and British influences, as reflected in the language, Bajan, which is recognized as an English creole. Its long sandy beaches make Barbados a popular tourist destination.

SURFING SPOT

Barbados is much loved by surfers, who travel from far and wide to try its near legendary waves. There are lots of great surfing spots on the south and west coasts of the island, but perhaps the most famous is the Soup Bowl on the east side. The fast, foamy barrel waves here challenge even the best break riders.

FLYING FOOD

The ingredients for Barbados's national dish can take some gathering. It's a combination of cou-cou (a mixture of corn meal and okra) and Bajan flying fish. That's right, fish that fly. Using their fins like wings, they launch themselves out of the water and travel through the air for up to 650 feet. There are many different species, which are common in local waters (and on local plates).

Crop Over is a vibrant harvest festival involving parades, colorful costumes, and lots of food and music.

"Cheese on bread!" —common Bajan phrase used to mark astonishment, like "Wow!"

Born Robyn Fenty, the pop star Rihanna is from Barbados. In 2017, the street where she grew up was renamed "Rihanna Drive."

BAFFLING BEARDS

Barbados means "The Bearded Ones" in Portuguese, although which particular beards are being referred to is up for debate. It could be the long, hanging roots of the island's fig trees, or the beards of the indigenous Carib people who once lived here, or even the beard-like sea-foam of the waves. No one really knows. It's also known as "Pork Chop Island" because of its shape, and locals often refer to it simply as "Bim."

TINY SNAKE

Owing to an introduced population of snake-eating mongooses, snakes are pretty rare on Barbados. Those that do remain are hard to spot, as the island is home to the world's smallest species, the Barbados thread snake. Like little brown pieces of spaghetti, an adult thread snake is just 4 inches long.

TRINIDAD AND TOBAGO

"Forged from the Love of Liberty"
—Trinidad and Tobago's national anthem

Just a short boat trip or flight from South America, the palm-tree-lined islands of Trinidad and Tobago are culturally very much part of the Caribbean. This nation has been responsible for some of the region's must famous musical exports, including calypso, soca, and steel drumming.

STEEL DRUMS

Steel drums were invented in Trinidad in the mid-20th century, making them the world's only acoustic instrument invented after 1900. Each drum is made from an old oil drum with the top (originally the bottom) beaten into dents of different sizes, each of which plays a different note.

OIL, GAS, AND ASPHALT

Unlike many other Caribbean countries, which rely on tourism for their income, the Trinidadian economy is mainly based on its large reserves of oil and natural gas. It also has the world's largest natural reservoir of asphalt (a substance used for making roads), known as Pitch Lake.

CALYPSO KINGS

Calypso is a highly rhythmic song-based music that emerged in Trinidad in the mid-1800s, gradually spreading across the Caribbean, and from there to the rest of the world. Some of the best known Trinidadian Calypso artists of the 20th century have included Lord Kitchener, the Duke of Iron, and Roaring Lion.

The bending-over-backward dance competition known as limbo was invented here.

WHAT'S IN A NAME?

The people from the main island of Trinidad are known as Trinidadians (or "Trinis" for short), while those from the smaller island of Tobago are referred to as Tobaganians. But if you want to refer to the people from both islands you should use the term Trinbagonians.

AME

SOUTH
RICA

COLOMBIA

The only South American country with both a Caribbean and a Pacific coastline, Colombia offers a wealth of natural environments: tropical beaches, volcanoes, grasslands, deserts, coffee plantations, and rainforests. The human experience is equally diverse, with festivals held throughout the year and a lively music scene.

KEY FACTS

Capital: **Bogotá**
Official Language: **Spanish**
Currency: **Peso**
Population: **49 million**
Area (land): **401,044 sq. mi.**

GREAT DIVERSITY

After Brazil, Colombia is believed to be the most biodiverse place on Earth. Its stretch of the Amazon is home to an estimated 10 percent of all Earth's species.

Colombia is the world's leading producer of emeralds, which are precious green gemstones. Around 70% of the world's entire supply is mined here.

GAMES WITH A BANG

Today soccer is by far the most popular sport here. But one traditional pasttime that has survived into the modern age is *tejo*. A bit like an explosive version of lawn bowling or pétanque, it involves throwing a metal puck at a small, triangle-shaped target, which is loaded with gunpowder. The aim is to hit the target directly and make it go bang!

RIVER OF COLORS

In the middle of the country is one of the continent's most unusual rivers, the *Caño Cristales* (Crystal Channel). The river water is clear and fast running, but the aquatic plants on the riverbed cause the water to change color during the second half of the year, swapping between yellow, green, blue, black, and a particularly intense red.

LAND OF GOLD

The indigenous peoples who inhabited Colombia at the time of the Spanish arrival in the 1500s were extremely skilled gold workers. They produced highly detailed jewelry and statues, and they even performed ceremonies using gold. One of these saw a leader being entirely covered in gold dust. This gave rise to tales of a place called El Dorado, a city of gold that the Spanish believed must lie somewhere deep in the jungle.

VENEZUELA

As the birthplace of Simón Bolívar, the revolutionary who led Venezuela and several other countries to independence, it could be claimed that this is where modern South America began. In the 20th century, Venezuela became one of the continent's richest countries thanks to its vast oil reserves.

KEY FACTS

Capital: **Caracas**
Official Language: **Spanish**
Currency: **Bolívar**
Population: **28.6 million**
Area (land): **340,561 sq. mi.**

PROTECTED ENVIRONMENTS

Venezuela protects around 54 percent of its territory against development—the most of any country. Within the protected zones are some incredible landscapes, including tabletop mountains, extensive cave systems, swaths of jungle, the vast Orinoco River, and an area of seasonally flooded grassland that is home to capybaras (the world's largest rodents), caimans, giant anteaters, and anacondas.

GIANT WATERFALLS

The Canaima National Park in eastern Venezuela is home to the world's highest waterfall, Angel Falls. It plunges down 3,212 feet, sending up a great cascade of spray that can produce several rainbows at once. The falls are named after the US aviator Jimmy Angel, who brought them to international attention when he became the first person to fly over them in 1933.

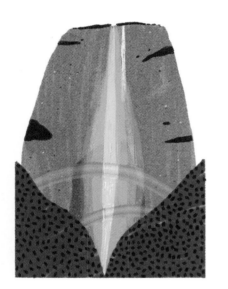

Venezuela has the largest oil reserves of any country on Earth.

Chévere, meaning "cool" or "great" is a common Venezuelan expression.

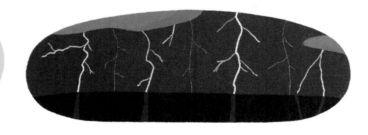

In the capital city, it's a tradition to travel to church services during the Christmas season on roller skates.

Most popular sports in Venezuela:
1. Baseball
2. Basketball
3. Soccer.

STORM WITHOUT END

If you're a fan of storms, then you should head to Lake Macaraibo at the mouth of the Catatumbo River, where a strange local weather phenomenon results in severe 10-hour electrical storms for around half the year. At these times, there can be as many as 100,000 lightning strikes over the course of a night.

GUYANA

Crisscrossed by rivers, streams, creeks, and waterfalls, Guyana is justly known as the "Land of Many Waters." But with much of the interior covered in dense, unspoiled rainforest, it could equally well be called the "Land of Lots of Jungle."

MASH IT UP

One of the country's biggest festivals is Mashramani, usually referred to simply as "Mash," held every year on February 23. It celebrates the country becoming a republic through parades, music, and food. A large proportion (over 40 percent) of the population is of Indian descent, and many Hindu festivals, such Diwali and Holi, are also celebrated here.

Drivers crossing the Takutu River Bridge from Guyana into Brazil need to have their wits about them, as it means swapping from driving on the left to driving on the right.

KEY FACTS

Capital: **Georgetown**
Official Language: **English**
Currency: **Guyanese Dollar**
Population: **750,200**
Area (land): **76,004 sq. mi.**

Kaieteur Falls is the world's largest single-drop waterfall, as measured by the amount of water going over it.

SURINAME

Many cultures have combined to create South America's smallest country. It's home to people descended from indigenous tribes, African slaves, Indian and Chinese laborers, and Dutch, Lebanese, and Jewish settlers. Around half the population is crammed into the busy coastal capital.

THE HOLE TRUTH

Suriname is home to a great wealth of wildlife. One of the most unusual species is the Surinam toad, which has a unique way of raising a family. A female's eggs become embedded in her back. The young then grow where they are, each in its own flesh hole. Once they've developed, the toadlets pull themselves out of their mother's back, hop off, and set off on their own.

KEY FACTS

Capital: **Paramaribo**
Official Language: **Dutch**
Currency: **Surinamese Dollar**
Population: **610,000**
Area (land): **60,232 sq. mi.**

Over 90% of Suriname is covered in forest, the highest proportion of any nation in the world. However, just 16% is officially protected in reserves.

ECUADOR

Straddling the equator, Ecuador enjoys a hot, tropical climate. Its landscapes change from towering snow-capped peaks to cloud forests to rainforests to pristine beaches. Wildlife watchers are spoiled for choice, particularly with the Galapagos Islands lying offshore.

INCREDIBLE ISLANDS

A group of islands lying about 600 miles due west of mainland Ecuador, the Galapagos are known around the world for their unique wildlife. The naturalist Charles Darwin visited the islands in the early 1800s, and the incredible biodiversity he encountered was one of the main inspirations for his theories of evolution by natural selection.

Around half the world's population of blue-footed boobies breed in the Galapagos Islands.

WILDLIFE

• marine iguana • flightless cormorant • Galapagos fur seal
• waved albatross • Galapagos hawk • Galapagos giant tortoise

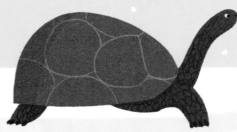

(ALMOST) OUT OF THIS WORLD

Because Earth is not a perfect sphere and bulges slightly in the middle, Ecuador's highest mountain, Mount Chimborazo, is actually about 1.5 miles farther from Earth's center than Mount Everest. That makes Ecuador officially the closest country to outer space.

CENTER OF THE EARTH

Ecuador is named after the equator, making it the world's only country named after a geographical feature. At the Middle of the World Monument in the capital, Quito, you can stand with one foot in the Northern Hemisphere and one foot in the Southern Hemisphere.

BRAZIL

Everything about Brazil seems larger than life. It's about the size of all the other countries in South America put together. It's home to the world's largest rainforest and the world's largest river. And its most populous city, São Paulo, is not just the largest in South America, but the largest in the entire Southern Hemisphere.

KEY FACTS

Capital: **Brasilia**
Official Language: **Portuguese**
Currency: **Real**
Population: **212 million**
Area (land): **3,227,096 sq. mi.**

Rio de Janeiro means "River of January." It was given its name by Portuguese explorers who first arrived on January 1, 1502, and mistook the great bay here for a river.

VIEW FROM THE TOP

Brazil's second-largest city, Rio de Janeiro, is one of the world's most popular tourist destinations. Every year, two million visitors pack its long, sandy beaches. The city is overlooked by one of the world's best-known statues, *Cristo Redentor* (Christ the Redeemer), which sits perched on a mountain some 2,300 feet up. Completed in 1931, the towering figure is 98 feet tall.

PARTY TIME

Rio has been hosting a carnival since 1723. What started as a simple celebration before a period of fasting in the lead-up to Easter has grown into a raucous five-day street party. It's centered on a glittering parade in which samba musicians and dancers perform alongside huge, elaborate floats.

FAVELAS

As in many countries, there is a great difference between the lives of rich and poor people in Brazil. While the wealthy enjoy large houses, many of the country's less fortunate inhabitants are crammed into shanty towns called favelas. Built quickly using cheap materials, favelas are particularly associated with Rio de Janeiro, where several line the hillsides surrounding the city's downtown.

SOCCER

Soccer is by far the most popular sport in Brazil, both to play and to watch. The country has also hosted the FIFA World Cup twice, in 1950 and 2014. The attendance of 199,854 for the final game of the 1950 tournament was the largest crowd ever for a soccer game.

SOCCER FANATICS

1958 • 1962 • 1970 • 1994 • 2002
—the five years in which Brazil has won the FIFA World Cup, more than any other country.

There are no bridges anywhere along the Amazon River. If you want get from one side to the other, you'll have to use a ferry . . . or swim! (Watch out for the piranhas!)

MIGHTY RIVER AND RAINFOREST

The Amazon River powers its way through northern Brazil. Surrounding it are the 2.1 million square miles of the Amazon Rainforest, around two-thirds of which lie in Brazil. Millions of incredible creatures lurk within—stealthy jaguars, schools of piranhas, colorful parrots, and bird-eating spiders the size of dinner plates. But many of its species are now under threat. Around 20 percent of the forest has been cleared, mainly for farmland and housing, since Europeans arrived in the 1500s.

The Amazon carries more water than the next three largest rivers (Nile, Mississippi, and Yangtze) combined.

NATIONAL SPECIALTIES

Typical Brazilian dishes include:

Pão d Queijo—a type of cheesy bread

Coxinha de Galinha—dumpling-like deep-fried chicken fritters

Feijoada—a stew made with pork, beans and rice, perhaps the country's most popular dish.

GRASSLANDS AND WETLANDS

Though best known for its rain-soaked jungles, Brazil boasts numerous other amazing habitats, including a vast stretch of grassland in the middle of the country known as the Cerrado. In the southwest is the Pantanal, the world's largest tropical wetland. Here, among a great patchwork of swamps, lagoons, and islands, you can find caimans (a relative of the crocodile), giant anteaters, and the world's biggest snake, the green anaconda.

PERU

Peru is so jam-packed with wonders, it's difficult to know where to start. There are the Andes Mountains, the Amazon Rainforest (which covers around half the country), coastal deserts, incredible remains of ancient civilizations, and much more.

KEY FACTS

Capital: **Lima**
Official Languages: **Spanish, Quechua, Aymara**
Currency: **Sol**
Population: **31.9 million**
Area (land): **494,209 sq. mi.**

INCAN INFLUENCE

Peru is a country with a deep connection to its past. It's where the great Incan state, which was the largest empire in the Americas prior to the arrival of Europeans, was centered. Today around a quarter of the population is indigenous, while over half has mixed ancestry.

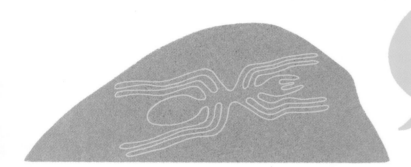

Al toque
common Peruvian expression meaning "right away"

The potato was first cultivated in Peru, from where it spread around the world after it had been discovered and exported by Spanish invaders. Today the country grows more than 3,500 varieties.

NAZCA LINES

About two thousand years ago, the local Nazca people created a series of giant pictures in the desert, some as large as 1,200 feet. They mainly depict animals such as hummingbirds, spiders, and monkeys. Nobody knows exactly why they were created, but it's presumed they played a part in the Nazca belief system—perhaps as messages for deities in the sky.

MACHU PICCHU

In the mid-1500s, many Incan cities, such as the capital, Cuzco, were taken over and rebuilt by the Spanish. One hilltop settlement, however, escaped detection. Probably built as an estate for the Incan emperor, Machu Picchu was abandoned shortly after the Spanish invasion, but it remained unknown to the outside world until being "rediscovered" by the American historian Hiram Bingham in 1911. Today it is one of the continent's most popular tourist attractions.

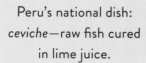

Peru's national dish: *ceviche*—raw fish cured in lime juice.

CHILE

Thin but very, very long, Chile winds down the west coast of South America for over 2,600 miles, all the way to the foot of the continent. Packed within is some extraordinary geography, including the world's driest desert and the continent's largest glaciers, not to mention countless mountains and forests.

KEY FACTS

Capital: **Santiago**
Official Language: **Spanish**
Currency: **Peso**
Population: **18.2 million**
Area (land): **287,187 sq. mi.**

Chile is just 40 mi. wide at its narrowest point, and no more than 221 mi. wide anywhere.

DRIEST DESERT

A large section of Chile is covered by the world's driest desert, the Atacama. The wettest parts receive just 0.6 inches of rain a year, but there are parts where no rainfall has ever been recorded. Some hardy species of plants and animals still manage to survive here. Penguins live on the coast, and flamingos can be found in high-altitude salt lakes.

GIANT FLYERS

Chile's mountains are home to the world's largest flying bird, the Andean condor, which can have a wingspan of up to 11 feet and weigh 33 pounds. It's a type of vulture, which means it feeds mainly on carrion (dead animals).

CLEAR SKIES

A lack of both rain clouds and light pollution makes the skies above the Atacama desert perfect for stargazing. A very large telescope made up of 66 linked radio telescopes is located here. Known as ALMA (Atacama Large Millimeter Array), it's provided valuable information about far-off galaxies and stars.

BIG HEADS

Chile's territory Easter Island (or Rapa Nui in the language of the native inhabitants) is famous for the more than 800 giant carved stone heads, known as *moai*, that dot the coast. Standing, on average, 13 feet high and weighing 14 tons, they were erected by the island's original settlers between the 1100s and 1600s for reasons that are no longer fully understood.

CHILEAN CUISINE HIGHLIGHTS

Completo—*hot dog with sauerkraut and tomatoes*

Curanto—*meat and seafood cooked over hot stones in a pit in the ground*

Pastel de choclo—*corn casserole with meat, vegetables, and hard-boiled eggs*

BOLIVIA

Landlocked Bolivia is named after Simón Bolívar, the revolutionary who led the breakaway of several South American countries from the Spanish Empire. Outside the cities, it's sparsely populated, with a landscape made up of swaths of fertile farmland, sterile desert, high-altitude forests, and enormous, shimmering salt flats.

KEY FACTS

Capital: **Sucre, La Paz**
Official Languages: **Spanish, Aymara, Quechua, Guarani, and 33 others**
Currency: **Boliviano**
Population: **11.6 million**
Area (land): **418,265 sq. mi.**

A LAKE WITH ALTITUDE

Lake Titicaca, on the border of Bolivia and Peru, is one of the highest large lakes. It was an important site for the Incas. Today the lake is inhabited by the indigenous Uro people, who live on about 120 floating islands constructed using reeds.

ANCIENT EMPIRES

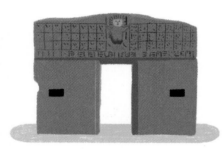

Bolivia has been home to many great civilizations, including the Incas of the 1400s and 1500s, as well as their predecessors, the Tiwanaku Empire (c. 550–900 CE). The Tiwanaku capital was centered on the banks of Lake Titicaca, and today numerous ruins can be seen on the southern shore.

Bolivia's rich human history is reflected in the languages of its many ethnic groups. The country has 37 official languages.

In La Paz, the clock on the main government building is backwards—the numbers are flipped, and the hands run counterclockwise. The arrangement is intended to represent the "southernness" of the Bolivian people.

LLAMA DRAMAS

The people who inhabit the mountains of Bolivia have long relied on llamas. Related to camels, llamas are good climbers and very strong, making them particularly useful as pack animals in tough terrain. They're also used as a source of meat and wool, and their dung can even be dried and burned as fuel.

SERIOUSLY SALTY

In southwestern Bolivia is a vast expanse of snow-like salt. The *Salar de Uyuni* is the world's largest salt flat, at over 4,000 square miles, stretching out as far as the eye can see. It was formed thousands of years ago when a giant salty lake dried out.

PARAGUAY

It might not get the same amount of international attention as its bigger neighbors, Brazil and Argentina, but Paraguay has just as much going on. Its landscapes range from cattle ranches and grassy plains to swamps, forests, caves, and semideserts.

KEY FACTS

Capital: **Asunción**
Official Languages: **Guarani, Spanish**
Currency: **Guaraní**
Population: **7.2 million**
Area (land): **153,399 sq. mi.**

The *lapacho*, or pink trumpet tree, is the national tree of Paraguay.

GIANT DAM

On the border of Paraguay and Brazil stands one of the great engineering marvels of the modern age, the Itaipu Dam. Built on the Parana River between 1971 and 1984 by around 40,000 workers, it is the world's second-largest producer of hydroelectric power, after the Three Gorges Dam in China. Standing 738 feet high and 4.5 miles long, it produces around 88 percent of Paraguay's electricity.

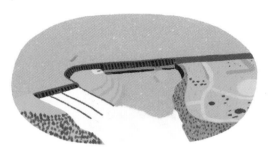

From 1864 to 1870, Paraguay engaged in the disastrous War of the Triple Alliance, which saw it lose around 50% of its territory to neighboring Brazil, Argentina, and Uruguay.

GRAN CHACO

The 1,675-mile-long Paraguay River divides the country into two rough halves from north to south. To the west is the most wildlife-rich region, the Gran Chaco. This semiarid terrain of low forests and savannas is populated by giant anteaters, jaguars, and capybaras.

THIRSTY WORK

If you want to cool off, do as the locals do and try a glass of *tereré*, a type of iced herbal tea made with the plant *yerba mate*. You'll sometimes see it served in a *guampas*, a cup made from cattle horn. Other local delicacies include *chimpas*, a type of cheese roll, and *sopa Paraguaya*, which despite its name (which means "Paraguayan soup") is actually a type of corn bread.

Paraguay is sometimes known as the *Corazón de Sudamérica* ("Heart of South America") because of its location right in the middle of the continent.

ARGENTINA

The European influence on Argentina is strong, particularly in Buenos Aires, home of the tango. Beyond the urban areas are the great mountains of the Andes, the grasslands and deserts of Patagonia, and the seemingly endless cattle ranches of the Pampas, the agricultural heartland.

KEY FACTS

Capital: **Buenos Aires**

Official Language: **None**

Currency: **Peso**

Population: **45.5 million**

Area (land): **1,056,642 sq. mi.**

WIDEST FALLS

On the border between Brazil and Argentina is one of the largest and most spectacular waterfalls on Earth. The Iguazu Falls are actually about 275 separate falls that together form a giant torrent of tumbling water stretching for 1.7 miles. The most intense stretch is a great curtain of water known as the *Garganta del Diablo* (Devil's Throat).

HIGHEST PEAK (ISH)

Standing 22,837 feet high, Aconcagua is the highest mountain anywhere outside of Asia. That said, there are so many tall mountains in Asia, particularly in the Himalayas, that it's only the 189th tallest on Earth.

Argentina has won the FIFA World Cup twice, (1978, 1986), and has produced two of the world's greatest soccer players ever, Diego Maradona and Lionel Messi.

SUPER DINOS

One of the biggest dinosaurs of all time was discovered in Argentina in 1987 and named after the country. A giant titanosaur with a long neck and legs like tree trunks, Argentinosaurus lived around 92 million years ago and may have measured 130 feet long and weighed 100 tons. However, as only a few bones have been found, it's difficult to say with certainty exactly what it looked like.

BE SURE TO DUCK

Argentina's national sport, *pato,* is a bit like basketball on horseback, with riders on opposing teams competing to throw a ball through a large basket. Incidentally, the name comes from the Spanish for "duck," as in the early days a live duck was used instead of a ball! (The poor duck!)

The intense partner dance and music known as tango originated in 19th-century Buenos Aires. Today performances are given every day at venues across the city.

URUGUAY

Much less mountainous than its neighbors to its west, Uruguay has also been in fewer wars. It's a peaceful place of vast fields and big skies. Much of the landscape is used for agriculture, the backbone of the economy. There are an estimated 3.5 cows for every person—the highest proportion in the world.

KEY FACTS

Capital: **Montevideo**
Official Language: **Spanish**
Currency: **Uruguayan Peso**
Population: **3.4 million**
Area (land): **67,574 sq. mi.**

Uruguay's national anthem is the longest in the world—over five minutes long.

BEEFY BATTLES

Every year, Uruguay and Argentina battle for the title of biggest consumer of beef. Huge cattle farms patrolled by horsemen known as gauchos are a distinct part of both the landscape and culture. An annual festival of horseriding, the *Fiesta de la Patria Gaucha*, is held in the northern city of Tacuarembó. It showcases music, poetry, and traditional dance, as well as rodeos.

Uruguay's motto is *Libertad o Muerte*, which means "Liberty or Death."

HAND IN THE SAND

Looking like a giant trying to escape from a beach, the *Mano de Punta del Este* (The Hand of the Eastern Point) is one of Uruguay's most distinctive landmarks. Made of concrete and plastic, and reinforced with steel bars, the sculpture of five fingertips poking through the sand is the work of the Chilean artist Mario Irarrázabal. It was created in 1982.

Uruguay won the very first soccer World Cup in 1930. They became champions again in 1950, but have failed to claim the title since.

GNOCCHI DAY

It's traditional in Uruguay to eat gnocchi on the 29th of each month. The practice began in the 1800s when people were generally paid on the 1st of the month. This meant that by the end of the month, many people had only basic ingredients left in their pantry, such as flour and potatoes—the main ingredients of the dish.

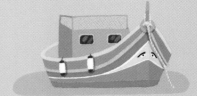

EUR

OPE

ICELAND

This country's name describes its cold, frozen surface well. But below the surface it's a different story. Here, bubbling volcanic activity has created volcanoes and geysers that provide some of the country's most spectacular sights. Iceland also gets most of its energy from geothermal (volcanically heated water) sources.

NEW (ICE) LAND

In 1963, Iceland got a little bit bigger when the eruption of an undersea volcano created a new island. Known as Surtsey, the island broke the surface on November 14 and kept on growing. By the time the eruption finally petered out in 1967, the island covered an area of 0.5 square miles and stood 509 feet above sea level.

SURROUNDING SEA LIFE

The snow-white Arctic fox is the island's only native mammal. Most large land animals, including reindeer, have been imported. But the seas surrounding the island are teeming with wildlife, including seals, whales, and seabirds, such as colorful puffins. When the seas freeze over, polar bears occasionally come over from Greenland.

Iceland's national dish is not for the faint-hearted. Known as *hákarl*, it's made of shark that's been fermented in the ground for up to 12 weeks, dried out, and served raw. It has a very powerful ammonia-like taste (apparently).

HIDDEN PEOPLE

Many Icelandic folk stories tell of the country's *Huldufólk* ("hidden people"), small elf-like creatures that live among the rocks and crags of the island. They are supposed to have supernatural powers, and people try to avoid disturbing them in case it brings them bad luck. In 2014, a road was diverted to prevent a supposed Huldufólk habitat from being destroyed.

Gaman að kynnast þér
*"Nice to meet you"
in Icelandic*

Founded in 930, Iceland's parliament —known as the Althing—is the oldest in the world.

WHAT'S IN A NAME?

Icelandic last names aren't carried down the generations. Instead, a child will take what's known as a patronym—an adapted version of their father's (or sometimes their mother's) first name—as their last name. So children named Stephen and Katy whose father was named Joseph would be named Stephen Josephson (son of Joseph) and Katy Josephdóttir (daughter of Joseph).

IRELAND

Out on Europe's western tip, facing the Atlantic, Ireland boasts a green, rain-soaked landscape of rolling fields and marshy peat bogs. In fact, it's so lush and green, it's been nicknamed the "Emerald Isle." The country takes up around 80 percent of the island of Ireland, with the rest given over to Northern Ireland, part of the UK.

KEY FACTS

Capital: **Dublin**

Official Languages: **Irish, English**

Currency: **Euro**

Population: **5.2 million**

Area (land): **26,596 sq. mi.**

There are no native snakes in Ireland. According to tradition, St. Patrick chased them all into the sea. (In truth, there have never been any snakes in Ireland.)

TALKING STATUES

Around 40 percent of the population lives in or around Dublin, which is famous for its cultural scene. Four of its writers have won the Nobel Prize for Literature over the past century. The city has erected a number of statues in their honor. If you download the "Talking Statues" app, you can hear the likes of James Joyce, Oscar Wilde, and George Bernard Shaw deliver monologues of their work as you pass them by.

POPULAR IRISH TEAM SPORTS

- Gaelic football —*like a cross between soccer and rugby*
- Hurling—*like a cross between hockey and lacrosse, played by men*
- Camogie—*like hurling but played by women.*

NATIONAL SYMBOLS

The shamrock, a type of three-leaf clover, has long been thought of as a national symbol of Ireland and features on the badge of many of its sports teams. Finding a rare four-leaf clover is said to be very lucky. However, despite popular belief, the shamrock is not the official national symbol of Ireland; that's the Celtic harp.

BLACK GOLD

Ireland's most popular alcoholic drink, Guinness, is now sold around the world. The dark, velvety beer was first produced in 1759 in a Dublin brewery, and the recipe has changed very little since. It's clearly proved a success: more than 10 million pints are poured (slowly) and drunk every day.

The Irish are actually the third-biggest consumers of Guinness, after people from Nigeria and the UK.

ST. PATRICK'S DAY

Saint Patrick, the man credited with introducing Christianity to Ireland in the 400s, is the country's patron saint. A celebration in his honor, held on March 17, has become Ireland's national day and public holiday. It's marked by parades and parties and is celebrated by many Irish communities around the world.

THE UNITED KINGDOM
A COUNTRY OF COUNTRIES

ENGLAND

For such a small country, England has had a huge global influence. Its language is spoken all over the world, and many of its cultural figures—particularly its writers and musicians—are iconic figures. But it's been around a while after all, with a history that stretches back thousands of years.

KEY FACTS

Capital: **London**
Official Language: **English**
Currency: **Pound Sterling**
Population: **56.3 million**
Area (land): **50,301 sq. mi.**

The Channel Tunnel, which connects England with France, was opened in 1994. It's 31 mi. long and cost over $15 billion to dig.

CAPITAL OF CULTURE

The city of London is home to around nine million people and is the site of many of the country's best known sights. Tourists can visit dozens of museums and hundreds of restaurants, not to mention unique attractions such as Buckingham Palace (the queen's official residence) and the Houses of Parliament (site of the iconic clock known as Big Ben).

KINGS AND QUEENS

Except for a brief period in the 1600s, England has always had a monarch. Although they continue to live in plush palaces, today's royals have little real power. But that wasn't always the case. Up until a few hundred years ago, the monarch's word was law. And they could even change that law if they wanted. That's what King Henry VIII did in the 1500s to allow him to marry six times.

England has produced some of the world's best-loved writers:

- **William Shakespeare**—*Macbeth, Hamlet, Romeo and Juliet*
- **Mary Shelley**—*Frankenstein*
- **Jane Austen**—*Pride and Prejudice, Emma*
- **Charles Dickens**—*Oliver Twist, David Copperfield*
- **Agatha Christie**—Hercule Poirot mysteries
- **J. R. R. Tolkein**—*The Hobbit* and *The Lord of the Rings*
- **Roald Dahl**—*Charlie and the Chocolate Factory, The Witches*
- **J. K. Rowling**—The Harry Potter books

MYSTERIOUS MONUMENT

Erected around 2500 BCE, about the same time as the Great Pyramids in Egypt, the stone circle of Stonehenge is very mysterious. Experts are unsure exactly what the arrangement of stones was for or even how they got there—some of the stones weigh over 24 tons and were brought from quarries more than 150 miles away by people without wheeled vehicles.

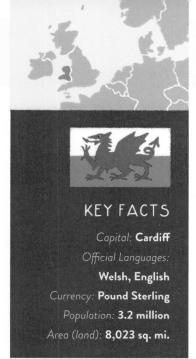

WALES

A land of mountains, castles, and age-old legends, Wales occupies the center-west of the island of Britain. This small country has worked hard to preserve its unique identity, as exemplified by the rich, melodious national language. Once on the verge of extinction, Welsh (or Cymraeg) is today spoken by around a fifth of the population.

KEY FACTS

Capital: **Cardiff**

Official Languages: **Welsh, English**

Currency: **Pound Sterling**

Population: **3.2 million**

Area (land): **8,023 sq. mi.**

Wales is home to the UK's deepest cave. *Ogof Ffynnon Ddu* (Cave of the Black Spring) is 900 feet deep and contains around 31 miles of subterranean passages.

MOUNTAIN RAILWAY

The highest peak in Wales and England is Mount Snowdon in Wales, at 3,560 feet. It's possible to walk to the summit in about five to seven hours, and many people do. Others prefer to take it easy and ride the rack railway service that runs to the top. It's the UK's busiest mountain, with over half a million visitors a year.

Home to the nation's soccer and rugby teams, the Principality Stadium in Cardiff seats over 70,000 people. If it starts to rain, the roof (the second-largest stadium roof in the world) can be closed.

CASTLE CRAZY

As well as providing plenty of exercise for walkers, Wales's mountains have throughout history proved very useful for another activity: castle building. During the Middle Ages, over 600 of them were built here—per square mile that's more than any other European country. Some of the best preserved and most visited include Caernarfon, Conwy, Harlech, and Pembroke.

NATIONAL DISHES

- Cawl—*a type of stew*
- Laverbread—*seaweed loaf*
- Bara brith—*fruit loaf*
- Welsh rarebit—*luxury cheese on toast with added mustard and ale*

Wales famously boasts one of the longest place names in the world: *Llanfairpwllgwyngyllgogerychwyrndrobwllllantysiliogogogoch,* which apparently means "Saint Mary's Church in the hollow of the white hazel near the rapid whirlpool and the Church of Saint Tysilio of the red cave."

THE UNITED KINGDOM

SCOTLAND

Covering the northern third of Britain, Scotland is a proud country with a long, rich history. Its rugged, weather-beaten landscape boasts heather-clad hills, mountains aplenty, deep mysterious lochs (lakes), and glens (narrow valleys). Its largest cities of Glasgow and Edinburgh enjoy vibrant cultural scenes.

CULTURAL COLOSSUS

Almost every year since 1947, Edinburgh has played host to the world's largest performing arts event: the Edinburgh Festival. Spread over 25 days, it involves more than 55,000 performances of everything from plays, musicals, and cabaret to circus, poetry, and comedy—in fact, comedy now accounts for around a third of all performances. More than 2.5 million tickets are sold annually, a number rivaled only by events such as the Olympics and the FIFA World Cup.

KEY FACTS

Capital: **Edinburgh**
Official Languages: **English, Scots, Scots Gaelic**
Currency: **Pound Sterling**
Population: **5.5 million**
Area (land): **30,090 sq. mi.**

It would take you over five years to watch all the performances at just one Edinburgh Festival.

LOCH NESS MONSTER

One of the world's most famous monsters is said to lurk in the depths of the lake called Loch Ness. There's a whole tourist industry based on looking for the creature, which is usually described as a long-necked prehistoric creature, such as a plesiosaur. There isn't any proof of its existence, but that doesn't stop people from coming to check for Nessie themselves.

National animal:
The Unicorn

BURNS NIGHT

People get together on January 25 to celebrate the life and work of the national poet, Robert "Rabbie" Burns. The festivities usually take the form of a traditional evening meal of haggis (a spicy meat pudding), neeps (swede), and tatties (potatoes), and performances of Burns's poems. His song "Old Lang Syne" is sung across the UK (and beyond) on New Year's Eve.

In the spring and summer, many people attend traditional Highland Games, which involve such Scottish sports as the caber toss (throwing huge wooden logs), tug of war, and hammer throwing.

The Royal and Ancient Golf Club of St. Andrew's, where the sport has been played since the 1400s, is one of the oldest courses in the world and is known as the "home of golf."

NORTHERN IRELAND

KEY FACTS

Capital: **Belfast**
Official Language: **English**
Currency: **Pound Sterling**
Population: **1.9 million**
Area (land): **5,456 sq. mi.**

Politically part of the UK, Northern Ireland's landscape has much in common with its southern neighbor, Ireland. Its countryside is dominated by drumlins—long hills carved out by glaciers during the last ice age. With a good deal of the population packed into busy Belfast, much of the countryside is sparsely populated.

GIANT'S CAUSEWAY

On the far north coast lies Northern Ireland's best known and most visited natural landmark, the Giant's Causeway. It consists of a mass of hexagonal stone columns covering an area of around 7.5 million square feet. Although they look manmade, they were actually formed naturally in volcanic eruptions. Of course, the first people to encounter them didn't know that, and many legends have grown up around them.

According to one legend, the Giant's Causeway was built by the giant Finn McCool as a pathway to Scotland so he could fight his rival giant, Benandonner.

TITANIC CONSTRUCTION

For much of the 20th century, Belfast was a major center of British shipbuilding, turning out giant tankers and liners. Its most famous ship was perhaps its least successful, the giant ocean liner RMS *Titanic*. Having been constructed here between 1909 and 1912, the ship sank during its maiden voyage when it struck an iceberg in the North Atlantic en route to New York.

Right in the middle of the country is Lough Neagh, the largest lake in the UK, which supplies Northern Ireland with 40% of its drinking water.

THE DARK HEDGES

In recent years, some of Northern Ireland's sites have been brought to a whole new audience. The Dark Hedges is an avenue of twisted interlocking trees that looks like the kind of road a witch might build—but was actually created in the 1700s as the approach to a mansion. It's achieved a new level of popularity since being featured in the hit TV series *Game of Thrones*.

FRANCE

Most years, France is the world's most visited country, with millions flocking here to sample the cuisine, wine, and culture. Its scenery includes mountains, Mediterranean beaches, big cities, giant chateaux (castles), traditional villages, and seemingly endless fields of lavender and sunflowers. *Vive la France!*

KEY FACTS

Capital: **Paris**

Official Language: **French**

Currency: **Euro**

Population: **67.8 million**

Area (land): **212,345 sq. mi.**

TACKLING THE TOWER

Almost everyone who goes to Paris finds themselves visiting the Eiffel Tower. The giant metal tower was built in 1889 to commemorate the French Revolution, which had overthrown the country's monarchy 100 years earlier. It's 1,063 feet high, and there are two elevators taking you up to platforms for great views out over the city. If you're feeling in shape, you could try the stairs, but be warned—there are 1,665 of them!

BREAD AND CAKES

The French are famous for their love of food. Paris alone boasts over 30,000 bakeries, and more than 40,000 restaurants, ranging from simple street corner bistros to high-end establishments. One thing that almost all French people have in common is their love of bread. 320 baguettes are eaten per second.

It's considered unlucky to place a baguette upside down on a table in France. Best to eat it instead.

POPULAR CAKES

- Mille-feuille *("thousand sheets") —layers of puff pastry and cream topped with chocolate and vanilla icing*
- Gateau St Honoré *—Caramel-coated cream puffs on a pastry layer, surrounding a whipped cream center*
- Fraisier *—Sponge cake layers filled with cream and sliced strawberries*

That staple of French cuisine, the croissant, was actually invented in Austria.

France is one of the world's largest wine producers, turning out around eight billion bottles a year.

BEGINNING OF BALLOONING

The hot-air balloon was invented by the Montgolfier brothers in the late 1900s. The French brothers tested their invention by sending a sheep, a duck, and a rooster up into the sky. When the (slightly confused) animals landed successfully, the brothers followed this experiment a couple of months later with the first successful manned flight.

Paris was founded in the 200s BCE by the Romans, who called it Lutetia, meaning "place by a swamp."

TOUR DE FRANCE

The world's most prestigious—not to mention arduous—bicycle race takes place across France every summer. First held in 1903, the Tour de France covers a 2,200-mile route across the country (and sometimes beyond), split into stages over 23 days. The winner, following the final stage in Paris, is awarded the iconic yellow jersey.

FRANCE OVERSEAS

France once controlled a large empire. Many of the countries that once formed that empire are now independent, but some have remained attached to France.
French Guiana—*South America*
Guadeloupe and Martinique islands—*Caribbean*
Réunion and Mayotte islands—*Indian Ocean*

FRENCH FILM FESTIVAL

Since 1946, France has held a film festival in Cannes, a resort on the country's sun-kissed southern coast known as the French Riviera. Hundreds of movies from around the world are shown during the two-week festival, which usually takes place in early summer. The one judged to be best is awarded the Palme d'Or (Golden Palm).

STACKS OF ART

The Louvre, housed in a former royal palace in the center of Paris, is the world's largest art museum. It covers an area of over 750,000 square feet— that's about as big as 280 tennis courts. It holds numerous priceless pieces, including what must surely be the most famous painting in the world, the *Mona Lisa*, created by the Italian artist Leonardo da Vinci in 1503.

ANDORRA

A mini mountainous country, Andorra is perched in the Pyrenees, sandwiched between France and Spain—although its official language is neither. Its many slopes and valleys attract hordes of hikers in the summer, and skiers and snowboarders in the winter.

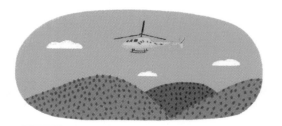

KEY FACTS

Capital: **Andorra la Vella**
Official Language: **Catalan**
Currency: **Euro**
Population: **77,000**
Area (land): **181 sq. mi.**

TAKE THE BUS

Andorra is the largest country not to have an airport. You can only arrive at this landlocked nation by wheeled transportation or by helicopter (there are a couple of heliports). And over the years, many people have. Only about a third of the people here are of Andorran nationality. The majority come from neighboring countries, with Spanish making up just over 40 percent of the population.

Andorra has two unelected heads of state: the French President and the Bishop of Urgell in Catalonia, Spain. The day-to-day running of the country is handled by the prime minister.

Set at 3,356 ft. above sea level, Andorra la Vella is Europe's highest capital city.

MONACO

If luxury yacht spotting is your thing, then head to Monaco, a millionaire's playground on the French Riviera, where the harbor is packed full of them. The tiny seaside state has a dense collection of upmarket restaurants, apartment complexes, and casinos. It's ruled by Prince Albert II, a member of the Grimaldi family, which has controlled Monaco since 1297.

KEY FACTS

Capital: **Monaco**
Official Language: **French**
Currency: **Euro**
Population: **39,000**
Area (land): **0.8 sq mi.**

STREET RACERS

Every year, the country plays host to the Monaco Grand Prix. But this motor race isn't held at a racetrack. Instead, Formula 1 drivers tear their way around the country's narrow streets at speeds of up to 160 miles per hour.

Monaco makes much of its money from casino gambling, but it's strictly foreign money only. Citizens are forbidden not just from gambling but from even entering a casino.

Monaco is smaller than New York's Central Park.

LUXEMBOURG

The smallest of the three "low countries" (along with Belgium and the Netherlands), Luxembourg is surrounded by Belgium, Germany, and France. It's a country defined by its thick forests, splendid castles, and money—as one of the world's major financial centers, the people here are the wealthiest in the European Union.

KEY FACTS

Capital: **Luxembourg City**

Official Languages: **Luxembourgish, French, German**

Currency: **Euro**

Population: **628,400**

Area (land): **998 sq. mi.**

One-third of Luxembourg is covered in forest.

THE OLD DUCHY

Once a fairly common type of European state, today Luxembourg is the world's last remaining Old Duchy (a country ruled by a Grand Duke). It's been that way for a while. Founded in 963, it became a duchy in 1354. In 1919, the people were asked to vote on whether they wanted to keep the Duke as head of state. They voted "yes," and so a duchy it has remained.

Luxembourg was one of the six founding nations of the European Union, along with France, Belgium, Germany, the Netherlands, and Italy.

LIECHTENSTEIN

Sandwiched between Switzerland and Austria, mountainous Liechtenstein is a small, prosperous, peaceful place. The crime rates are low, the standard of living high, and the skiing plentiful throughout the winter. It's one of the world's only double-landlocked countries—meaning there are at least two countries between it and the sea in every direction.

KEY FACTS

Capital: **Vaduz**

Official Language: **German**

Currency: **Swiss Franc**

Population: **39,100**

Area (land): **62 sq. mi.**

ALL WELCOME

The country was founded by, and named after, the Austrian prince Johann von Liechtenstein. It's still ruled by a prince. Since 1989, this has been Prince Hans-Adam II, who resides in Vaduz Castle, which sits on a hill overlooking the capital. It's generally closed to the public, but each year on August 15, all the country's residents are invited to a party on its grounds to celebrate the country's national day. (Thankfully, they don't all show up!)

A Liechtenstein company, Ivoclar Vivadent, is the world's leading manufacturer of false teeth, accounting for around a fifth of global sales.

NETHERLANDS

The Netherlands is a very flat place, with much of the land barely three feet above sea level. It also covers a fairly small area, although it's grown significantly over time. Around 17 percent of the land here has been reclaimed from the sea.

KEY FACTS

Capital: **Amsterdam**
Official Language: **Dutch**
Currency: **Euro**
Population: **17.3 million**
Area (land): **13,019 sq. mi.**

TULIP MANIA

Tulips are so closely associated with the Netherlands that it's surprising to discover they didn't originate here. They were first grown in Turkey, arriving in the Netherlands in the 1500s, and since then have become hugely popular. In the spring, the country's parks and gardens are full of these colorful blooms, and the farms here produce more than a billion bulbs a year for sale around the world.

LIKING BIKING

No one loves riding bikes as much as the Dutch. The country's 17 million inhabitants own 23 million bicycles between them—that's more per person than any other country. In Amsterdam, bikes outnumber cars by two to one.

CANALS AND BRIDGES

Two wheels aren't the only way to get around. Amsterdam is crisscrossed by a network of canals. There are 165 of them in total—linked by 1,281 bridges—and boat trips are one of the most popular ways of seeing the capital.

There may not be many hills, but you may still find yourself looking up a lot, as the Dutch are on average the tallest people in the world. The average height is 6 ft. for a man and 5 ft. 7 in. for a woman.

WINDMILLS & DYKES

Much of the land that has been reclaimed from the sea was drained by pumps operated by wooden windmills. Many of these still stand and have become symbols of the country. A network of more than 1,500 miles of dykes (walls) is in place to hold back the water and prevent the sea from flooding back over the land.

KEY FACTS

Capital: **Brussels**

Official Languages: **Dutch, French, German**

Currency: **Euro**

Population: **11.7 million**

Area (land): **11,690 sq. mi.**

POPULAR BELGIAN DISHES

(in French and Flemish):

- *Frites/Frieten*—fluffy, twice-cooked fries
- *Moules-frites/mosselen-friet*—mussels and fries
- *Gaufre/wafel*—waffles
- *Croquettes aux crevettes grises/garnalen krokketten*—gray shrimp croquettes
- *Anguilles au vert/paling in 't groen*—eel in green herb sauce.

BELGIUM

Belgium is all about trying to make differences work. It's officially bilingual, with mostly French speakers in the south and mostly Flemish (Dutch) speakers in the north. Its capital is home to the European Parliament, where politicians from all over the continent come to make decisions. What everyone can agree on is the country's many charms: its beautiful architecture and drool-worthy cuisine.

THE ATOMIUM

The center of Brussels is dominated by grand old stone buildings. But on the outskirts of the city is something a little more unusual. Created for the 1958 Brussels World Fair, the Atomium is a shiny steel structure of giant balls connected by tubes that is intended to represent an iron crystal magnified 165 billion times. Today the building houses a museum and restaurant and has become an icon of the country.

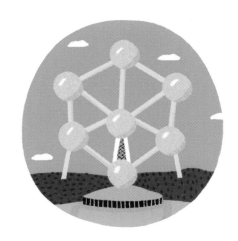

CUISINE AND CHOCOLATE

Belgium is justly famous for its cuisine. Some of its most famous dishes include *moules* (mussels) and steak, both served with the country's distinctively delicious double-cooked fries. In fact, you could just go for the fries on their own, which are sold from mobile shops called *Fritkots*. Belgium is also known as one of the continent's main producers of luxury chocolates.

DIAMOND DISTRICT

A small area of the city of Antwerp has become the center of the global diamond trade. Filled with hundreds of workshops, over 80 percent of the world's rough diamonds, or approximately $16 billion worth, are processed here every year. If you want to pick up a diamond ring, you'll have plenty of choice.

The big bang theory of the universe was devised by the Belgian physicist (and priest) George Lemaître, although he referred to it as the "Cosmic Egg."

The country gets its name from the Belgae tribe who lived here around 2,000 years ago.

GERMANY

Lying at the heart of Europe and bordered by nine countries, Germany's influence extends across the continent and beyond. Its landscape encompasses everything from the beaches and plains of the north to the deep, dark forests of the center and the towering Alps of the south.

KEY FACTS

Capital: **Berlin**
Official Language: **German**
Currency: **Euro**
Population: **80.2 million**
Area (land): **134,623 sq. mi.**

PRINTING PRESS

In the 1450s, the German inventor Johann Gutenberg came up with a contraption that changed how information is distributed forever: the printing press. By creating movable type, he made it possible for books to be produced quickly and simply in large quantities for the first time.

Germany is the most populated country in the European Union.

FAIRY-TALE CASTLES

Germany boasts several castles, but perhaps none stand out quite like the Disney-esque Neuschwanstein Castle in Bavaria. Constructed on a rugged hilltop by King Ludwig II, the castle's design became ever more ambitious and expensive, resulting in its completion being repeatedly delayed. Begun in 1869, it was still unfinished at the time of the king's death in 1886.

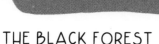

BROTHERS GRIMM

In the early 1800s, two German brothers, Jacob and Wilhelm Grimm, began collecting folktales and legends from across German-speaking lands (and beyond), which they turned into a book. The hugely successful collection helped popularize tales that are now known the world over, including "Cinderella," "Beauty and the Beast," "Hansel and Gretel," "Little Red Riding Hood," and "Rapunzel."

THE BLACK FOREST

In the country's southwest corner is its largest nature reserve, the Black Forest. This mountainous region, with its dense canopy of evergreen trees (from which the forest gets its name), features quaint villages, ruined castles, meadows, and age-old gnarly trees. The whole place has the air of a Grimms' fairy tale.

OKTOBERFEST

Since 1810, the nation's favorite alcoholic drink has been celebrated at a huge 16–18 day autumn festival called Oktoberfest. Over six million people attend, sitting in tents at long tables, where they consume traditional snacks such as *Schweinshaxe* (roasted pork knuckles), *Brezel* (pretzels) and, of course, lots of beer—around 2 million gallons.

POETS, THINKERS, AND MUSICIANS

Germany is often referred to as *Das Land der Dichter und Denker*, "The Land of Poets and Thinkers." It has produced numerous acclaimed writers over the years, including Johann Wolfgang von Goethe and Günter Grass, not to mention many acclaimed musicians. Some of the country's best-known classical composers include Bach, Brahms, Wagner, and Beethoven.

THEY'VE HAD WURST

There are more than 1,500 varieties of German sausages, including:
- *Mettwurst*—pork and beef sausage
- *Bockwurst*—veal and pork sausage
- *Leberwurst*—spreadable liver sausage
- *Weisswurst*—white sausage traditionally eaten for breakfast
- *Currywurst*—a popular fast food of sausage slices with curry ketchup.

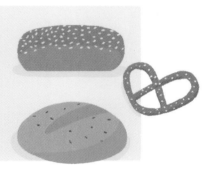

Germany has over 300 varieties of bread, and the country also boasts at least two museums dedicated to baked goods.

WARS AND REUNIFICATION

Germany's recent history has been particularly turbulent. In the 20th century, it was the initiator—and loser—of two world wars. After World War II, Germany was divided into separate countries: a capitalist West and a communist East, with a fortified border between them. A huge wall split the city of Berlin in two. Following reunification in 1990, the country has enjoyed a peaceful existence and has grown into Europe's largest economy.

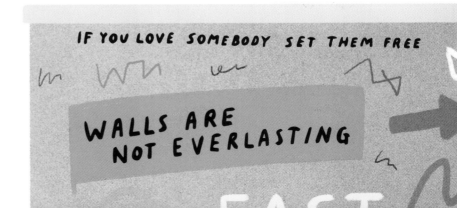

IF YOU LOVE SOMEBODY SET THEM FREE

WALLS ARE NOT EVERLASTING

EAST

AUSTRIA

From its great Alpine mountains to its lush rolling hills, Austria has a landscape that seems to inspire music. Its peaks provide the backdrop to the movie *The Sound of Music*, while its cities have nurtured some of classical music's most famous names. Today visitors come for the country's castles, cakes, and concert halls.

KEY FACTS

Capital: **Vienna**
Official Language: **German**
Currency: **Euro**
Population: **8.5 million**
Area (land): **31,832 sq. mi.**

ALPINE ADVENTURES

Over half of Austria is covered in mountains, which visitors can explore through cross-country skiing tours and high-altitude train journeys. At 12,461 feet, *Grossglockner* ("Big Bell") is the tallest peak and is known for its High Alpine Road—a twisting mountain pass full of hairpin bends and heart-stopping views.

The warbling style of singing known as "yodeling" is believed to have originated with farmers communicating to one another across Austria's alpine hilltops.

MUSIC IN THE AIR

The capital city, Vienna, has long been one of the major centers of European classical music, where world-class composers such as Beethoven, Mahler, and Johann Strauss once performed. Wolfgang Amadeus Mozart (1756–91), perhaps the most famous classical composer of all time, spent much of his career in Vienna.

Austria is home to the largest ice cave in the world, the 26 mi. long *Eisriesenwelt*, which means "World of the Ice Giants."

Mozart began to play and compose his own music at just four years of age.

CAKE CULTURE

Austrian sweet treats sold in pâtisseries, bakeries, and cafés in every town include:

Cremeschnitte—custard creme cake
Sachertorte—chocolate sponge cake
Topfentorte—cheesecake
Apfelstrudel—apple pastry
Kardinalschnitte—sponge and meringue cake.

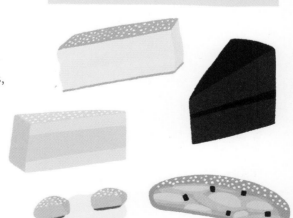

KEY FACTS

Capital: **Bern**
Official Languages:
**German/Swiss German,
French, Italian, Romansh**
Currency: **Swiss Franc**
Population: **8.4 million**
Area (land): **15,443 sq. mi.**

The Swiss athlete
Roger Federer is one
of the most successful
tennis players of all time,
winning 20 Grand Slam
tournaments, including
eight Wimbledon titles.

The multipurpose
penknife known as the
Swiss Army knife was
first produced here in 1891.

SWITZERLAND

The popular image of the Swiss landscape is of endless mountains capped with snow, which isn't too far from the truth. But there's much else besides, including flower-filled meadows, icy lakes, and prosperous cities. Positioned in the heart of Europe, Switzerland is an important headquarters for many international organizations.

MOUNTAINS THAT MATTER

Switzerland may be small, but it is packed full of land with hundreds of mountains. The craggy, pointed peak of the Matterhorn is one of the highest in the Alps. You need to be a real expert to tackle it, as it's notoriously difficult to climb. A safer journey past spectacular views can be enjoyed on a train to the continent's highest station, Jungfraujoch, sitting 11,332 feet up a mountainside.

CLEAR OF CONFLICT

Switzerland is a fiercely independent nation that long ago made the decision to stay out of other nations' business. The country is not a member of the European Union and has remained neutral in all major international conflicts, including both world wars. Many international organizations that favor that neutrality have their headquarters here, such as the World Health Organization and the Red Cross.

CRAFTY CHOCOLATIERS

The Swiss population loves chocolate: the country consumes the most amount per person in the whole world. And they're not bad at making it, either: their milk chocolate is renowned for its quality.

SMASHING TIMES

Deep beneath the Swiss-French border sits one of the world's largest machines, the Large Hadron Collider. Scientists use it to send subatomic particles crashing into each other at incredible speeds, creating conditions similar to the big bang. It's believed that this machine will help us find out more about how the universe was created.

ITALY

More than 2,000 years ago, boot-shaped Italy gave rise to the Roman Empire, which had a major influence on the development of Western civilization. Italy continues to capture attention with wonders that range from Renaissance masterpieces, world-famous pizzas, and palace-lined canals.

KEY FACTS

Capital: **Rome**
Official Language: **Italian**
Currency: **Euro**
Population: **62.4 million**
Area (land): **113,568 sq. mi.**

MACHINES AND MASTERPIECES

Born in 1452, artist, engineer, inventor, and all-around brainiac Leonardo Da Vinci is one of Italy's most celebrated figures. Famous for his masterpiece paintings, such as the *Mona Lisa*, he was a major player in the Renaissance. This was a period of intense artistic and scientific activity in Italy (and beyond) between the 1300s and 1600s.

The world's largest pizza was produced in Rome in 2012. It measured 131 feet across and used almost 20,000 lb. of cheese.

FAMOUS ITALIAN RENAISSANCE ARTISTS

Michelangelo *(1475–1564)*
Raphael *(1483–1520)*
Botticelli *(1445–1510)*
Titian *(1490–1576)*
Leonardo da Vinci *(1452–1519)*

A CITY ON WATER

In Venice, the transportation system is a little different from the norm. The city is built on a network of islands, so instead of using roads, people travel on canals. Motorboats called *vaporetti* and long black rowboats called gondolas get people where they need to go. Venice was once one of the richest and most powerful cities in Europe, and many of its canals are lined with grand, historic palaces.

THEATER IN THE ROUND

Built in the first century CE, the Roman Colosseum is the largest amphitheater (circular stone arena) in the world. It once staged large, bloodthirsty public events—including gladiator fights, wild animal battles, and naval reenactments—and could host up to 80,000 people.

Italy has more UNESCO World Heritage sites than any other country.

PRESERVED IN ASH

In 79 CE, the volcano Mount Vesuvius erupted violently. It buried the nearby Roman city of Pompeii in tons of ash, killing its inhabitants but preserving the buildings. Over the past few hundred years, the city has been excavated, giving a fascinating insight into how ordinary Romans lived.

The Italian island of Sicily boasts Europe's highest active volcano, Mount Etna.

SAN MARINO

Tucked away in the hills of eastern Italy, the microstate of San Marino claims to be the world's oldest republic. It's built along the ridge of the 2,425-foot-high Mount Titano, where castles and fortress walls lead up to panoramic views. Traveling to and from Italy to San Marino is easy, as there are no borders dividing the two nations.

KEY FACTS

Capital: **San Marino city**
Official Language: **Italian**
Currency: **Euro**
Population: **399,600**
Area (land): **8,805 sq. mi.**

If you want to get your passport stamped in San Marino, it will cost you €5.

MOUNTAINOUS MICROSTATE

Founded in the 300s CE, San Marino is entirely mountainous. The capital occupies the highest point, where medieval stone walls surround three ancient stone castles—these are depicted on the San Marino flag and coat of arms. The highest castle is Rocca Cesta, home to a museum of ancient weapons.

San Marino is completely surrounded by Italy. This makes it an enclave—a country that sits within another country. The only other enclaves are Vatican City and Lesotho.

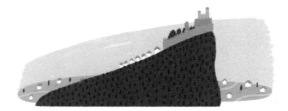

VATICAN CITY

The world's smallest country is situated right in the center of Rome, Italy's capital city. The Vatican City is ruled by the pope—the leader of the Catholic Church—and is home to many grand religious buildings and countless artistic masterpieces. There's a huge amount of culture and history crammed into this tiny territory.

KEY FACTS

Official Language: **Italian**
Currency: **Euro**
Population: **1,000**
Area (land): **0.17 sq. mi.**

At any given time, most of the Vatican's citizens are abroad, representing the church in nations around the world.

PACK A PUNCH

The pope and his predecessors have been protected by a team of soldiers from Switzerland called the Swiss Guard for over 500 years. Adorned in colorful striped uniforms, they form the smallest army in the world. Don't be fooled by their cheery outfits—these soldiers are highly trained.

When visiting the 15th-century Sistine Chapel, it's important to look up—the ornate ceiling, painted by artist Michelangelo, depicts dense biblical scenes and is regarded as a masterpiece.

SPAIN

Just a stone's throw from North Africa in Europe's southwest, Spain is a vibrant mixture of cultures that have been carried all across the globe. Divided into 17 regions, the country is renowned for its colorful architecture, long beaches, fiestas, flamenco, and the small sharing plates of food known as *tapas*.

KEY FACTS

Capital: **Madrid**
Official Language: **Spanish**
Currency: **Euro**
Population: **50 million**
Area (land): **192,657 sq. mi.**

AMAZING ARCHITECTURE

Antoni Gaudí (1852–1926) was a Spanish architect whose influence can be seen all over Barcelona, Spain's second-largest city. His most famous creation is the still unfinished church known as the *Basílica de la Sagrada Família*. With 18 curving towers, a mass of twisting statues, and colorful stained glass windows, there's no other building quite like it.

TYPICAL TAPAS DISHES

Patatas bravas—*fried potato cubes in spicy tomato sauce*

Albondigas—*meatballs*

Calamares—*battered squid*

Pinchos morunos —*meat skewers*

Tortilla de patatas —*potato omelette*

FLAMENCO FEVER

Flamenco is an important part of Spanish culture. It's a performance that's made up of four elements: singing, dancing, acoustic guitar, and percussion—usually provided by hand clapping, foot stomping, and cheering. The fastest flamenco dance ever recorded was performed by Rosario Varela in 2009, who managed to stamp out 1,274 foot taps in just one minute.

SOCCER FAVORITES

Spain is home to two of the world's best-supported teams:

Barcelona
Established 1899
Stadium capacity 99,354

Real Madrid
Established 1902
Stadium capacity 81,044.

MOORISH MARVELS

Situated overlooking the city of Grenada, the Alhambra is a grand complex famous for its intricate Moorish designs of patterned tiling and fountain-filled gardens. Originally constructed as a fortress in 889 by the Islamic Moors of North Africa, it was later converted into a palace. Today it is a fantastic mix of different styles.

Every year in the town of Buñol in eastern Spain, thousands of people take part in *La Tomatina*, the biggest food fight on the planet. Crowds take to the streets to launch over 100 tons of tomatoes at each other.

PORTUGAL

Standing alongside the Atlantic Ocean, Portugal is Europe's westernmost country. With most of its population living on the coast, the nation is well equipped with beaches and laid-back portside cities. The country has a long history of ocean exploration, and the Portuguese navy is one of the oldest in the world.

KEY FACTS

Capital: **Lisbon**

Official Language: **Portuguese**

Currency: **Euro**

Population: **10.3 million**

Area (land): **35,317 sq. mi.**

THE GREAT NAVIGATORS

1488
Bartolomeu Dias
First European to sail around southern tip of Africa.

1498
Vasco da Gama
First person to sail from Europe to India.

1500
Pedro Álvares Cabral
First European to reach Brazil.

1522
Ferdinand Magellan
Led first round-the-world voyage.

The oldest bookstore in the world, Livraria Bertrand, is located in Lisbon, and has been in business for almost 300 years.

SAILING THE SEAS

The first European to cross the Pacific Ocean and give it its name (meaning "peaceful sea") was the Portuguese explorer Ferdinand Magellan. In 1522, his ship became the first to circumnavigate (sail all the way around) the world, although he died before the ship returned to Portugal.

SWELL SURFING

The conditions along Portugal's Atlantic coastline are ideal for year-round surfing. The seas here produce some big waves. In fact, the records for the biggest waves surfed by both a man and a woman were set off Portugal's coast.

TRADITIONAL TILES

Decorative painted tiles known as *azulejos* are a popular art form in Portugal. You'll see them everywhere—making up murals and mosaics on the walls of churches, metro stations, cafés, shops, and houses. Traditional tiles depict scenes in a blue and white glaze, but today there are many different colors and styles.

Cristiano Ronaldo, one of the world's best and most famous soccer players, is from the Portuguese island of Madeira in the Atlantic Ocean.

GREECE

Greece is Europe's sunniest country—averaging over 250 sunny days a year—and perhaps its most influential. Its ancient civilization came up with mythologies, philosophies, artistic styles, sporting competitions, and political systems that spread around the whole world.

KEY FACTS

Capital: **Athens**
Official Language: **Greek**
Currency: **Euro**
Population: **10.6 million**
Area (land): **50,443 sq. mi.**

MYTHS AND LEGENDS

Greek mythology is still a huge part of popular culture today. Stories of heroes and gods, first written down in epic poems, have been retold through the generations. These tales center on the soap-opera-like lives of a group of gods living on Greece's highest mountain, Mount Olympus.

ICONIC ARCHITECTURE

There are countless ancient ruins spread across Greece's mainland and islands. The most visited is the 2,500-year-old Parthenon, a temple built on a hill known as the Acropolis in central Athens. Built to honor the goddess Athena, the Parthenon is famous for its symmetrical columns and intricate carvings.

GREEK GODS AND GODDESSES

Zeus *the sky*
(and all the other gods)

Hera *women and family*

Poseidon *the Sea*

Athena *wisdom*

Ares *war*

Demeter *agriculture*

Hephaestus *craftsmanship and volcanoes*

Artemis *hunting*

Apollo *music and the arts*

Aphrodite *love*

Hades *the dead*

Hermes *travel and communication (messenger of the gods)*

The Olympic Games were a Greek sporting competition held every four years between 776 BCE and 393 CE in honor of Zeus. In 1896 they were revived (with a few more sports added) as the event that we know today.

ISLAND DIVERSITY

Greece's 6,000-plus islands are very popular with tourists. On the largest, Crete, are the ruins of Greece's oldest city, first settled around 7000 BCE. Here the twisting passageways of the palace of Knossos gave rise to the legend of the labyrinth—and the half-human, half-bull minotaur that lurked at its center.

CYPRUS

KEY FACTS

Capital: **Nicosia**

Official Language: **Greek**

Currency: **Euro**

Population: **1.2 million**

Area (land): **3,568 sq. mi.**

Set in the far eastern corner of the Mediterranean Sea, the island of Cyprus is divided into two halves: the Turkish-governed north and the Greek-operated south, and there are ongoing tensions between the two communities. Cyprus is known for its sunny climate, resorts, long stretches of sand, and fabulous food.

DIVINE ORIGINS

Cyprus was formed as a result of volcanic eruptions millions of years ago. In Greek mythology, the island was the birthplace of the goddess Aphrodite. An imposing sea stack known as Aphrodite's Rock, near the city of Paphos, supposedly marks the spot where the goddess first rose out of the foamy water.

The popular—and very squeaky when grilled—cheese known as halloumi can only officially be referred to as such if it's produced in Cyprus. Halloumi is a combination of goat's and sheep's cheese.

MALTA

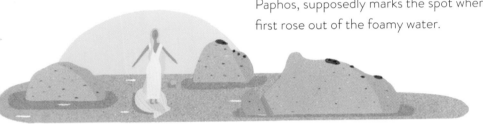

The small nation of Malta is made up of just three islands—Malta, Gozo, and Comino—that sit beneath Italy. Ownership of Malta has been disputed over the centuries, but it gained independence in 1964. It's famous for its fortresses, rugged coastlines, diving spots, and *luzzu*—colorful fishing boats with "lucky" eyes painted on their sides.

KEY FACTS

Capital: **Valletta**

Official Language: **Maltese**

Currency: **Euro**

Population: **457,267**

Area (land): **122 sq. mi.**

ANCIENT FINDS

Malta is home to some of the oldest religious sites in the world. The imposing stone temples of Ħaġar Qim and Mnajdra are relics of the past that date back over 5,000 years. They sit atop a hill overlooking the sea on the main island's southwest coast. Both have been named UNESCO World Heritage sites.

Malta is one of the most densely populated countries in Europe, but only two of its islands are inhabited. The smallest, Comino, is a nature reserve.

"Bonġu"
*"Good Morning"
in Maltese*

SLOVENIA

Slovenia is keen to go green. Named the world's first "green nation" by the European environmental organization Green Destinations, it has passed numerous laws designed to protect its wealth of outdoor attractions. These include mountains, forests, and lakes, which sit alongside neatly laid-out cities and rugged castles.

LUCKY STEPS

The most famous of Slovenia's many lakes is the postcard-perfect Lake Bled, which has an island right at its center. If you were to take a rowboat across, you'd find a small church with a very tall, ancient staircase leading up to it. It's a popular spot for weddings, with local tradition stating that a husband must carry his new bride up all 99 steps to guarantee good luck for their married life.

KEY FACTS

Capital: **Ljubljana**
Official Language: **Slovenian**
Currency: **Euro**
Population: **2.1 million**
Area (land): **7,780 sq. mi.**

Slovenia is the only country in the European Union that has given the honeybee protected status.

CROATIA

Stretched out along the Adriatic Sea, crescent-shaped Croatia offers a coastline dotted with hundreds of islands, many of them popular with tourists who come for the sun, sailing, and seafood. Inland, waterfalls tumble down mountains into dark forests. Croatia has been at peace since 1995.

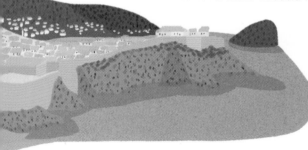

ANCIENT WALLS

Once a powerful trading state, the coastal city of Dubrovnik was founded in the 600s. The Old Town is surrounded by 6.5-foot-thick stone walls that tower over the landscape. Constructed in the 1300s, the sturdy walls preserved the city from attack. Today visitors can take a stroll along the walls from tower to tower, gazing out over the city's rooftops and beyond to the sea.

The iconic black-and-white spotted Dalmatian dog is native to Croatia— its name comes from the country's Dalmatian Coast.

KEY FACTS

Capital: **Zagreb**
Official Language: **Croatian**
Currency: **Croatian kuna**
Population: **4.2 million**
Area (land): **21,612 sq. mi.**

Croatia's national animal is the pine marten.

BOSNIA AND HERZEGOVINA

The country suffered greatly in the Bosnian War of 1992–95, as its people tried to break free of Yugoslavia—the former country made up of what is now Bosnia & Herzegovina, Croatia, Kosovo, Montenegro, North Macedonia, and Serbia. Today it's a peaceful place of rivers and lakes, mosques, markets, and coffee shops.

KEY FACTS

Capital: **Sarajevo**

Official Languages:
Bosnian, Serbian, Croatian

Currency: **Bosnian Mark**

Population: **3.8 million**

Area (land): **19,763 sq. mi.**

ICONIC BRIDGE

The Stari Most ("Old Bridge") in the city of Mostar was originally built in the mid-1500s. Sadly, the arched construction was destroyed in 1993 during the war. But with the help of international donations, it has since been rebuilt, using building techniques similar to those of the 16th century. In the summer, a competition is held when daredevil divers plunge the 65 feet from the top of the bridge down into the icy Neretva River below.

Locals speak three official languages: Bosnian, Serbian, and Croatian. Each is a variant of the same language.

SERBIA

Serbia has had a troubled history, including periods of communism and conflict with neighboring nations. Today it is a country of diverse Slavic cultures. With ancient thermal spas, ski resorts, and thriving cities, Serbia ties ancient traditions with modern living.

KEY FACTS

Capital: **Belgrade**

Official Language: **Serbian**

Currency: **Serbian dinar**

Population: **7 million**

Area (land): **29,913 sq. mi.**

ELECTRIC INVENTIONS

We can thank Serbian-American inventor, engineer, and all-around futuristic thinker Nikola Tesla (1856–1943) for many of the electronic gizmos of the modern world. He was a pioneer of wireless electricity, which eventually led to such modern technology as WiFi, drones, and smartphones. Thousands of his invention-filled journals, as well as photos, plans, and sketches, can be seen at the Nikola Tesla Museum in Belgrade.

Serbia is speckled with over 200 ornate medieval Orthodox monasteries, typified by domed roofs, curved archways, and colorful wall paintings.

Belgrade is believed to be one of the oldest cities in Europe, having been first inhabited around 5700 BCE.

MONTENEGRO

With a name that translates as "Black Mountain," Montenegro is one of the world's newest nations, only gaining its independence in 2006. Its small confines are packed with dense, dark forests, as well as snow-capped mountains in the north and sun-drenched old towns and bays in the south.

MYSTERIOUS MONASTERY

Set into a near-vertical cliff face in a way that seems to defy gravity, the Ostrog Monastery has been puzzling visitors for hundreds of years. It was constructed in the 1600s in two large caves, although no one is entirely sure how. That it stays where it is rather than falling to the valley floor seems almost miraculous.

The Montenegran city of Stari Bar is home to what is believed to be one of the most ancient olive trees in the world, at around 2,000 years old.

KEY FACTS

Capital: **Podgorica**

Official Language: **Montenegrin**

Currency: **Euro**

Population: **609,859**

Area (land): **5,194 sq. mi.**

"Zdravo"
(pronounced "zdrah-voh")
"Hello" and "Goodbye"
in Montenegrin.

KOSOVO

Since declaring its independence in 2008, Kosovo has been recognized by the majority of the world as Europe's newest country. Following the destructive Kosovo War of 1998, the small nation is now focused on its future. It's home to many wonders, from craggy canyons and magnificent mosques to bustling bazaars and a sanctuary for bears.

GOING UNDERGROUND

One of Europe's longest canyons—and one of Kosovo's most spectacular sights—the Rugova Canyon carves its way through the mountains near the border with Montenegro. It's scattered with waterfalls, springs, and hundreds of stalactite-filled caves, some of which have yet to be fully explored.

KEY FACTS

Capital: **Pristina**

Official Languages: **Albanian, Serbian**

Currency: **Euro**

Population: **1.9 million**

Area (land): **4,203 sq. mi.**

Kosovo has Europe's youngest population—over half of its people are under the age of 25.

ALBANIA

Albania is a unique country with a unique way of communicating—its language isn't closely related to any other language. It spent much of the 20th century under strict communist rule and was isolated from the rest of the world. But it has now emerged into the international spotlight and is welcoming visitors to its many natural attractions.

KEY FACTS

Capital: **Tirana**
Official Language: **Albanian**
Currency: **Albanian Lek**
Population: **3 million**
Area (land): **10,578 sq. mi.**

XHIRO HOURS

In towns and cities across Albania, people make a point of taking a leisurely stroll, known as a *xhiro*, in the early evening. It's seen as a time to wind down after a day's work and catch up with friends.

WONDROUS WILDLIFE

Albania is a biodiversity hotspot. Its mountain-fringed forests and long beaches are home to:
brown bears • Eurasian lynx • Eurasian otters • golden eagles (the country's national animal) • greater flamingos • gray wolves • jackals • loggerhead turtles.

NORTH MACEDONIA

Landlocked North Macedonia is extremely mountainous, with peaks covering 80 percent of the country. Its culture (and cuisine) is a distinctive combination of Mediterranean and Turkish influences, the latter being the result of the 500 years it spent as part of the Ottoman Empire (which was centered on Turkey).

KEY FACTS

Capital: **Skopje**
Official Language: **Macedonian**
Currency: **Macedonian Denar**
Population: **2.1 million**
Area (land): **9,820 sq. mi.**

ANCIENT OHRID

The historic city of Ohrid is packed full of well-preserved historic architecture: grand churches, monasteries, an ancient Greek theater, and—overlooking it all—an imposing medieval castle. The city sits on the shores of sparkling, sprawling Lake Ohrid, one of Europe's deepest and oldest lakes. It's believed to have formed over five million years ago.

Twice a year, Macedonians hold a tree-planting day across the nation, with people helping restore the damage caused by forest wildfires in 2006 and 2007.

BULGARIA

Bulgaria first came into being as the Bulgarian Empire in 681 CE and went on to dominate the region for the next few hundred years. It was eventually taken over by the Ottoman Empire and spent much of the 20th century as part of the communist world. Modern Bulgaria offers a diverse landscape of ski slopes, black sand beaches, and everything in between.

KEY FACTS

Capital: **Sofia**
Official Language: **Bulgarian**
Currency: **Bulgarian Lev**
Population: **6.9 million**
Area (land): **41,888 sq. mi.**

OLD GOLD

Bulgaria is the proud owner of the world's oldest gold treasure. Found in the 1970s in a necropolis (cemetery) in the city of Varna, the jewelry dates back over 6,000 years. It once belonged to warriors who were buried wearing their finest and most precious possessions. Since then, over 3,000 pieces of intricately worked gold have been found here.

In northern Bulgaria, the Belogradchik Rocks are a collection of oddly shaped formations. From "the mushrooms" and "the cuckoo" to "the horseman," each outcrop has been given a name and a legend to describe its creation.

SUPER SCRIPT

In the 800s CE, the Bulgarian leader Simeon the Great ordered the creation of a new, written alphabet. The result, the Cyrillic script, is now used by over 250 million people in many countries across eastern Europe and Asia, including Bulgaria, Ukraine, and Russia.

SWEET SMELL OF SUCCESS

Bulgaria is the world's leading provider of rose oil, which is widely used in the perfume industry. An area known, appropriately enough, as Rose Valley, is planted with millions and million of blooms—which is just as well, because it takes roughly 250,000 rose petals to make just 0.17 ounces of rose oil. Most roses are still harvested in the traditional way, by hand—watch out for the thorns!

Bulgaria's national animal is the lion.

ROMANIA

Romania is a land of imposing mountains, deep forests, and winding rivers, dotted with traditional villages. Legends and myths seem to seep from the ground—with none more potent than that of the world's most famous vampire, Count Dracula, and his brooding, medieval home, Transylvania.

KEY FACTS

Capital: **Bucharest**
Official Language: **Romanian**
Currency: **Romanian leu**
Population: **21.3 million**
Area (land): **88,761 sq. mi.**

There are around 6,000 wild bears in Romania—more than any other country in Europe.

VAMPIRIC INSPIRATION

Perched precariously on a peak, the turrets and towers of Bran Castle welcome you (spookily) to Transylvania. The castle is believed to have been the inspiration for Count Dracula's castle in Bram Stoker's 1897 novel. The vampire shares his name with a real-life 15th-century Romanian figure—Vlad Dracula, also known as "Vlad the Impaler." Vlad got his nickname from skewering up to 80,000 of his enemies on long spikes.

In 2013, a small village near Bucharest unfurled the world's largest flag, measuring 850,000 sq. ft. An enormous version of the Romanian national flag, it was laid on the ground and held in place by sandbags.

BIGGEST BUILDING

The award for the largest building in Europe—as well as being the world's heaviest—goes to Bucharest's Palace of Parliament. The enormous structure has over 3,000 rooms, and beneath it is a parking garage that can hold 20,000 cars. It weighs an estimated 770,000 tons.

At the 1976 Olympics, the Romanian gymnast Nadia Comăneci became the first competitor to be awarded a perfect "10" by the judges.

ROCK STAR

In 2004, a giant rock sculpture was unveiled in Romania on the banks of the Danube River. Depicting Decebalus, the ancient king of Dacia (an area more or less corresponding to modern-day Romania and Moldova), it's the tallest rock sculpture in Europe, at 180 feet high.

POLAND

Poland has a busy past. Its borders have moved countless times, and for 123 years, from 1795 to 1918, Poland as we know it didn't even exist. Today it's a thriving land that is proud of its national treasures—from grand churches and modern cities to its rich cuisine celebrated during Christmastime feasts.

KEY FACTS

Capital: **Warsaw**
Official Language: **Polish**
Currency: **Polish Złoty**
Population: **38.2 million**
Area (land): **117,474 sq. mi.**

POLISH PIONEER

Born in 1867 in Warsaw, Marie Sklodowska Curie was a groundbreaking Polish scientist. The prejudices of her day meant that as a young woman in Poland, she was forced to study in secret. She later moved to France, where she became the first person to win two Nobel prizes. Her discovery of two elements—radium and polonium—and her work on radioactivity make her a key figure in the history of modern science.

FIERY LEGEND

Krakow, Poland's second-largest city, boasts numerous intriguing sights, including *Rynek Główny* ("Old Square"), Europe's largest medieval town square. Overlooking the old town is Wawel, a gigantic castle that was supposedly once the home of Smok, a dragon that terrorized the locals until it was slain by a prince named Krakus, after whom the city was then named.

TRADITIONAL POLISH DISHES

Bigos—*stew with chopped sausage and sauerkraut*

Gołąbki—*cabbage roll*

Kielbasa—*meat sausage*

Kotlet schabowy —*breaded pork cutlet*

Zupa ogórkowa —*sour cucumber soup*

Poland's Krzywy region is home to the "Crooked Forest," which is filled with hundreds of strange trees that have grown into a "C" shape—but nobody knows exactly how or why.

DEVASTATING HISTORY

Set up during the German occupation of Poland, Auschwitz was the largest Nazi concentration and extermination camp of World War II. Over 1.3 million people were sent here—most of them Jews—of which 1.1 million were killed. As one of the most harrowing reminders of the atrocities conducted by the Nazis, Auschwitz is now a museum and a memorial to those who lost their lives.

CZECH REPUBLIC (CZECHIA)

Formerly the single nation of Czechoslovakia, the Czech Republic and Slovakia peacefully parted ways in 1993. Indeed, the split was conducted so smoothly that it became known as the "Velvet Revolution." The Czech Republic is now known for its fairy-tale castles, historical cities, picturesque towns, and (great) love of beer.

KEY FACTS

Capital: **Prague**
Official Language: **Czech**
Currency: **Czech Koruna**
Population: **10.7 million**
Area (land): **29,825 sq. mi.**

The people of the Czech Republic consume more beer per person than any other nation on Earth.

TIME WILL TELL

The astronomical clock on Prague's Old Town Hall was installed in 1410. Since then, it's been taken apart, destroyed, and pieced back together again numerous times, but it keeps on ticking. Today it's the oldest clock in the world still in use. As well as telling the time, it also represents the positions of the Sun and Moon and the passing of the Zodiac signs, and it has mechanical figures that pop out to mark the hours.

SLOVAKIA

Though officially one of Europe's newer nations, this mountainous land has been around for a long time. It was under Hungarian rule for almost a thousand years, and it was briefly joined to the Czech Republic as Czechoslovakia. Slovakia has stood alone since 1993.

KEY FACTS

Capital: **Bratislava**
Official Language: **Slovak**
Currency: **Euro**
Population: **5.4 million**
Area (land): **18,933 sq. mi.**

Sitting next to both Austria and Hungary, Slovakia's capital, Bratislava, is the only capital city in the world that borders two other countries.

COOL CAVES

Slovakia may be small, but there are believed to be more caves here per person than in any other country on Earth. Over 6,000 subterranean caverns hide a range of secret attractions, from giant bat colonies to some of the planet's tallest stalagmites and stalactites. Perhaps the most fascinating is Dobšinská, Europe's largest ice cave, where the ice can grow up to 80 feet thick.

HUNGARY

With the Danube River winding its way down the middle of the country, Hungary is a peaceful place known for its grand old buildings, warming thermal baths, and comforting national dish—the hearty stew known as goulash. The people here call themselves Magyars, which is also the name of the language.

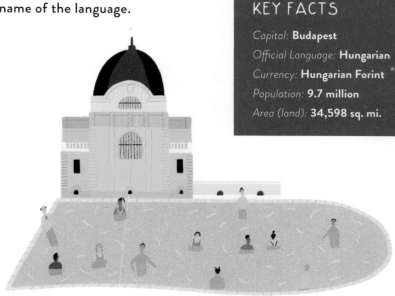

KEY FACTS

Capital: **Budapest**
Official Language: **Hungarian**
Currency: **Hungarian Forint**
Population: **9.7 million**
Area (land): **34,598 sq. mi.**

THERMAL HOT SPOTS

There are a whopping 1,500 hot springs and around 450 spas in Hungary. The country's love of bathing dates back to Roman times, and was enthusiastically continued in the form of the Turkish bath when Hungary was part of the Ottoman Empire (1541–1699). Today locals flock to public bathing spots, such as Széchenyi Thermal Bath in the capital and Lake Hévíz in the western part of the country, where spring water bubbles from the ground at over 158°F.

Current record for solving a Rubik's Cube:
3.47 seconds by Chinese puzzler Yusheng Du.

PUZZLE CRAZY

One of the world's most popular (and fiendishly difficult) puzzles is Hungarian. The Rubik's Cube—the plastic colored cube that can be twisted into almost any combination, but solved using just one—was invented by and named after the Hungarian professor Ernő Rubik in 1974.

The language spoken in Hungary is more closely related to Finnish than to the languages of its neighbors.

A TALE OF TWO CITIES

The Danube River runs through the middle of Hungary's capital, Budapest, dividing it in two. Once upon a time, the two halves were separate cities—Buda in the west and Pest in the east—which were unified in 1873. Both have their fair share of grand buildings, with Buda Castle atop a hill in the west and the lengthy Hungarian Parliament Building in the east.

UKRAINE

Ukraine is the largest country located entirely in Europe. Much of its vast area is given over to the growing of wheat and other grains, from which it gets its nickname the "Breadbasket of Europe." But there's room for plenty more, including the Carpathian Mountains, mineral springs, and ancient cities.

KEY FACTS

Capital: **Kyiv**
Official Language: **Ukrainian**
Currency: **Ukrainian Hryvnia**
Population: **43.9 million**
Area (land): **223,681 sq. mi.**

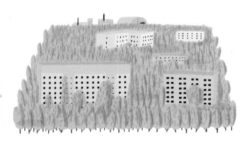

NUCLEAR ACCIDENT

In 1986, the worst nuclear accident in history took place at a nuclear power plant in Chernobyl. Following an explosion, deadly radioactive materials were released into the air and were soon spread across Europe by the wind. The residents of the nearby town of Pripyat fled, never to return. Though some wildlife has since thrived there, it's estimated that Chernobyl may be inhospitable for humans for up to 20,000 years to come.

SUNNY DISPOSITION

Ukraine is one of the largest producers of sunflowers in the world. The sunflower is the national flower, and its image is seen throughout the country on everything from furniture to clothes.

MOLDOVA

Only a small number of intrepid tourists make it to landlocked Moldova each year, but few come away disappointed. It boasts a beautiful landscape of vineyards, lavender fields, ancient ruins, and rivers—although not the Moldova River itself (after which it's named), which is now part of Romania.

KEY FACTS

Capital: **Chişinău**
Official Languages:
Romanian/Moldovan
Currency: **Moldovan Leu**
Population: **3.3 million**
Area (land): **12,699 sq. mi.**

CAVE MONASTERY

Tucked away in a wild and remote part of the country is the fascinating historical complex of Orheiul Vechi, parts of which date back over 2,000 years. The highlight is the cave monastery, made up of chapels and churches cut directly into limestone cliffs around 800 years ago.

The world's largest wine collection is located in the Moldovan town of Milestii Mici. It contains an estimated two million bottles.

BELARUS

Belarus's resilient capital, Minsk, has been around for ten centuries, during which it's been destroyed and rebuilt eight times. Outside its ever-changing confines, almost half the country is carpeted in lush forest containing age-old castles, thousands of rivers and lakes, and villages where traditional ways of life are still practiced.

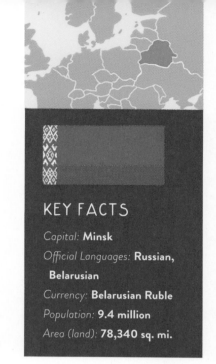

KEY FACTS

Capital: **Minsk**

Official Languages: **Russian, Belarusian**

Currency: **Belarusian Ruble**

Population: **9.4 million**

Area (land): **78,340 sq. mi.**

ANCIENT FOREST

The immense Białowieża Forest is one of the last remaining stretches of the primeval forest that once covered much of northern Europe. It's home to an abundance of wildlife, including European bison, as well as ancient trees.

BELARUSIAN BANYAS

The traditional bathing method in bathhouses, called *banyas*, involves steaming yourself in a sauna, then submerging yourself in ice-cold water, after which you're slapped with birch twigs. It's very good for the skin—apparently.

In 1991, Belarus, Russia, and Ukraine met in Białowieża Forest to sign an agreement that dissolved the Soviet Union.

LITHUANIA

Welcome to the center of Europe, geographically speaking. In 1989, a group of scientists determined that the small village of Purnuškės marked the exact middle of the continent. Lithuania has a breezy Baltic coastline, huge freshwater lakes, wildlife-filled forests, large expanses of flat farmland, and plenty of picturesque villages.

KEY FACTS

Capital: **Vilnius**

Official Language: **Lithuanian**

Currency: **Euro**

Population: **2.7 million**

Area (land): **24,201 sq. mi.**

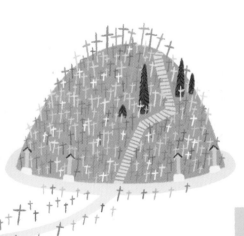

CRUCIFIX HILL

One of the country's top attractions, the Kryžių Kalnas ("Hill of Crosses") emerged as a sign of defiance when the country was under the control of the Soviet Union from 1944 to 1990. Citizens began planting wooden crosses on the hill—the site of an ancient burial ground—as a way of showing their national identity. Today there are over 200,000 crosses of all kinds of shapes, sizes, and styles.

Basketball is the most popular sport in Lithuania; they have won three bronze Olympic medals.

Labas rytas!
"Good morning!" in Lithuanian

LATVIA

Latvia is a watery world. Its west coast is lapped by the icy Baltic Sea, while the interior contains some 12,000 rivers and 3,000 lakes. On land, the country is known for its beautiful capital, Riga—the so-called "Paris of the North"— and its many traditional festivals and celebrations.

KEY FACTS

Capital: **Riga**
Official Language: **Latvian**
Currency: **Euro**
Population: **1.8 million**
Area (land): **24,938 sq. mi.**

Europe's largest market is housed in five converted airship hangars in the center of Riga.

AMBER FINDS

Fragments of amber—ancient, fossilized tree sap—regularly wash up on Latvia's coastline, where they're turned into jewelry and decorations. Some pieces of amber are tens of millions of years old.

WIDE WONDER

Latvia is home to Europe's widest (if not tallest) waterfall, the Venta Rapid. It's 817 feet wide— but just 6.5 feet high.

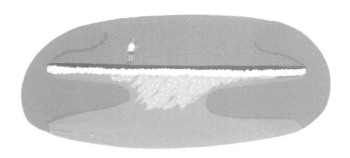

ESTONIA

Roughly the same size as Switzerland, Estonia is as full of trees as its central European equivalent is of mountains. Forests cover half of the land, which makes it a fairly quiet place. Most years, tourists outnumber residents! Estonia is known for its quirky sports and long, rocky coast dotted with islands.

KEY FACTS

Capital: **Tallinn**
Official Language: **Estonian**
Currency: **Euro**
Population: **1.2 million**
Area (land): **16,366 sq. mi.**

2,355
Number of islands off Estonia's Baltic coast.

METEORITE MAGIC

Estonia has suffered the most meteorite impacts of any country. The last one landed in Kaali on the island of Saaremaa around 7,500 years ago. The impact was huge—the equivalent of a nuclear bomb—and left behind a water-filled crater.

IT'S ELECTRIC

St. Olaf's Church in the center of Tallinn has been struck by lightning at least 10 times since its construction in the 1100s. It's burned to the ground three times but has been rebuilt every time.

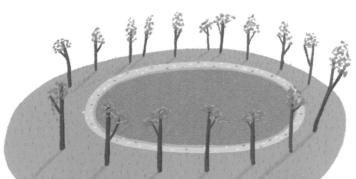

RUSSIA

Countries don't come any bigger than Russia. More than twice as large as the United States, it stretches across 11 time zones and two continents. As you'd expect, it's a place of endless variety, with packed cities, epic empty landscapes of rolling plains called steppes, and frozen snowy forests where wildlife reigns supreme.

LAKE DISTRICT

Russia has around 100,000 rivers, as well as the two largest lakes in Europe, Ladoga and Onega. But even these are dwarfed by Lake Baikal on the Asian side. The world's largest freshwater lake, and the deepest lake of any kind, it contains around 20 percent of all the world's nonfrozen freshwater.

SUPER TRAINS

Perhaps unsurprisingly, the world's largest country is the location of the world's longest passenger railroad service. Trains run from the capital, Moscow, to the port of Vladivostok on the country's eastern coast, a distance of 5,753 miles—or almost a quarter of the way around the planet. It takes seven days to complete the whole journey.

Europe's highest mountain is Russia's Mount Elbrus (18,510 ft.).

GIANT DOMES

The country is famous for its distinctive architecture. Many of its buildings are topped with round, onion-shaped domes painted in bright colors. One of the country's most visited sites, the domes of St. Basil's Cathedral in Moscow, have supposedly been arranged to resemble the shape of a bonfire.

WILDLIFE

Arctic foxes • Baikal seals • bearded vultures • brown bears • gray wolves • imperial eagles • lynx • polar bears • sable • Siberian tigers • snow leopards • walruses • wolverines

THE TSAR

From 1547 to 1917, Russia was ruled by a powerful figure known as a tsar. The first was Ivan IV, also known as Ivan the Terrible because of the cruelty of his reign. The last was Nicholas II, who was overthrown in World War I.

The last two tsars commissioned the Russian jeweler Peter Carl Fabergé to create elaborate Easter eggs made of gold and precious stones. Each of the remaining eggs are worth millions of dollars.

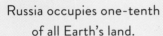

Russia occupies one-tenth of all Earth's land.

ONE INSIDE THE OTHER

Matryoshkas (also known as Russian dolls or nesting dolls) are sets of wooden carvings that fit one inside the other, and they are one of the country's most popular souvenirs. First created in 1890, the figures typically depict a woman in traditional Russian dress. However, there are many different types, in the shape of animals, politicians, pop stars, and more.

ST. PETERSBURG

The world's northernmost big city, St. Petersburg was founded by the tsar Peter the Great in 1703. He had several large and lavish buildings erected, including the Winter Palace, which became the official residence of the tsar. Today it houses the Hermitage Museum, one of the world's largest museums.

The Ural Mountains, which run north to south through the middle of Russia, are usually regarded as marking the boundary between Europe and Asia.

FEMALE RULERS

Uniquely among the great powers of the time, Russia was ruled by several women in the 1700s, including Catherine I (1725–27), Anna Ioannovna (1730–40), Anna Leopoldovna (1740–41), and Elizabeth (1741–62). The final ruler in this line was Empress Catherine II (1762–96), also known as Catherine the Great, who oversaw a great flourishing of arts and science.

The village of Oymyakon is the coldest permanently inhabited place on Earth, where temperatures in winter can drop below −49°F.

FINLAND

Finland is one of the most northern countries in the world. This mainly flat land is peppered with lakes, earning it the nickname "land of a thousand lakes"—though there are in fact 187,888 of them, as well as 178,947 islands. It is also the most densely forested country in Europe, being 70 percent covered in thick, wild woods.

KEY FACTS

Capital: **Helsinki**

Official Languages: **Finnish, Swedish**

Currency: **Euro**

Population: **5.6 million**

Area (land): **117,304 sq. mi.**

The author Tove Jansson was born in Helsinki in 1914. Her most famous creations were the Moomins, a family of hippopotamus-like trolls.

POLAR NIGHTS

Winter is the longest season in Finland—in the northern regions of Lapland it lasts for six freezing months, from mid-October to the end of April. Some northern parts of Finland experience 24-hour-long polar nights (called *kaamos* in Finnish). The Sami village of Utsjoki doesn't receive any daylight for almost two months of the year. In contrast, much of Finland receives almost 24 hours of sunlight each day in the summer.

Spring and autumn are the best times to visit Finland if you want to see the spectacular *aurora borealis*, or northern lights, dance across the night sky.

Many Finns have a sauna in their home. They are traditionally constructed from birch wood.

NATURAL WONDERS

Much of Finland's forests, lakes, and hills are contained within 40 national parks. If you're lucky, you may spot creatures such as elk, gray wolves, wolverines, lynx, and brown bears roaming a Finnish forest. Its lake district is also home to the endangered Saimaa ringed seal—one of just three species of lake seals in the world.

DENMARK

The most southerly Scandinavian country, Denmark is situated between the Baltic and North seas. It consists of the Jutland peninsula—an area that sticks out from the top of Germany—and roughly 400 islands, about 300 of which are uninhabited. This lively yet relaxed nation is regularly listed as one of the happiest countries in the world.

KEY FACTS

Capital: **Copenhagen**
Official Language: **Danish**
Currency: **Danish Krone**
Population: **5.9 million**
Area (land): **16,384 sq. mi.**

Hygge
(pronounced "hooga")
is the feeling of coziness
and contentment that is
at the heart of Danish life.

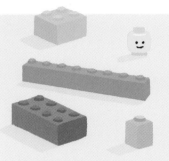

PLAYING WELL

One of Denmark's most famous exports is LEGO ®. These simple plastic building blocks were invented by Ole Kirk Christiansen in 1949. He came up with the now world-famous brand by taking the first two letters from the Danish words *"Leg godt,"* which means "play well."

The Danes certainly know how to do that. Founded in 1583, the world's oldest amusement park is the Dyrehavsbakken, just outside Copenhagen. You don't have to go far to find the second-oldest theme park: Tivoli Gardens in the city center opened its gates in 1843 and still draws over four million visitors a year.

COMFORTING CUISINE

Danish food is hearty and comforting. For a tasty lunchtime snack, try a smorrebrod, a slice of rye bread topped with endless combinations of meat, cured fish, cheese, and pickles. Or stop by a local bakery to pick up a flaky, sweet *wienerbrod* (Danish pastry).

GO GREEN

Copenhagen is aiming to be the world's first carbon-neutral city by 2025. To achieve this, it is ditching fossil fuels and switching to carbon-neutral alternatives, such as biomass, wind, and solar. Buses are powered by biogas or electricity, and developments to the city's bicycle network have seen a big uptake in bike use, with almost half of all trips in the city now made by bike.

National Anthem:
"Der er et yndigt land"
*(There was a
lovely country)*

The fairy tales of Danish author
Hans Christian Andersen are loved around
the world and were the inspiration behind
two of Disney's best-loved movies,
The Little Mermaid and *Frozen*.

NORWAY

Once the land of Vikings, this long, thin Scandinavian country is today a place of thick pine forests, polar bears, and midnight Sun. Its coast is thronged with sea deep inlets known as fjords that were carved out over millions of years by glaciers. It can get very cold here, but visitors are always warmed by the wondrous sights.

MIDNIGHT SUN

For several weeks in the summer, the Sun doesn't set in northern Norway at all but just hangs low on the horizon. In the far north, between late April and late August, it's possible to go bike riding, kayaking, or even have a round of golf in the middle of the night. This phenomenon comes about because of the way Earth is tilted toward the Sun in the summer.

At 15.2 mi., Norway's Laerdal Tunnel is the world's longest road tunnel.

On the island of Svalbard, in the far north, is a giant store of plant seeds from across the world known as the World Seed Bank. It can hold up to 2.5 billion seeds.

SAMI PEOPLE

The north of Norway is home to the Sami people, who traditionally live a nomadic lifestyle, herding reindeer. The Sami eat reindeer meat, use reindeer fur and leather to make clothes and shoes, and form tools from reindeer antlers and bones. When traveling with their herds, Sami people will sleep in traditional tents called *lavvos*.

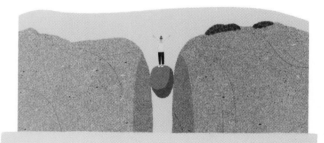

DON'T LOOK DOWN

The Kjeragbolten is an enormous boulder wedged tight in a mountain crevasse. It's possible to walk onto the boulder, although you need to be careful, as it's set above a 3,228-foot abyss.

WINTER CHAMPIONS

Norway is a nation of winter sports fanatics, and it has the awards to prove it. Norwegian athletes have won more medals at the Winter Olympic Games than any other country, with over 360 in total (including more than 130 golds). The country has been less successful at the summer games, where it's failed to reach the top 20 medal winners.

SWEDEN

The largest of the Scandinavian countries, Sweden is traditionally divided into three areas. In the south is the most densely populated part, Götaland. In the middle of the country is Svealand, where the capital is located. And in the north is Norrland, which is thick with forests and mountains.

KEY FACTS

Capital: **Stockholm**
Official Language: **Swedish**
Currency: **Swedish Krona**
Population: **10.2 million**
Area (land): **158,431 sq. mi.**

Swedes eat more than 20 million *semlor* (traditional cream buns) every year.

ORESUND BRIDGE

Sweden and Denmark got even closer in 2000 following the opening of the Øresund Bridge. This combined rail and road crossing links the Swedish coastal city of Malmö with the Danish capital, Copenhagen. The bridge part stretches for 5 miles from the Swedish coast to an artificial island in the middle of the sea. The rest of the crossing is via a 2.5-mile-long tunnel.

A BOOM IN PRIZES

The Swedish inventor Alfred Nobel became very rich from his invention of dynamite in the 1800s. However, he was worried about how he would be remembered when a newspaper accidentally printed his obituary while he was still alive. Its description of him as a "merchant of death" led him to set up a fund to establish five prizes to be awarded annually in Stockholm after his death.

ICE HOTEL

In the far north of the country, the town of Jukkasjärvi plays host to a remarkable annual construction: the Ice Hotel. This real hotel is made entirely of ice harvested from a nearby river. All the walls, furniture, and even the glasses are made of ice. It's built every December and lasts till April, when it melts away.

SHOP LIKE A VIKING

In the summer, at the Foteviken Museum, you can visit a reconstructed Viking settlement. All the houses have been made using traditional materials and techniques and are inhabited by volunteers—who must live as the Vikings did without modern technology. Viking battle reenactments are staged, and a large Viking market is held in the middle of the summer.

Nobel Prizes:
Physics
Chemistry
Medicine
Literature
Peace (awarded in Oslo)

AFR

ICA

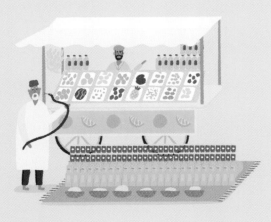

MAURITANIA

Mauritania is a ruggedly beautiful place of vast sand dunes (known as ergs) and mountains, punctuated by the occasional oasis and ancient village. Most of the population is crammed into the small portion that isn't desert. There are even some patches of tropical forest along the Senegal River that marks the country's southern boundary.

KEY FACTS

Capital: **Nouakchott**
Official Language: **Arabic**
Currency: **Ouguiya**
Population: **4 million**
Area (land): **397,955 sq. mi.**

GIANT IRON TRAIN

Iron mining is one of the Mauritania's main businesses. The main mines are located far inland in the northern part of the country around the town of Zouérat. From here, the ore is transported 435 miles to the coast on the country's only railroad. Each train can be up to 1.8 miles long, making them the longest and heaviest in the world. Passenger cars are sometimes attached to the trains for people to ride in.

CAREFUL WITH YOUR COMPASS

Just west of the iron mining hub of Zouérat is Kediet ej Jill, a mountain with a mind of its own. It's composed mainly of magnetite, a rock so packed with iron that it gives the peak a shiny, bluish tinge. It's also magnetic, which means that compasses won't work here and will simply point at the rocks rather than north—making it easy to get lost.

The port city of Nouadhibou, where the iron-ore trains arrive, has around 300 shipwrecks and abandoned ships lining its shore, making it the world's largest ship graveyard.

GIANT EYE

Mauritania's stretch of the Sahara contains several giant craters formed by meteorite impacts. At about 30 miles across, the biggest crater, known as the Richat Structure, looks like a giant eye gazing out from the desert floor. However, scientists believe this structure was formed underground by volcanic activity, rather than any impact.

The sand dunes here can be 500 feet high.

COASTAL CAPITAL

Nouakchott was little more than a village of a few thousand people when it was chosen to be the country's new capital in 1960. The decision marked Mauritania's new independence from the former colonial power of France. Severe droughts in the 1970s and 1980s saw many people move here from the countryside, and it is now a major metropolis.

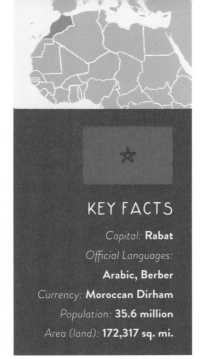

MOROCCO

Just 6 miles from Europe at its northernmost point, Morocco is scattered with ancient *casbahs* (castles) that once defended the inhabitants from attack and now often provide dramatic setting for *souks* (markets) and cafés. It can be busy and bustling in the cities, but life is lived at a much slower pace farther away.

KEY FACTS

Capital: **Rabat**

Official Languages: **Arabic, Berber**

Currency: **Moroccan Dirham**

Population: **35.6 million**

Area (land): **172,317 sq. mi.**

Built of rust-colored sandstone, Marrakech is known as the "red city."

AT THE MARKETPLACE

The souks of the former capital of Marrakech are famous the world over. The huge open square of Jemaa el-Fna is filled with stalls selling colorful, fragrant spices, traditional carpets, leatherwork, clothes, hats, and sizzling street food. As well as tradespeople, the square also attracts performers such as musicians, acrobats, magicians, fortune tellers, and snake charmers.

DON'T BE BLUE

The small city of Chefchaouen in northwest Morocco has become a major tourist attraction for one main reason: its color. Almost all the houses are painted in shades of blue. As to why the city has adopted the color with such enthusiasm, no one is quite sure. Suggested reasons include to keep cool, to keep mosquitoes away, to represent water, or possibly to remind people to live a pure life.

The university of al-Qarawiyyin in the city of Fez was founded in 859 CE, making it the world's oldest continuously operating place of education.

TRADITIONAL MOROCCAN DISHES

- Couscous—*Small crushed balls of wheat, usually served with meat or vegetable stew.*
- Tagine—*Slow-cooked stew named after the clay dish in which it's served.*
- Bastilla—*Savory pie traditionally made with pigeon meat.*
- B'sarra—*Broadbean soup.*
- Harira—*Highly seasoned tomato soup with chickpeas and lentils, traditionally served during Ramadan to break the day's fast.*

GREEN TEA

The country's most popular drink is green tea, which is usually prepared with spearmint leaves and sugar. Served in a clear glass and poured from a height to create froth (known as a crown), it forms a central part of Moroccan social life. It's drunk throughout the day and is invariably offered to guests to show hospitality.

ALGERIA

It may be Africa's largest country by area, but much of Algeria is pretty empty—at least of people. Almost everyone lives in a narrow, fertile band near the Mediterranean coast, but some brave the harsh conditions of the Sahara. Algeria's economy is largely based on extracting and exporting its huge oil and gas reserves.

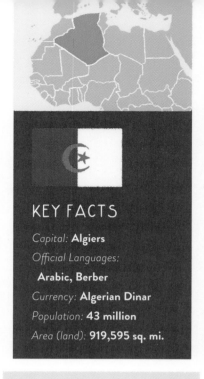

KEY FACTS

Capital: **Algiers**
Official Languages:
Arabic, Berber
Currency: **Algerian Dinar**
Population: **43 million**
Area (land): **919,595 sq. mi.**

VAST DESERT

The Sahara, the world's largest hot desert, stretches across North Africa, with the biggest portion of it sitting in Algeria. Despite its popular image as an enormous inland beach, only about a fourth of the Sahara is sand dunes. The rest is made up of mountains, stony plateaus, dry valleys called *wadis* (which may flow during rare periods of rain), and a few fertile areas known as oases.

The Sahara covers an area of 3,552,140 sq. mi., approximately the same size as the United States.

ROCK ART RECORDS

Tassili n'Ajjer National Park in southeast Algeria holds a fascinating collection of prehistoric cave art. Begun around 12,000 years ago, when this area was still lush grassland, the earliest pieces show only wild creatures, such as gazelles, giraffes, and elephants. Around 4500 BCE, cattle start to appear, representing the beginning of farming. Horses show up around 2000 BCE. The later pictures even show horse-drawn chariots.

LIFE IN THE DESERT

The Sahara supports over 2,800 plants, which are experts at rooting out tiny amounts of water stored underground. The desert also provides a home to several hardy animals, including:

- fennec fox
(*the national animal of Algeria*)
- dorcas gazelle
- Saharan cheetah
- deathstalker scorpion
- Saharan silver ant
- Saharan horned viper.

OASES

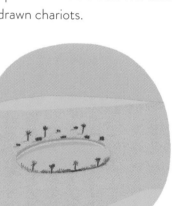

Algeria's great stretch of desert holds several oasis cities—settlements that have grown up around rare sources of desert water. Many of these sources are located deep underground in water-bearing rock layers called aquifers. The inhabitants dig boreholes (vertical tunnels) to gain access to the water, both for drinking and to irrigate crops such as dates.

Opened in 2019, the Djamaa el Djazaïr mosque in the capital, Algiers, has the world's tallest minaret, at 870 feet.

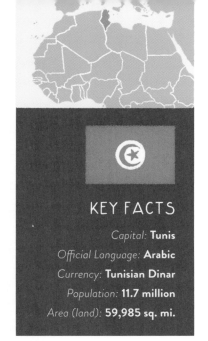

KEY FACTS

Capital: **Tunis**

Official Language: **Arabic**

Currency: **Tunisian Dinar**

Population: **11.7 million**

Area (land): **59,985 sq. mi.**

Following periods of Roman, Arab Muslim, Ottoman, and French rule, the country has been independent since 1957.

TUNISIA

Tunisia is a relatively small country surrounded by much larger neighbors. In ancient times, the city of Carthage on its northern coast controlled a mighty empire, and today Tunisia has one of the continent's highest standards of living (according to the United Nations). Most of the population is of Berber descent.

MIGHTY EMPIRE

The city of Carthage was founded back in the 800s BCE by Phoenician settlers from Lebanon. By the 200s BCE it had established an empire stretching across the Mediterranean. That brought it into conflict with the region's other growing power, Rome. Over three brutal conflicts, known as the Punic Wars, ending in 146 BCE, Rome defeated Carthage and took over its lands.

The most famous event in the Punic Wars saw the Carthaginian general, Hannibal, march his troops and a group of war elephants through Spain and over the Alps to launch a surprise raid on Roman territory.

ROMAN TUNISIA

Roman rule of Tunisia lasted for about 800 years. The old city of Carthage was destroyed and rebuilt in a Roman style, and numerous other Roman settlements were established. These included Thysdrus—now known as El Djem—where one of the empire's largest amphitheaters was constructed. Built around 238 CE, much of the structure survives today, making it one of the continent's best-preserved Roman ruins.

A GALAXY NOT THAT FAR AWAY

Light sabers at the ready. Various scenes from the early *Star Wars* movies were filmed in Tunisia, and many of the locations can still be visited (preferably in full *Star Wars* costume). These include the home of Luke Skywalker's family in the first movie (in reality the Sidi Driss Hotel, a traditional subterranean Berber settlement), plus the set for the spaceport of Mos Espa created for *The Phantom Menace*.

The Festival of the Sahara takes place at the end of December. Events include camel races, poetry readings, and musical performances.

LIBYA

This has been a volatile land shaped by many different civilizations, including Greeks, Romans, Vandals, Arabs, Berbers, Ottomans, and Italians. And there have been two civil wars in the past decade. But whatever the current political situation, its natural wonders remain undimmed, including mountains, great seas of sand, and scatterings of oases.

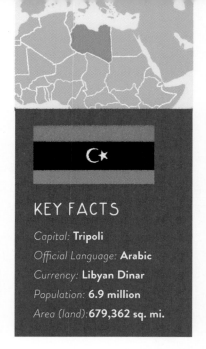

ANCIENT RUINS

Numerous remnants of Libya's long and varied past remain, preserved by the dry air and baking heat. The 2,500-year-old ruins of Cyrene, a Greek city that once rivaled Athens for magnificence, can be seen near the coastal town of Shahhat. In the northwest is Leptis Magna, one of the best preserved of all ancient Roman cities, with many of its original buildings still standing.

KEY FACTS

Capital: **Tripoli**
Official Language: **Arabic**
Currency: **Libyan Dinar**
Population: **6.9 million**
Area (land): **679,362 sq. mi.**

SALTY SAND SEAS

Libya's desert interior is home to several oases, but not all desert waters are life-giving. In Ubari, in the southwest, there are several picturesque, palm-tree-fringed lakes. To any parched traveler staggering out of the desert, the water would look delicious. But be warned: it's five times saltier than seawater. However, this does make it very good for swimming, because it's easier to float in salty water.

TRADITIONAL LIBYAN DISHES

- **Salata mishwiya** —*spicy salad.*
- **Shakshuka**—*a breakfast dish of eggs poached in a spicy tomato and onion sauce.*
- **Shorba**—*lamb and vegetable soup.*

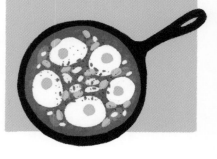

Parts of Libya's desert can go decades without rainfall, so the people here are skilled at locating underground water sources.

DESERT EXPERTS

Libya has many towns and cities, but not everyone chooses to live in them. In the southwest, there are many Tuareg, a seminomadic people related to the Berbers. They are known for their traditional blue veils and turbans, and live by trading and herding animals. In total, there are around two million Tuaregs living across several Saharan countries.

SUDAN

Following the end of a 30-year dictatorship in 2019, Sudan looks to be heading toward a more peaceful, democratic future. Its history goes back thousands of years, to ancient kingdoms that were once rivals to Egypt. Much of the country has a harsh terrain of desert and mountains, but the mighty Nile flows through its center.

KEY FACTS

Capital: **Khartoum**

Official Language: **Arabic**

Currency: **Sudanese Pound**

Population: **45.6 million**

Area (land): **668,602 sq. mi.**

RED SEA LIFE

Lying between Africa and Asia, the Red Sea is a unique marine environment. Its many coral reefs provide a home to hundreds of fascinating creatures, including sea turtles, hammerhead sharks, and many types of nudibranchs, strange mollusks that look a little like multitentacled sea slugs.

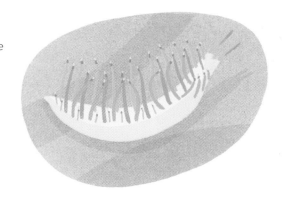

255—the number of pyramids in Sudan; almost twice as many as in Egypt.

NUBIAN PHARAOHS

Thousands of years ago, as a civilization was growing in Egypt alongside the Nile, another civilization, called Kerma, was flourishing farther south in Sudan in a region known as Nubia. It was eventually taken over by Egypt, but the Nubian kingdom controlled Egypt for almost a century, with its rulers becoming their pharaohs. Like the early Egyptians, the Nubians buried their rulers in pyramids.

TWO INTO ONE

The country's capital, Khartoum, is located at the point where two great rivers, the Blue Nile and the White Nile, merge. Together they form the Nile itself, the world's longest river. The waters support a great abundance of life, including one of the continent's most iconic animals, the giant Nile crocodile.

Haboobs
—the name for the fierce sandstorms that whip up in Sudan's driest regions.

1,000 mi.—length of the giant pipeline pumping oil, which is Sudan's main export, from wells to the coast.

EGYPT

Egypt is one of the hottest, driest, sunniest places on Earth. It would be almost uninhabitable if it weren't for one thing: the Nile River. Running from south to north through the country, the river allowed one of the world's great ancient civilizations to flourish here for over 3,000 years and still supports cities full of bustle and life.

KEY FACTS

Capital: **Cairo**
Official Language: **Arabic**
Currency: **Egyptian Pound**
Population: **104 million**
Area (land): **384,345 sq. mi.**

4,130 miles—*the length of the Nile, the world's longest river.*

THREE SEASONS OF THE NILE

In ancient times, the people here divided their year into three seasons based around the Nile River. The most important time was *Akhet* (June–September), when the river flooded, depositing nutrient-rich soil on the land around it. Next came *Peret* (October–February), the growing season, when farmers planted and raised crops, followed by the harvest season of *Shemu* (March–May).

ANCIENT EGYPT

By 3100 BCE, a civilization had emerged in Egypt that would be led by a succession of rulers known as pharaohs. It would last for over 3,000 years, during which enormous cities were constructed on the banks of the Nile. They were filled with great temples and statues of gods and pharaohs, many of which still stand and are visited by millions of people each year.

MANY MUMMIES

The Egyptians believed it was possible to live on after death in the afterworld. But to get there, the body first had to be preserved—or mummified—using bandages and a natural salt called natron. Before being wrapped up, the body's internal organs were removed and stored in special vessels called canopic jars. It wasn't just people who were mummified; the Egyptians also preserved animals, including cats, birds, snakes, and even crocodiles.

EGYPTIAN GODS & GODDESSES

The Egyptians worshipped more than 2,000 gods. Many were depicted with a human body and an animal's head.

God/Goddess	Head of a	Responsibilities
Osiris	human	the underworld
Thoth	ibis	writing and knowledge
Isis	human	marriage, motherhood, good fortune
Sobek	crocodile	crocodiles
Sekhmet	lioness	war, disease, medicine
Ra	hawk	the Sun
Anubis	jackal	the dead

THE PYRAMIDS

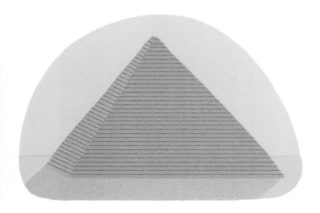

Egypt's famous pyramids were basically giant tombs where pharaohs were laid to rest. The biggest was constructed over a 20-year period for the pharaoh Khufu. Containing more than two million stone blocks, the Great Pyramid of Giza still stands today and is the largest stone structure ever built.

The ancient Egyptian written language used picture symbols known as hieroglyphs.

1 mi.—the length that the unwrapped bandages of a pharaoh could stretch.

KING TUT

The tombs of pharaohs were filled with precious objects for use in the afterlife. This made them a magnet for robbers, and over time almost all the pyramids' grave goods were stolen. Eventually, rulers were buried in secret underground tombs in a place known as the Valley of the Kings. Most of these tombs were also robbed, but in the 1920s, the tomb of a minor pharaoh called Tutankhamen was discovered intact. Its rooms were packed with objects made of gold and precious stones.

THE SUEZ CANAL

Until the mid-1800s, ships traveling between Europe and Asia had to go all the way around the southern tip of Africa, a journey that could take weeks. Opened in 1867 (and expanded in 2015), the Suez Canal runs through Egypt and links the Red Sea with the Mediterranean Sea. It reduced a trip of several thousand miles to just 120 miles.

12%—amount of the world's shipping trade that passes through the Suez Canal.

Cairo is home to one of the world's busiest metro systems—it racks up over a billion passenger rides each year.

WAITING FOR INDEPENDENCE

Egypt has one of the longest recorded histories of any country, stretching back over 5,000 years. However, in the past 2,500 years, it's only been truly independent for a handful of them. It was taken over by series of foreign powers, including the Greeks, Romans, Arab Muslims, Ottomans, French, and British. It finally achieved independence in 1952.

CAIRO

Home to around 21 million people, Egypt's capital is the largest city in the entire Arab world (and the second-largest in Africa). It didn't exist in ancient Egyptian times but was formally founded in 969 CE on the site of earlier Roman and Christian settlements. Over time, it has expanded greatly, and the Great Pyramids of Giza can be found on its outskirts.

ERITREA

One of North Africa's smaller nations, Eritrea is nonetheless packed with diversity. There are nine recognized ethnic groups, who speak nine official languages. In the north it's hot and arid, while the southern highlands are more lush and provide a home to plenty of wildlife, including elephants, hyenas, and antelope.

ANCIENT PEOPLES

One of the oldest hominids—the ancestors of *Homo sapiens* —dating back around one million years was found in Eritrea in the 1990s.

Eritrea is dotted with ancient remains from the time when this land was part of the Aksumite Kingdom, a powerful empire that dominated the region from around 80 BCE to 800 CE. Sites include the major city of Matara and the port of Adulis, which traded with the major civilizations of the time, including the Roman Empire and India.

Eritrea was formerly controlled by Ethiopia but gained independence in 1993 following a war.

DJIBOUTI

Djibouti may not have many people, but they've been around a long time. Located near the meeting point of the Atlantic Ocean and the Red Sea, the capital city is a major port, welcoming shipping from around the world. Inland there are mountains as well as fields of fumaroles—vents caused by underground volcanic activity where steam and gas escape from Earth's surface.

LAKE ASSAL

Lake Assal in west Djibouti is the lowest point in Africa. A crater lake without an outflow (such as a river or stream), it is the third-saltiest body of water in the world, ten times saltier than standard seawater. This salt forms great white fields on the side of the lake, which are mined commercially and have become one of the country's major exports.

Over half of the country's population lives in the capital.

Residents of Djibouti are known as Djiboutians.

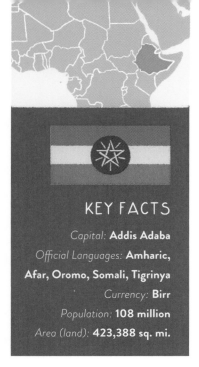

ETHIOPIA

Huge, landlocked Ethiopia has a long past. It's the continent's oldest independent state, with a rich recorded history going back thousands of years. Many scientists believe the very first humans emerged here before spreading out across the world. Today's country boasts almost equal numbers of historical and natural treasures.

The Mercato in Addis Ababa is the continent's largest street market, covering an area of several square miles.

ETHIOPIAN DISHES

• **Injera**—*spongy flatbread that acts as a plate onto which other dishes are served.*
• **Wat**—*the national dish, a spicy meat stew.*
• **Tibs**—*stir-fried meat and vegetables.*
• **Kifto**—*ground raw beef with butter and spices.*
• **Azifa**—*salad of lentils, tomatoes, and onions.*

EARLY HUMANS

Remains of some of the earliest human-like species, known as hominins, have been found in Ethiopia. The most famous is Lucy, a 3.2-million-year-old hominin. Although Lucy would have looked ape-like when alive, crucially she would have walked on two legs—one of the key developments that saw hominins evolve into humans. Her skeleton is preserved in the National Museum of Ethiopia in Addis Ababa.

BLEEDING HEARTS

Monkeys known as geladas live in the Ethiopian highlands and have bright red markings on their chests, from which they get the nickname "bleeding heart monkeys." In fact, the markings are just patches of skin that the monkeys use to signal to one another. Most other monkey species signal with their bottoms, but the geladas spend so much time sitting on theirs that they've evolved another strategy.

ROCK-CUT CHURCHES

The city of Lalibela in northern Ethiopia holds one of the country's greatest architectural wonders: a collection of eleven churches that have been carved directly out of volcanic rock. Created between the 600s and 1100s CE, most have been carved downward, directly into the ground.

GATEWAY TO HELL

Parts of Ethiopia are highly volcanically active. The Danakil Depression in the far northeast is an otherworldly place of volcanoes, hot sulfurous springs, and extreme heat. In places, heat-loving bacteria known as extremophiles have created a strange rainbow-colored landscape in the hot springs.

SOMALIA

Located at the eastern tip of the continent, an area known as the "Horn of Africa," Somalia has had a troubled recent history and is experiencing an ongoing civil war. But outside of wartime, there are many things to enjoy here, including prehistoric art and a long coast that is rich with marine life.

KEY FACTS

Capital: **Mogadishu**
Official Languages: **Somali, Arabic**
Currency: **Somali Shilling**
Population: **11.8 million**
Area (land): **242,216 sq. mi.**

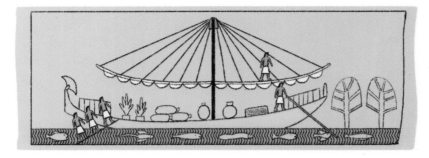

LAND OF PUNT

Many scholars identify Somalia as the fabled "Land of Punt," a great trading nation mentioned in ancient Egyptian writings. These tell of several Egyptian boat expeditions to Punt to obtain precious objects such as gold, ivory, and wild-animal skins. Although the Egyptians never stated exactly where Punt was, Somalia seems to match their description—today there's even a region there called Puntland.

2,071 mi.—*the length of Somalia's coastline, the longest in mainland Africa.*

CAVE PAINTINGS

Somalia has been inhabited since the Stone Age. Twenty thousand years ago, the people here created elaborate paintings on the walls of the Laas Geel caves in the northwestern part of the country. The colorful images depict people, wild animals, and aurochs—the ancestors of modern cattle. The images lay undisturbed for many thousands of years and were only discovered in 2002.

There are believed to be more camels in Somalia than any other country— about seven million.

PIRATES

The civil war that engulfed Somalia in the 1990s created huge problems for the country. Rising poverty combined with a collapse of the Somali navy led to a rise in piracy in the 2000s. Armed groups began seizing ships passing by the coast and then holding their crew as hostages until a ransom was paid by the ships' owners. After hundreds of ships were targeted in this way, an international navy began patrolling the waters in 2008, and the problem has now largely been stamped out.

TANZANIA

When you think of Africa, you probably think of the landscape of Tanzania: sweeping plains where lions and leopards prey upon herds of wildebeests and zebras, while the great summit of Mount Kilimanjaro looms in the background. But there's much more, including busy cities, giant lakes, and tropical islands.

KEY FACTS

Capital: **Dodoma**

Official Languages: **Swahili, English, Arabic**

Currency: **Tanzanian Shilling**

Population: **55.6 million**

Area (land): **342,009 sq. mi.**

To show respect to their elders, Swahili speakers in Tanzania use the greeting *Shikamoo,* meaning "I am beneath your feet."

SERENGETI

The Serengeti National Park, along with the adjacent Maasai Mara Reserve in Kenya, holds one of the world's great concentrations of wildlife. These vast, grassy plains—known as savannas—are home to over 300 species of mammals and 500 species of birds. More wild lions live here than anywhere else on Earth.

KILIMANJARO

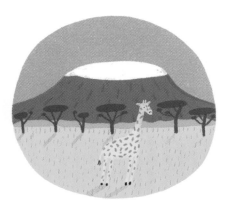

Towering over the Tanzanian landscape, Kilimanjaro stands alone. At 19,341 feet, it's the tallest mountain in the world that doesn't form part of a chain. Once an active volcano, Kilimanjaro has been calm for around 150,000 years, although gas-emitting vents at its peak are a reminder that it could possibly erupt again. Its foothills are covered in forest, while much of its summit is covered in ice.

MAMMAL CHECKLIST

Here are just some of the many mammals that can be spotted on Tanzania's great plains:

- African elephants
- black rhinoceroses
- blue wildebeests
- Cape buffalo
- giraffes
- Grant's gazelles
- leopards
- lions
- spotted hyenas
- warthogs
- zebras

ANCIENT PEOPLES

The Hadza, a people of around 1,300 individuals in northern Tanzania, are one of the continent's last hunter-gatherer tribes, and one of its most ancient. They are believed to have inhabited this area for many thousands of years, and they speak a language utilizing clicks and pops that is unrelated to any other.

Tanzania is bordered by three of Africa's largest lakes: Lake Malawi, Lake Victoria, and Lake Tanganyika.

KENYA

Kenya has everything: long stretches of coast, deep lakes, big cities, mountains and highlands, tea and coffee plantations, more than 40 ethnic groups, and 60 languages. But it's known above all for one thing: animals. It's one of the world's most popular safari destinations, where people flock to see the country's most iconic creatures.

THE GREAT MIGRATION

Every year, Kenya's Maasai Mara reserve stages the most incredible wildlife show on Earth, known as the "Great Migration." Millions of zebras, wildebeests, and gazelles follow the rains on a circular journey across the savannas of Kenya and Tanzania in search of the best grass to eat. On the way, they must deal with attacks by predators, including lions and leopards, as well as crocodiles lying in wait when the herds are forced to cross rivers.

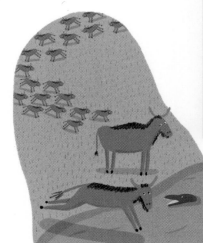

Kenya has
24 national parks,
15 national reserves,
and six marine parks.

FLAMINGO LAKE

Flamingos thrive in environments that other animals would find toxic. Lake Bogoria in southwest Kenya is so salty almost nothing can live in it—except for tiny single-celled creatures called cyanobacteria, and the flamingos that feed on them, filtering these microorganisms from the water with their beak. The lake supports one of the world's largest populations of lesser flamingos.

Speak Swahili like a Kenyan:
Habari   Hello/Hi
Asante   Thank you
Mini ni   My name is/I am. . .

MAASAI PEOPLE

One of the largest ethnic groups in Kenya, and certainly the best known internationally, are the Maasai people. They've been living a seminomadic existence, herding cattle, for around 500 years. They're famous for their colorful traditional clothing, jumping dance known as the *adumu*, and warrior skills. In fact, a Maasai shield and crossed spears appear on the Kenyan flag.

RECORD-BREAKING RUNNERS

Kenya's runners are in a league of their own. Kenya has won over 100 medals at the Summer Olympics, almost all of them for running. In 2019, Eliud Kipchoge became the first man to run a marathon in under two hours, while in the same year his fellow Kenyan Brigid Kosgei became the first woman to run it in under two hours and 15 minutes.

BURUNDI

Although it is today one of Africa's poorest nations, Burundi has a proud history. It first emerged in the 1600s and would go on to become a powerful kingdom. Periods of European colonization and civil wars (following its achieving independence in 1962) weakened the country, but its rich culture and natural wonders remain.

KEY FACTS

Capital: **Gitega**

Official Languages: **Kirundi, French**

Currency: **Burundian Franc**

Population: **11.9 million**

Area (land): **9,915 sq. mi.**

BURUNDI DRUMMERS

The percussion group known as the Royal Drummers of Burundi have toured the world extensively over the past few decades, introducing people to traditional Burundian music. Using drums made of animal skins stretched over hollowed-out tree trunks, the performers put on complex, energetic performances. In Burundi, drums are used in ceremonies such as births, marriages, and funerals.

LAKE TANGANYIKA

Although Burundi is landlocked, the 418-mile-long, sea-like Lake Tanganyika provides a coastline along its southwestern border. It's a record-breaking body of water: the second-oldest, the second-deepest, the second-largest by volume, and the longest freshwater lake in the world. It's home to many large animals, including Nile crocodiles, as well as several unique ones. Over 250 species of a type of fish called cichlid live here and are rarely found elsewhere.

Lake Tanganyika is supposedly home to a giant killer crocodile named Gustave that has eaten over 300 people.

GROUPS OF THREE

Burundi's flag is made up of three colors: white, representing peace; red, symbolizing the past suffering of the country; and green, representing hope for the future. The stars in the center stand both for the country's three main ethnic groups—Hutu, Tutsi, and Twa—and Burundi's motto, "Unity, Work, and Progress."

Amasho
—a traditional Burundi greeting meaning "may you have many head of cattle."

RWANDA

Today Rwanda is largely at peace, following years of devastating conflict at the end of the 20th century. The economy is growing, largely based on the export of tea and coffee, and the country is welcoming more and more tourists. Many visitors are drawn to its mountain forests and the elusive gorillas that lurk within.

KEY FACTS

Capital: **Kigali**

Official Languages: **English, French, Kinyarwanda, Swahili**

Currency: **Rwandan Franc**

Population: **12.7 million**

Area (land): **9,524 sq. mi.**

DAZZLING DANCES

Music and dance have long been major parts of Rwandan culture. Traditional dances, as regularly performed by the country's National Ballet, are usually made up of three parts. These are the *Umushshagiriro*, a dance by women, which has graceful fluid movements; the *Ngoma*, a display of traditional drumming; and the *Intore*, the dance of warrior heroes, performed by men in grass wigs carrying spears.

660 lb. —*the weight of a male "silverback" mountain gorilla.*

GENOCIDE

In 1994, ethnic tensions exploded between the country's two main peoples, Hutus and Tutsis. The assassination of Rwanda's Hutu president led to genocide—an attempt by the Hutus to completely wipe out the Tutsis. Hundreds of thousands were massacred before a civil war ended the slaughter. The country is still living with the memory and legacy of those times.

GORILLAS IN THE MIST

Some of the continent's rarest and most incredible animals can be found in the misty cloud forests of Rwanda's Virunga volcanoes: mountain gorillas. These gentle, long-haired giants live in family groups and spend most of their time feeding on forest vegetation. There are believed to be only around 1,000 mountain gorillas left in the wild.

RECYCLED ART

Imigongo is a traditional art form in which large geometric pictures are created using an unusual material: cow dung. The dung is treated with ash to kill bacteria and stop it from smelling, and then natural dyes are added. Red, black, white, and gray are the colors that are most often used.

Over 60% of the politicians in Rwanda's parliament are female—the highest proportion in the world.

UGANDA

Uganda is a potent mixture of colorful street life—as epitomized by the busy streets and markets of the capital, Kampala, one of the fastest-growing cities on the continent—and awe-inspiring nature: great lakes, winding rivers, and forests filled with exotic creatures.

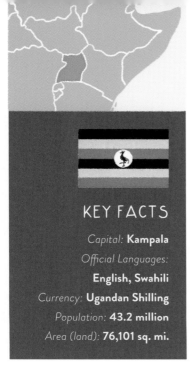

KEY FACTS

Capital: **Kampala**
Official Languages:
English, Swahili
Currency: **Ugandan Shilling**
Population: **43.2 million**
Area (land): **76,101 sq. mi.**

UGANDAN STREET FOOD

The country is well known for the wide range of tasty snacks sold at roadside stalls, including:

• Matooke—*steamed, mashed plantains wrapped in banana leaf.*

• Rolex—*omelet and vegetables wrapped in a chapati (the name is derived from "roll eggs").*

• Nsenene
—*Pan-fried grasshoppers.*

Uganda has 10 national parks and more than 60 protected areas.

BUGANDA

The history of Uganda is closely tied to that of Buganda, a kingdom that by the 1700s had become one of East Africa's most powerful states. Taken over by the British in the late 1800s, the kingdom was abolished after Uganda's independence in 1962. However, it was reinstated as a kingdom in the 1990s, although it remains part of Uganda and the role of the king is largely ceremonial. The tombs of four 19th-century Bugandan kings are preserved in giant thatched buildings in Kasubi, a World Heritage Site.

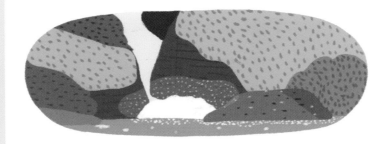

FAST-FLOWING FALLS

The country's largest national park is centered on the Murchison Falls. Here the Nile River is squeezed through a narrow gorge and over a 130-foot drop, creating a dramatic cascade of water and mist. The park is a refuge for many water-dwelling creatures, including the country's largest population of crocodiles.

Popular Ugandan girls' names:
Namono
Dembe
Masiko

Popular Ugandan boys' names:
Adroa
Balondemu
Kaikara

IMPENETRABLE FOREST

The aptly named Bwindi Impenetrable Forest is a protected park in the country's southwest, running along the border with the Democratic Republic of Congo. One of the most biodiverse places on the continent, the dense, ancient jungle is home to 120 species of mammals, 220 species of butterflies, 350 species of birds, and over 1,000 flowering plants.

SOUTH SUDAN

South Sudan is one of the world's newest countries. It broke away to become independent from Sudan in 2011 following a war of independence. It then entered a period of civil war, from which it has only recently emerged. The future looks more hopeful, as the people move toward peace.

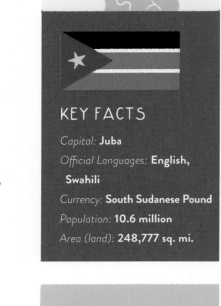

KEY FACTS

Capital: **Juba**
Official Languages: **English, Swahili**
Currency: **South Sudanese Pound**
Population: **10.6 million**
Area (land): **248,777 sq. mi.**

GIANT SWAMP

The middle of the country is dominated by the Sudd, one of the world's largest swamps. With dense, waterlogged ground and thick vegetation, it's an extremely difficult area to travel through or build on—which has made it a haven for wildlife. More than 70 species of fish and 400 species of birds are found here, as well as larger species such as Nile crocodiles and hippopotamuses.

South Sudan has one of the youngest populations of any country, with over half the people under 18 years of age.

GIANT BULLS

Much of this landlocked landscape is made up of grasslands, where the country's distinctive long-horn cattle, known as Ankole, graze. Many Dinka people, the country's largest ethnic group, own herds of these cattle. However, they don't keep them for meat or leather, but for their milk, as a form of currency, and for use in their cultural rituals.

MEGA MIGRATION

One of the world's biggest animal migrations takes place in Bandingilo National Park in the southern part of the country. At least a million antelope—made up of species called tiang and white-eared kob—undertake an epic journey across the land in search of fresh grass. On the way, they have to avoid attacks by some of Africa's fiercest predators, including lions, cheetahs, and African wild dogs.

WRESTLING MANIA

Traditional forms of wrestling have long been practiced in Sudan, and today national competitions are held that draw large crowds. It's believed that the popularity of wrestling is helping bring the country together after its devastating civil war.

CHAD

This huge landlocked country right in the middle of North Africa is dominated by the shifting sands of the Sahara. In fact, the desert is slowly taking over, covering the land and shrinking the country's largest lake. Most of the people here work as farmers or herders, or in the cotton and oil industries.

KEY FACTS

Capital: **N'Djamena**

Official Languages:
Arabic, French

Currency:
Central African CFA Franc

Population: **16.9 million**

Area (land): **486,180 sq. mi.**

THREE REGIONS

The country is divided into three distinct climate zones. The north is dry, harsh, and sparsely populated desert. This gives way to the slightly more fertile Sahel region in the middle—the location of Lake Chad—before transitioning to the lush savanna and forests of the south.

THE MORE OR LESS LAKE

Lake Chad, from where the country gets its name, is an unpredictable body of water. A huge but shallow lake surrounded by swamps and wetlands, it shrank significantly between the 1960s and 2000 because of both climate change and overuse of the water by local people for farming. However, it's believed that the lake has started growing again in the past couple of decades.

The ancient Romans carried out expeditions to Lake Chad, which they named the "Lake of Hippopotamus" because of the great numbers of the animals they found wallowing there.

LIFE IN THE DESERT

The Ennedi Plateau in the country's northwest contains unusual rock formations created by thousands of years of wind erosion. A dry and mostly barren place, it boasts a number of oases, called *gueltas*, where rare animals thrive, far from civilization. The Guelta d'Archei, an ancient pool of water lying deep in the desert, is one of the last strongholds of the West African crocodile.

CENTRAL AFRICAN REPUBLIC

The Central African Republic (CAR) is located, as its name suggests, pretty much right at the heart of the continent. The country's current borders were only established in the 1800s when it became a French colony. Its recent history has been troubled, and much of the population lives in poverty, but CAR has many natural resources, as well as reserves of oil, uranium, gold, and diamonds.

KEY FACTS

Capital: **Bangui**
Official Languages:
French, Sango
Currency: **Central African CFA Franc**
Population: **5.9 million**
Area (land): **240,535 sq. mi.**

HONEY GATHERERS

The people in CAR have a sweet tooth: more honey is consumed here than in any other country! Some of this is farmed and some is collected from wild hives. The Baka people of the southwest (who also live in neighboring Cameroon, Gabon, and the Republic of Congo) are particularly skilled at climbing trees and removing honey from bees' nests without harming either the bees or themselves.

The CAR is home to around 600 species of butterflies.

LOWLAND WILDLIFE

Much of the country's southwest is given over to thick, steamy rainforest. A large section of this is preserved in the Dzanga-Sangha Forest Reserve, which provides a home to numerous large endangered species, including forest elephants, bongo antelopes, and western lowland gorillas.

MAGNETIC MAYHEM

If you were to look at a compass almost anywhere on Earth, it would point north, but not in the Central African Republic. Owing to a strange phenomenon known as the Bangui magnetic anomaly, compasses here basically go haywire. Scientists are not entirely sure why. One theory suggests that it was caused by an enormous meteor striking Earth around a billion years ago, heating the rock and causing the iron within it to become magnetic.

In the wet season, from June to September, there are rainstorms almost daily. The rest of the year is dry and hot.

DEMOCRATIC REPUBLIC OF CONGO

Easily confused with the neighboring Republic of the Congo to the west, this used to be known as Zaire and today is commonly referred to as the DRC. It's a place of great diversity, both in terms of its people—more than 700 languages are spoken here—and the wildlife found in its great stretch of Congo jungle, which is the world's second-largest rainforest.

KEY FACTS

Capital: **Kinshasa**
Official Languages: **French**
Currency: **Congolese Franc**
Population: **102 million**
Area (land): **875,312 sq. mi.**

Kinshasa is the world's second-largest French-speaking city.

THE CONGO

The Congo River runs in a loop around the center of the country. Surrounding it is a dense mass of moist rainforest fed by some of the continent's highest rainfall. Much of the forest is protected in national parks, five of which have been named as UNESCO World Heritage sites. The trees provide a refuge for an abundance of wildlife, including three types of great apes: chimpanzees, eastern gorillas, and bonobos.

HIDDEN IN THE JUNGLE

Some of the country's animals are extremely skilled at hiding. A relative of the giraffe, the okapi is so good at secreting itself in the jungle that it remained unknown to western science until the early 20th century—although local people have known about it since ancient times. The okapi looks a little like a cross between a giraffe and a zebra, with a long neck and a striped backside.

Plunging to 720 feet in places, the Congo is the world's deepest river.

RUMBLE IN THE JUNGLE

One of the most famous boxing matches in history took place here in 1974. In front of 60,000 fans in a stadium in Kinshasa, the American boxer Muhammad Ali regained the title of heavyweight champion of the world by beating George Foreman. The fight, which Ali called the "Rumble in the Jungle" was watched by an estimated one billion people around the world.

TERRIBLE LEGACY

From 1885 to 1908, King Leopold II of Belgium took control of this part of Africa as his own personal property, called the Congo Free State. He became very rich by exploiting the local population, who were forced to grow rubber and could be killed or mutilated if they failed to harvest fast enough. An estimated 10 million people died during this time. Eventually, the Belgian government forced him out, taking over the colony before the country finally achieved independence in 1960.

ANGOLA

This coastal land spent much of the late 20th century in conflict. First it battled for independence from its colonial ruler, Portugal. Then in 1975 it entered a long civil war that only came to an end in 2002. Since then, the country has been at peace, and its economy has been rapidly growing thanks to its large mineral and oil reserves.

KEY FACTS

Capital: **Luanda**
Official Language: **Portuguese**
Currency: **Kwanza**
Population: **32.5 million**
Area (land): **481,354 sq. mi.**

SHIPWRECK BEACH

About 20 miles north of the capital, the otherwise empty coast suddenly becomes filled with over 20 giant rusting ships, including cargo ships, oil tankers, and fishing vessels. These ghostly remains are not accidental shipwrecks, but crafts that have been deliberately abandoned and that are being broken slowly apart by the relentless beating of the waves.

ANGOLAN DANCE

Music and dance have long been a major part of Angolan culture. The traditional music and dance known as *semba* is very popular here and has given rise to other related forms in recent decades, including *kizomba* and *kudoro*.

At 345 feet high and 1,300 feet wide, the Kalandula Falls in northern Angola is one of the largest waterfalls in Africa.

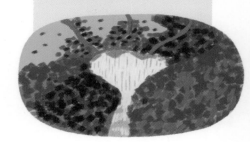

VIEWPOINT OF THE MOON

About 25 miles south of the capital, a section of soft sandstone rocks has been eroded by wind and rain into a bizarre collection of multicolored pinnacles and pillars. Their appearance is so strange and otherworldly that they've been nicknamed the *Miradouro da Lua* (Viewpoint of the Moon).

Angola is the world's second-largest Portuguese-speaking country, after Brazil.

UPSIDE-DOWN TREE

The Angolan national tree is the *imbondeiro*, the local name for the African baobab. Local legends say that it looks the way it does, with strange root-like branches, because the gods planted it upside down after it started complaining about other trees.

REPUBLIC OF THE CONGO

Lying on the equator, the Republic of the Congo (ROC) enjoys a warm, wet climate throughout the year. It's been inhabited by Bantu people for over 3,000 years. Following a period of French rule, the country became independent in 1960 and has grown wealthy on the back of its large oil reserves.

KEY FACTS

Capital: **Brazzaville**

Official Languages: **French**

Currency: **Central African CFA Franc**

Population: **5.3 million**

Area (land): **131,854 sq. mi.**

SPEAK KONGO

Mbote—Hello

Sala kia mbote—Goodbye

THE KONGO PEOPLE

The Bantu people who inhabit the forests of the country are also known as Kongo—which is also the name of their language. It was the language of many of the people transported to the Americas during the time of the Atlantic slave trade, from the 1600s to the 1800s. As such, many Kongo words are used across the world, including "zombie," "funky," and "mambo."

Kinshasa, the capital of the DRC, and Brazzaville, the capital of the Republic of the Congo, are the world's two closest capital cities, facing each other across the Congo River.

KEEPING THE BEAT

Performances of drumming are very important in Kongo culture and are used to mark special events such as births, marriages, and deaths. The drums are known as ngoma and are made of wood covered in cow skin. They can be played with either the hands or sticks.

MOKOLÉ MBEMBE

Legends tell of a mysterious monster lurking in the Congo jungle. Named Mokolé Mbembe, it is supposed to be huge and terrifying, capable of killing and eating anything that crosses its path, even elephants. While some have speculated that it might be a dinosaur that has somehow survived to the modern age, it is generally assumed to be just a legend. (Or is it?)

BRAZZAVILLE MARKET

Poto-Poto Market in the heart of the capital is filled with stalls selling all kinds of goods, including colorful textiles, bags, clothing, shoes, jewelry, street foods, and more.

GABON

With an estimated 85 percent of the country covered in forest, you're never far from nature in Gabon. It's one of the most prosperous nations in sub-Saharan Africa, with plentiful reserves of gold, uranium, and—perhaps the most precious reserve of all—wildlife.

KEY FACTS

Capital: **Libreville**
Official Language: **French**
Currency: **Central African CFA Franc**
Population: **2.2 million**
Area (land): **99,486 sq. mi.**

WILDLIFE ON THE BEACH

Many large animals hide away in Gabon's jungles, including forest elephants, buffalo, antelope, monkeys, leopards, crocodiles, and more. Wildlife-spotting opportunities are sometimes best at the forest edge. Loango National Park has 100 miles of uninhabited coast where, in places, the forest comes right down to the shoreline. It's occasionally possible to see gorillas strolling along the beach or hippos playing in the surf here.

Gabon is home to around 80% of the world's entire wild gorilla population.

MAKING MASKS

Gabon is well known for its carved wooden masks, which are used for religious ceremonies and during festivities to mark major life events, such as births, marriages, and funerals. Each of the country's 40 ethnic groups has its own style and traditions of mask making.

LÉCONI CANYONS

Perhaps the country's most famous geological landmarks are the peaks and pinnacles of the Cirque de Léconi, a circular red rock canyon in the country's southeastern corner. The rocks here have been weathered into bizarre shapes over millions of years.

EQUATORIAL GUINEA

KEY FACTS

Capital: **Malabo (current), Ciudad de la Paz (future)**

Official Languages: **Spanish, Portuguese, French**

Currency: **Central African CFA Franc**

Population: **836,200**

Area (land): **10,831 sq. mi.**

There are two parts to the small nation of Equatorial Guinea: the forested mainland, sandwiched between Cameroon and Gabon, and five offshore islands. The largest of these islands, Bioko, actually lies closer to Cameroon and is the site of the capital (for now). The discovery of oil in the 1990s has brought much wealth to the country.

NEW CAPITAL

In the 2010s, work began on a new mainland capital to be called Ciudad de la Paz (City of Peace). Carved out of the rainforest about 105 miles inland, the plan is for it to have a presidential palace, a parliament building, an opera house, a five-star hotel, a university, and streets of housing, as well as a hydroelectric plant to supply it with electricity. As yet, only a handful of buildings have been completed, so it remains a capital-in-waiting.

GOLIATH FROG

Equatorial Guinea is home to the world's largest frog species, the Goliath frog. Growing up to 1 foot long and weighing over 6 pounds, these slippery giants spend their days lurking in the country's many rivers and streams. At night, they emerge onto land to feed on insects, worms, and spiders.

Equatorial Guinea is the only country in Africa to have Spanish as an official language.

RICH VS. POOR

Oil revenues have turned Equatorial Guinea into one of the richest countries in Africa. However, the money is not divided evenly, so many people continue to live in poverty. It has one of the greatest income inequalities in the world.

DON'T FORGET YOUR UMBRELLA

The village of San Antonio de Ureca on the island of Bioko, just south of the capital, receives an astonishing 34 feet of rain per year. This makes it the wettest place in all of Africa, and one of the wettest locations in the world.

CAMEROON

This country's varied landscape includes deserts in the north, beaches and mountains in the middle, and extremely wet rainforests in the south. All three regions are home to unique wildlife. Living alongside the natural wonders are more than 200 ethnic groups speaking 260 national languages.

KEY FACTS

Capital: **Yaoundé**
Official Languages: **English, French, English**
Currency: **Central African CFA Franc**
Population: **27.8 million**
Area (land): **182,514 sq. mi.**

BAMILEKE BEADS

The largest ethnic group in Cameroon is the Bamileke people. They're famed for their traditional crafts, particularly beadwork, which they use to create colorful masks. Worn during festivals, these masks often depict animals, such as elephants, leopards, and buffalo, and are made of a range of materials, including shells, seeds, pearls, corals, and colored glass.

Cameroon is one of the only countries where you can see the world's largest monkey, the blue-and-red-faced mandrill.

DEADLY LAKE

Lying high on the side of a volcano, calm Lake Nyos holds a deadly, invisible secret—its water is full of carbon dioxide that escapes from the volcano. In 1986, the lake suddenly released a great cloud of the gas, which killed thousands of people and animals. To prevent a recurrence, tubes have been inserted into the lake to release the gas slowly and safely.

DIVIDED NATION

The country of Cameroon is formed from two colonies, one French-speaking, one English-speaking. Tensions between the two have led to an English-speaking area declaring itself an independent state, called Ambazonia. Its independence isn't recognized by the Cameroon government or any other nation.

NATIONAL PARK WILDLIFE

Cameroon is a hugely biodiverse place, with 9,000 plant species, 900 bird species, and more than 300 species of mammals. Some of the many animals to be spotted in Cameroon's 19 national parks include:
• African wild dogs • bushpigs • cheetahs • elephants • gazelles • giraffes • gorillas • hippos • hyenas • leopards • ostriches.

CAMEROONIAN DELICACIES

• **Puff-Puff** —*deep fried dough*
• **Ndolé**—*stew with peanuts, bitter greens, and beef or fish*
• **Kati Kati**—*spiced grilled chicken.*

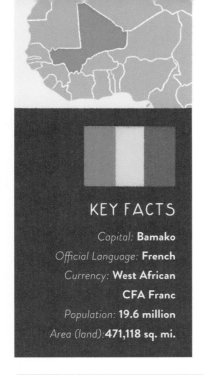

MALI

Once one of the world's major trading centers, Mali is now better known as a cultural hub, famous for its musicians and craftspeople. The landscape here ranges from dry desert in the north down to the more fertile south, where the Niger and Senegal Rivers flow, and most of the population lives.

KEY FACTS

Capital: **Bamako**
Official Language: **French**
Currency: **West African CFA Franc**
Population: **19.6 million**
Area (land): **471,118 sq. mi.**

MUSIC

Many different genres of music are played here on instruments including:
- Kora—*a large instrument, somewhat like a cross between a lute and harp, with 21 strings.*
- Xalam—*small lute-like stringed instrument with one to five strings.*
- Balafon—*a xylophone-like instrument with gourds used as resonators (sound boxes).*

TIMBUKTU

In the Middle Ages, Mali was one of the dominant players in world trade. At its peak, the Mali Empire stretched across West Africa. Its cities were major trading points, controlling the flow of goods between sub-Saharan African and Europe. The greatest city, Timbuktu, grew into a major center of learning and culture and was revered as a near legendary place in the West. However, as the trade routes dried up, so the city went into decline. Today it is slowly being swallowed up by the surrounding desert.

In the Middle Ages, goods were moved across the desert using long lines of camels known as caravans. Each caravan could have several thousand camels.

RICHER THAN RICH

Musa I (also known as Mansa Musa), who was king of the Mali Empire in the early 1300s, is believed to have been one of the richest people who ever lived. His wealth was mainly made up of gold. In 1324, he undertook a pilgrimage to Mecca accompanied by 60,000 followers dressed in finest cloths and carrying bags of gold dust, which they handed out to poor people along the route.

Mali means "hippopotamus" in Bambara, one of the country's main languages.

GREAT MOSQUE OF DJENNÉ

One of the most distinctive sights of Africa, the Great Mosque in the town of Djenne is the largest mud-brick building in the world. Constructed of earth and straw held in place by wooden beams, the huge, spiky building looks like the ground has come to life. It was constructed in 1907 and is constantly being repaired and upgraded to prevent it from being damaged by rain.

NIGER

Niger is a beautiful but largely empty place. Most of the country is made up of great sand dunes and rocky plateaus because the Sahara takes up 80 percent of the territory. The majority of the population lives in the southwest, where the capital Niamey is situated. The economy is based mainly on agriculture.

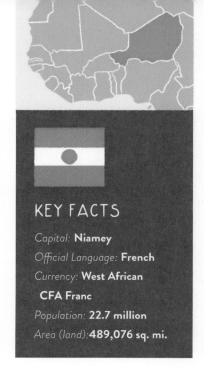

THE LONELIEST TREE

Niger was once home to the loneliest, most isolated tree on Earth. A spiny leafed acacia, the Tree of Ténéré was located in the middle of the harshest stretch of Niger's Sahara Desert, over 250 miles from any other tree. It was used as a landmark by people traveling through the desert and appeared on many maps—before being accidentally knocked down by a drunk truck driver in 1973.

PROTECTING THE W

Around 17 percent of the country is protected from development. Much of it lies within the W National Park, an area that also stretches into neighboring Benin and Burkino Faso. It gets its name because it surrounds a W-shaped meander of the Niger River, and it is home to a great variety of wildlife, including several large mammal species, such as:
• aardvarks • baboons • caracal • cheetahs
• elephants • hippopotamus.

The country is named after the Niger River, the third-largest river in Africa, which stretches for 2,600 miles.

DUSTY DINOSAURS

Millions of years ago, this barren land was full of life. The remains of numerous dinosaurs and prehistoric reptiles have been found in the central Agadez desert region, including:
• Afrovenator, *a two-legged predator a bit like an African T. rex*
• Sarcosuchus, *a giant crocodile that could grow over 30 feet long*
• Nigersaurus, *a long-necked sauropod that was named after the country.*

EYES AND TEETH

Every year, the Wodaabe people of Niger hold a weeklong courtship ritual known as the *Guerewol.* It involves young unmarried men dressing in traditional costumes and painting their faces before forming lines to sing and dance to attract the attention of unmarried young women. The men concentrate on showing off the physical characteristics most prized by the Wodaabe, particularly white eyes and teeth, so the dances feature lots of eye-rolling and smiling.

NIGERIA

Nigeria has got it all going on. As Africa's most populous country, it's teeming with life and culture. It's also West Africa's richest nation, with much of its economy based on sales of oil, rubber, and cacao. It also boasts a fascinating landscape of savannas, mountains, rainforests, and huge urban centers.

KEY FACTS

Capital: **Abuja**
Official Language: **English**
Currency: **Nigerian Naira**
Population: **214 million**
Area (land): **351,649 sq. mi.**

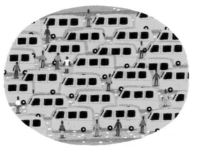

BIG COUNTRY—BIG NUMBERS

Nigeria is the world's seventh-largest country by population. It's also the leading producer of oil in Africa. The country's former capital, Lagos, is the largest city in Africa, with an estimated population of over 23 million people.

Nigeria's movie industry, nicknamed "Nollywood," is the third largest in the world, producing around 2,500 movies a year.

BRONZE MASTERS

From the 1000s to the late 1800s, southern Nigeria was dominated by the mighty kingdom of Benin (not to be confused with the modern country of Benin). The people were skilled bronze workers, creating many pieces to decorate the royal palace. When the British invaded and took over the city in 1897, they took the bronzes with them. Most of the pieces ended up in European museums. Nigeria has been asking for them back, but only a few have been returned.

FABULOUS FESTIVALS

Hundreds of festivals are held in Nigeria throughout the year. Some of the biggest include:

- New Yam Festival—*an Igbo harvest celebration.*
- Osun-Osogbo Festival—*a celebration of the traditional Yoruba goddess of the river.*
- Eyo—*a Yoruba celebration to welcome a new ruler, performed by dancers in distinctive costumes of robes, masks, and wide-brimmed hats.*
- Argungu Fishing Festival—*a four-day celebration in which men compete to catch the largest fish.*

ETHNIC GROUPS

There are around 250 ethnic groups in Nigeria. The three largest are:
- Hausa-Fulani (27%)—*who live mainly in the north*
- Yoruba (21%)—*who live mainly in the west*
- Igbo (18%)—*who live mainly in the east.*

The small Nigerian town of Igbo-Ora has been named the "twin capital of the world" for the high number of twins born there—over 150 pairs for every 1,000 births.

BENIN

The site of the former Kingdom of Dahomey, Benin has a long history. It also has a long, thin shape, stretching for 400 miles through grasslands, forests, and mountains. Most of the population lives in bustling coastal towns. Outside of these, much of the land is given over to agriculture, particularly the production of cotton.

ROYAL PALACES

From 1625 to 1904, when it was annexed by the French, southern Benin was dominated by the Kingdom of Dahomey, one of the most powerful West African kingdoms. Some of the restored mud-brick royal palaces from this period can still be visited in the town of Abomey, the former royal capital. They're decorated with designs depicting the history of the kingdom.

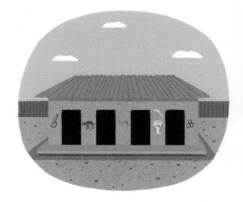

KEY FACTS

Capital: **Porto-Novo**
Official Language: **French**
Currency: **West African CFA Franc**
Population: **12.9 million**
Area (land): **42,711 sq. mi.**

SLAVE COAST

Dahomey was a major player in the devastating transatlantic slave trade. For around three centuries, until the late 1800s, the rulers of Dahomey sold their prisoners of war to Portuguese slave traders. The area where the slave ships departed became known as the Slave Coast. Benin's capital, which means "New Port" in Portuguese, was developed as a port for the export of slaves.

Benin's national parks are one of the last refuges for the endangered West African lion.

STILT VILLAGE

Benin boasts numerous towns and villages *by* bodies of water, but just one built *on* a body of water—Ganvie. Like Venice on stilts, it consists of thousands of wooden buildings raised up above the waters of Lake Nokoué, near the country's south coast. The town was constructed in the 17th century by the Tofinu people to avoid being captured by Fon warriors and sold into slavery. Relying on fishing, fish farming, and tourism for its income, it's still a thriving place today.

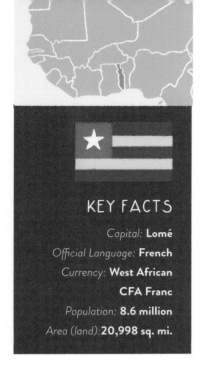

TOGO

One of the world's narrowest countries, Togo looks like a thin ribbon sandwiched between Ghana and Benin. It is just 100 miles across at its widest point. Nonetheless, it's an extremely varied place, with sandy beaches; marshes; mangroves; lagoons; and yam, cassava and millet plantations; plus mud castles and voodoo markets.

KEY FACTS

Capital: **Lomé**
Official Language: **French**
Currency: **West African CFA Franc**
Population: **8.6 million**
Area (land): **20,998 sq. mi.**

Togo has been ruled by the same family for over 50 years.

VODUN

The ancient religion known elsewhere as voodoo, and locally as *vodun*, has its origins in this part of the world. It is still practiced by around a third of the population. Vodun is centered on the belief that the world and everything in it is controlled by spirits. These are worshipped through a range of rituals often involving singing and dancing. Vodun markets are common in Togo, selling animal skulls that can be crushed up to create potions to ward off evil spirits.

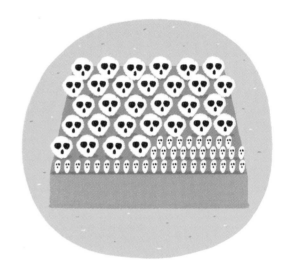

MUD FORTRESSES

Stretching into neighboring Benin, the Koutammakou region is home to some remarkable architecture, the work of the local Batammariba people. Houses called *takienta* are made of mud and grass, with towers and pointed turrets that make them look a little like medieval European castles. A symbol of Togo, the houses have become a UNESCO World Heritage site.

The former president, Gnassingbé Eyadéma, who ruled from 1967 to 2005, had a comic book written about him in which he appears as a superhero. He also ordered all civil servants to wear a watch on which his face would appear every 30 seconds.

TOGOLESE DISHES

- Ablo—*Bread made with fermented corn flour*
- Fufu—*Dough made from pounded cassava and plantains*
- Kokonte —*Stew made with dried cassava, often served with peanuts.*

GHANA

Sandwiched between the Côte d'Ivoire, Togo, and Burkino Faso, Ghana has a long, proud history. Much of it once formed part of the Ashanti Empire that dominated the region between the 1600s and 1800s. It became the first country in sub-Saharan Africa to gain independence after World War II as the colonial era came to an end.

KEY FACTS

Capital: **Accra**
Official Language: **English**
Currency: **Ghanaian Cedi**
Population: **29.3 million**
Area (land): **87,851 sq. mi.**

ASHANTI EMPIRE

In the 1700s and early 1800s, the Ashanti people built a powerful empire. The British went to war four times with the Ashanti before finally defeating them in 1902. In 1957, four British colonies united to form the new, independent nation of Ghana. Today the Ashanti Kingdom survives as a region of Ghana and is still ruled by a king.

VOLTA FOR VOLTAGE

Between 1961 and 1965, the huge Akosombo Dam was built across the Volta River to provide electricity for the country. It created a vast new lake that swallowed up entire villages—around 80,000 people had to be relocated. Today the dam still supplies most of the country's electricity, and Ghana also sells excess electricity to neighboring countries.

Shells were once used as currency in Ghana, which is why today's currency is called the *cedi*, a local word meaning "cowry shell."

COLORFUL CLOTH

Ghanaians are known for a colorful woven cloth known as *kente*. Originally worn by royalty, it's now popular with all of Ghanaian society, both at home and abroad. The finest and most expensive cloth, worn on special occasions, is hand woven by skilled weavers.

Ghana's jungles are home to over 650 species of butterflies, including one of the world's largest, the giant African swallowtail, which can be 8 in. across.

WALKING WITH BIRDS

At Ghana's Kakum National Park, you can tour the upper reaches of the rainforest along a 1,150-foot-long treetop walkway, one of just three such walkways in all of Africa. Animals to look out for in the branches include monkeys, gray parrots, and hornbills.

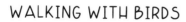

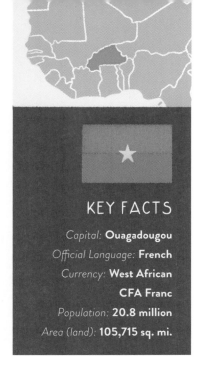

BURKINA FASO

Burkina Faso is a sun-baked land of scorched pavements and painted mud-brick houses. The capital and largest city, Ouagadougou, is located in the center, with dry areas to the north, near the Sahara, and lusher areas of grasslands and forests to the south. Eighty percent of the population works in agriculture.

KEY FACTS

Capital: **Ouagadougou**
Official Language: **French**
Currency: **West African CFA Franc**
Population: **20.8 million**
Area (land): **105,715 sq. mi.**

The national animal of Burkino Faso is the white stallion.

A MOUTHFUL OF MOORÉ

Although French is the official language, about half the people speak the indigenous language Mooré (also known as Mossi). Here are a couple of useful Mooré phrases:

• *Yam Kibaré?*
—How are you?
• *Laafi Bala, La Yamba?*
—I'm fine, and you?

AT THE MOVIES

Held in the capital, the biennial (held every two years) Pan-African Film and Television Festival is one of the hottest tickets around. Over five days, more than 150 movies by African filmmakers are shown. The festival culminates with the awarding of the top prize, the *Étalon de Yennenga* (Stallion of Yennenga). It's named after a legendary princess and supposed mother of the Mossi people, the country's largest ethnic group.

PAINTED HOUSES

The houses of the small village of Tiébélé in southeastern Bukina Faso are made traditionally, using earth, wood, and straw. Hordes of tourists are attracted each year by the houses' incredible decorations. Each is adorned with a unique collection of intricate geometric patterns created using mud and chalk.

SHARP SANDSTONE PEAKS

Burkino Faso is an overwhelmingly flat place, but that doesn't mean it's completely featureless. The Sindou Peaks are a collection of gnarled sandstone formations in the far western part of the country that jut jaggedly out of the surrounding landscape. They were originally formed on the ocean floor but have gradually been pushed above sea level over millions of years.

There are many ethnic groups in Burkino Faso, including the Mossi (who make up just under half the population), the Lobi, the Mande, and the Gurunsi.

CÔTE D'IVOIRE

Côte d'Ivoire (Ivory Coast) was a peaceful, prosperous place until it endured two devastating civil wars between 2002 and 2011. Thankfully, peace has returned, as have visitors, who come to experience the skyscraper-filled cities, tropical beaches, and dense forests where elephants, pygmy hippos, and chimps roam.

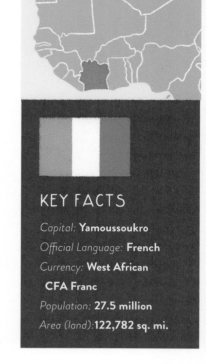

KEY FACTS

Capital: **Yamoussoukro**
Official Language: **French**
Currency: **West African CFA Franc**
Population: **27.5 million**
Area (land): **122,782 sq. mi.**

ELEPHANT EXCELLENCE

Soccer is Côte d'Ivoire's most popular sport. The country has produced numerous famous players over the years, including Serge Aurier, Didier Drogba, and Yaya Touré, who was voted African Player of the Year every year between 2011 and 2014. Many people follow the fortunes of the national team, nicknamed *"Les Eléphants"* (The Elephants), which has won the African Cup of Nations twice, in 1992 and 2015, and has qualified for several World Cups.

THE BIGGEST BASILICA

For many years, St. Peter's Basilica in Vatican City was the world's largest church. But that record was surpassed in the early 1990s with the construction of the Basilica of our Lady of Peace in the capital Yamoussoukro. With a domed roof not unlike the one on top of St. Peter's, the enormous church has space for up to 18,000 worshippers.

WHAT'S IN A NAME?

The country is named after the ivory—the tusks of elephants—that were once one of the region's most important exports. The ivory trade has now been banned, and the authorities are doing their best to protect the country's remaining population of forest elephants from poachers.

CHOCAHOLIC COUNTRY

Côte d'Ivoire is by far and away the world's largest producer of cocoa beans—the main ingredient in chocolate. Every year, its farms turn out around 1.9 million tons of beans, enough to create a giant chocolatey mountain, and amounting to 40 percent of the world's total supply.

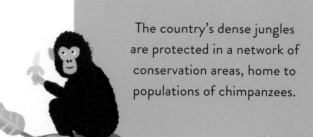

The country's dense jungles are protected in a network of conservation areas, home to populations of chimpanzees.

LIBERIA

Liberia was Africa's first republic and the continent's first country to elect a female head of state, in 2006. Its recent history has been difficult, featuring a civil war and a deadly outbreak of Ebola from 2013 to 2016. But brighter times hopefully lie ahead for this land of coastal plains, rubber plantations, and tropical rainforests.

KEY FACTS

Capital: **Monrovia**
Official Language: **English**
Currency: **Liberian Dollar**
Population: **5.1 million**
Area (land): **37,189 sq. mi.**

FREEDOM AND CONFLICT

Liberia was founded in 1821 as a new country for both freed slaves and free-born people of color from the United States. It was felt that they would have better lives on the continent of their ancestors rather than in the US, where slavery was still legal. However, disagreements between the settlers and the indigenous ethnic groups led to tensions that lasted decades.

RUBBER GIANT

Rubber production has been a major industry in Liberia since the 1920s. Today the tire company Bridgestone operates the world's largest rubber plantation in Harbel, western Liberia. It covers an area of around 260 square miles, which is almost the same size as the city-state of Singapore! About 8,000 people work there, making Bridgestone the country's largest private employer.

PROTECTING PANGOLINS

Sapo National Park, the country's first and largest national park, protects a great mass of rainforest. The densely packed trees are a home to many species, including several rare creatures, such as:
• African golden cat (first photographed in 2002)
• Diana monkey
• three species of pangolins (white-bellied, black-bellied, and giant).

FIRST LEADERS

Liberia is not only the first African country to elect a female head of state—Ellen Johnson Sirleaf, who served as president from 2006 to 2018—it's also the first country in the world to be ruled by a former soccer World Player of the Year. Elected in 2018, George Weah was a striker who played for several top European clubs, including Paris St. Germain, AC Milan, and Chelsea.

FLAGS OF CONVENIENCE

Shipping is one of the most valuable sectors of the Liberian economy, though it's not because Liberia has a lot of ships. By law, ships have to be registered somewhere, and many ships owners choose Liberia, where the taxes are lower and the labor laws are less strict. This is known as using a "flag of convenience." About 11 percent of all the world's ships are registered in Liberia, including about 33 percent of all oil tankers.

SIERRA LEONE

With its recent problems—including a civil war in the 1990s and an outbreak of Ebola in the mid 2010s—behind it, Sierra Leone can look forward to enjoying its abundance of natural resources. These include large reserves of gold and diamonds, long stretches of tropical coast, dense mangroves, and rainforest that covers around a third of the land.

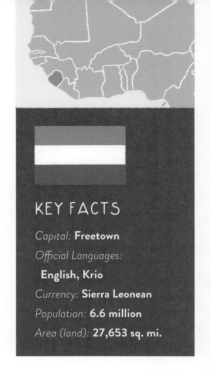

FREEDOM TREE

In 1792, the settlement of Freetown was established as a home for freed slaves, and it has since grown into a major city of more than a million inhabitants. The early settlers in Freetown used to gather to pray around a giant cotton (or kapok) tree. It still stands near the city's Supreme Court building and has become a symbol of the country. The tree is believed to be at least 250 (and possibly over 300) years old.

KEY FACTS

Capital: **Freetown**
Official Languages:
  English, Krio
Currency: **Sierra Leonean**
Population: **6.6 million**
Area (land): **27,653 sq. mi.**

Sierra Leone means "Lion Mountains."

DIAMOND DEPOSITS

Diamonds are big business in Sierra Leone, accounting for most of the country's wealth, and diamond fields cover much of the east and southeast of the country. So Sierra Leone should be a very rich country. Unfortunately, during the civil war, mines were often used as a source for "blood diamonds" (gems exchanged for weapons), and today a lot of diamonds are smuggled out of the country.

SPEAK LIKE A SIERRA LEONEAN

Most people here speak both English and Krio, an English-based language developed by the descendants of the freed slaves of Freetown. Here are a couple of useful phrases:
• Aw di bodi? *"How are you?"* (literally: *"How is the body?"*)
• Di bodi fayn (*"I'm fine"*).

The country's name is often shortened to *"Salone"* in the local Krio language.

GIANT SNACKS

Giant snails are a popular snack in Sierra Leone and several neighboring countries. These slimy creatures, which can be 7 inches long and 4 inches wide, are often sold at street stalls, where they're grilled and served on skewers.

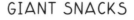

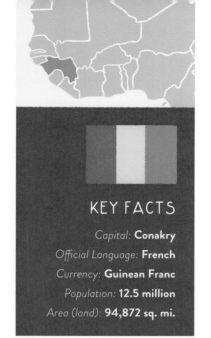

GUINEA

Guinea forms a rough crescent shape, stretching inland from the Atlantic coast. It's divided into four main regions: the baking coastal plains; the cooler highlands of the interior; the grasslands of the northeast; and the rainforests of southeast. It has huge reserves of diamonds and metal, as well as a rich musical heritage.

KEY FACTS

Capital: **Conakry**
Official Language: **French**
Currency: **Guinean Franc**
Population: **12.5 million**
Area (land): **94,872 sq. mi.**

CIRCUS CULTURE

Founded in 1998 but drawing on a tradition going back centuries, Circus Baobab is a proudly African take on a circus. It stages performances in Guinea and around the world in which dancers, acrobats, and trapeze artists perform energetic, daredevil routines to the accompaniment of traditional drumming. Many of the routines tell stories based on traditional Guinean legends.

LAND OF WATER

The middle of the country is taken up by the Fouta Djallon, a collection of giant sandstone plateaus punctuated by deep canyons and covered in lush grassland and forest. With an extremely damp climate, the Fouta Djallon boasts numerous waterways and waterfalls and is the source of two of the region's major rivers, the Gambia and the Senegal.

LAND OF METAL

Aluminum is the most common metal on Earth, making up around 8 percent of our planet's crust. However, it is rarely found in its pure form and generally has to be extracted from metal-holding minerals called ores. Guinea has around a quarter of all the world's reserves of bauxite—the main ore from which aluminum is extracted. This metal accounts for over 60 percent of all the country's exports.

Guinea is sometimes called Guinea-Conakry to avoid confusing it with the two other nearby countries with "Guinea" in their name: Guinea-Bissau and Equatorial Guinea.

Guinea's national animal is the African forest elephant.

THE GAMBIA

The smallest nation on mainland Africa by area, The Gambia is a long thin slice of land surrounded on three sides by Senegal. Around 300 miles long but less than 30 miles wide, it winds inland following the course of the Gambia River. It's known for its glorious beaches, traditional music, and abundance of birdlife.

Until recently, people in The Gambia voted by dropping marbles into a bucket representing their candidate rather than by marking a ballot or using a voting machine.

LIVING HISTORY

Griots are important figures in The Gambia and across West Africa. A combination of historian, poet, and musician, the griot has been around since at least the Middle Ages. Originally acting as living history books, preserving stories and traditions through songs, the griot's main role today is as a performer. Many griots play instruments, such as the kora (an instrument with 21 strings, somewhat like a giant lute), and some even tour internationally.

KEY FACTS

Capital: **Banjul**
Official Language: **English**
Currency: **Gambian Dalasi**
Population: **2.2 million**
Area (land): **3,907 sq. mi.**

The country's national sport is a type of traditional wrestling called *boreh*.

GUINEA-BISSAU

Guinea-Bissau is made up of two distinct parts. There's the mainland, which is thick with mangroves and swamps and, in the east, areas of grassland and rainforest. Then there are the Bijagós Islands, which lie to the southwest and are famous for their beautiful beaches and unique wildlife.

SALTWATER HIPPOS

The stunningly pretty Bijagós Islands are the country's main tourist draw. There are 88 in total, 20 of which are populated, and between them they boast a range of habitats, including palm forests, grasslands, and sandy beaches, as well as various marine environments. The Bijagós' most famous animal residents are a group of rare saltwater hippos, which can sometimes be seen wallowing in the waters around the largest island, Orango.

KEY FACTS

Capital: **Bissau**
Official Language: **Portuguese**
Currency: **West African CFA Franc**
Population: **1.9 million**
Area (land): **10,857 sq. mi.**

A popular style of music here and in many neighboring countries is *gumbe*. Named after the drum that provides the main rhythm, gumbe music combines vocals with percussion instruments to produce an upbeat, danceable sound.

SENEGAL

Occupying the most westerly part of the African mainland, Senegal's influences are a mix of African and French. Just south of the Sahara, its landscape consists largely of savanna and shrubland, interspersed with lively cities—and there are few livelier than the capital, Dakar, with its vibrant music scene.

KEY FACTS

Capital: **Dakar**
Official Language: **French**
Currency: **West African CFA Franc**
Population: **15.7 million**
Area (land): **74,336 sq. mi.**

The country gets its name from the Senegal River that borders it to the north and east.

EAT (AND DRINK) LIKE A SENEGALESE

• Thiéboudienne—*Fish, rice, and vegetables cooked in tomato sauce; it's considered the national dish.*
• Yassa—*Chicken or fish cooked with caramalized onions, lemon, and mustard.*
• Bissap—*Tangy, citrusy drink made from hibiscus flowers.*

GIANT STATUE

Perched on a hill on Dakar's outskirts is the continent's largest statue, the African Renaissance Monument. Completed in 2010 to celebrate the 50th anniversary of the country's independence from France, it depicts a 170-foot-high African family gazing up toward the sky. An elevator whisks visitors up to the top, where they can enjoy the views from the father's crown.

DOOR OF NO RETURN

For hundreds of years, until the 1800s, people were shipped to the Americas as slaves. Many people believe that a building known as the House of Slaves on Gorée Island was an 18th-century slave market. It's said that thousands of people were taken through a gateway known as "The Door of No Return" to a life of servitude. It's a powerful monument to the inhuman transatlantic slave trade.

LIVELY CITY

Dakar was first settled in the 1400s. For many years, it remained small and sparsely populated, until the arrival of the French in the 1800s, which saw it grow into a major port. Today it's a thriving metropolis of over two million people, known for its numerous venues where you can hear the popular style of dance music called mbalax.

NATIONAL MUSIC

The title of Senegal's national anthem is an invitation for people to make music: "*Pincez Tous vos Koras, Frappez les Balafons,*" which means everyone strum your koras, strike the balafons). The kora is a stringed instrument, a bit like a large lute, while the balafon resembles a xylophone but with gourds used as resonators to project the sound.

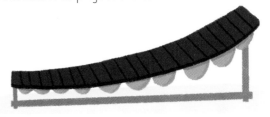

SÃO TOMÉ
AND PRÍNCIPE

Africa's second-smallest country is made up of two islands off the mainland's western coast. It was once known as the "Chocolate Islands" after the cocoa plantations established by Portuguese colonists. Today it's fringed by sandy beaches, dotted with volcanic towers, and covered with thick rainforest across around 30 percent of the land.

STORY TELLING

The dramatic musical dance performances known as Tchiloli, which often retell stories of medieval Europe, are one of the most important parts of São Tomé culture. Every year in mid-August, the country stages an epic piece of street theater called the *Auto de Floripes*, in which the island's entire population participates to reenact a medieval battle between Christians and Moors.

Around 96% of the population lives on the larger island of São Tomé.

CAPE VERDE

This group of ten volcanic islands lies off west coast of Africa and enjoys a blend of Portuguese and African cultural influences. The Verde ("green") landscape is well named, with forests blanketing much of the land alongside volcanoes, canyons, sandy beaches, and bright blue expanses of ocean.

Cape Verde's beaches are a major nesting site for loggerhead sea turtles.

NATIONAL DISH

The national and most famous dish of Cape Verde is a slow-cooked stew called *cachupa*. It's made from corn, beans, sweet potato, cassava, a type of blood sausage called *morcela,* and either meat or fish. Each island has its own unique take on the recipe.

Some of the island's volcanoes are still active. Pico do Fogo erupted in 2014, destroying several houses that had been built nearby (although thankfully no one was injured).

MALAWI

Nicknamed the "Warm Heart of Africa" because of the friendliness of its people, Malawi is dominated by the huge lake that stretches down its eastern side. The country is a wildlife watcher's paradise, with a vast array of animals inhabiting the varied landscape, including elephants, lions, and rhinos lurking in its grasslands.

KEY FACTS

Capital: **Lilongwe**

Official Languages: **English, Chewa**

Currency: **Melawian Kwacha**

Population: **21.2 million**

Area (land): **36,324 sq. mi.**

FISH BY THE THOUSAND

Lake Malawi is the fifth-largest freshwater lake in the world, taking up around a third of the country's total area. It contains more species of fish than any other lake in the world—over 1,000. Around 700 of those are cichlids, a small tropical fish that comes in a range of dazzling colors.

LAKE OF STARS

Since 2004, a major music and cultural celebration has been held on the banks of Lake Malawi—the Lake of Stars Festival. The name is a reference to the lanterns of the fishing boats that often patrol the lake at night, making it look as if it's covered in stars.

MALAWI'S FLAG

Malawi's flag, adopted when the country became independent from Britain in 1964, consists of three horizontal bands of color: black, representing the country's people; red, representing the blood of their struggles; and green, representing nature. In the black section is a red rising sun, representing freedom and hope.

CHEWA PEOPLE

Malawi's main ethnic group, making up a third of the population, is the Chewa. One of their traditional practices, dating back at least 300 years, is a dance known as the *Gule Wamkulu*. Performed to mark special occasions (and for the benefit of tourists), it often takes the form of a morality play designed to promote good behavior. Dancers wear wooden masks representing a range of characters, including wild animals and spirits of the dead.

The country's name is believed to derive from an old Chewa word meaning "flames."

SPEAK CHEWA (OR CHICHEWA) LIKE A MALAWIAN

- Muli bwanji?
  —"*How are you?*"
- Ndiri bwino, kaya inu?
  —"*I'm fine, and you?*"
- Chonde—"*Please*"
- Zikomo—"*Thank you*"

ZAMBIA

Despite being far from the coast, this landlocked country is dominated by water. The Zambezi River floods the lowlands each year. The great Bangweulu wetland system of lakes and swamps spreads out across the northeast, while in the south are the mighty Victoria Falls. On land, there's a wealth of wildlife and numerous bustling cities.

KEY FACTS

Capital: **Lusaka**
Official Language: **English**
Currency: **Zambian Kwacha**
Population: **17.4 million**
Area (land): **287,028 sq. mi.**

VICTORIA FALLS

Many people believe the vast collection of waterfalls on the border between Zambia and Zimbabwe are the world's largest. Part of the Zambezi River, the Victoria Falls are 5,604 feet wide and 354 feet high, which makes them over twice the height of Niagara Falls. Every minute, more than 132 million gallons of water pours over the edge, creating a constant eruption of spray.

Victoria Falls, named after the 19th-century British queen, is known locally as *Mosi-oa-Tunya*, which means "The Smoke that Thunders" in the Lozi language.

WINGED VISITORS

Every year between October and December, the skies above Kasanka National Park turn dark as around 10 million fruit bats arrive here following their migration from the Congo rainforest. These winged mammals fill the trees of the swamp forest, feasting on the fruits that come into season at this time. There are so many roosting bats that the trees' branches sometimes snap under their weight.

The country's economy has long been dominated by the mining of copper.

CELEBRATING WATER

The traditional Kumoboka ceremony takes place every year in Zambia to mark the rainy season, when the Zambezi River bursts its banks and floods the surrounding area. The celebrations involve moving the king of the Lozi people from his compound near the river up to higher ground. He's transported in a ceremonial black-and-white barge, powered by rowers, on top of which sits a statue of a giant black elephant.

ZIMBABWE

The country's political and financial difficulties have dominated the headlines in recent years, but with the situation improving, it's time to focus more on the charms of Zim (as it's known locally). There's plenty of choice, including wildlife-filled national parks, logic-defying rock formations, and the giant stone cities of ancient empires.

KEY FACTS

Capital: **Harare**
Official Languages: **English, Chewa, Shona, Kalanga, and 12 other languages**
Currency: **Zimbabwean Dollar**
Population: **14.5 million**
Area (land): **149,362 sq. mi.**

GREAT ZIMBABWE

In the 1300s, the country's southeast was dominated by a giant city of stone known today as Great Zimbabwe. Created by the local Shona people, it sat at the center of a great trading network. At its peak, it would have been home to many thousands of people, but it was abandoned around 1450 for reasons that are not fully understood. The modern country was named in honor of this medieval metropolis, and the national flag features a stone bird (known as a "Zimbabwe Bird") discovered at the site.

ROCKS AND WILDLIFE

Matobo National Park in the southern part of the country is famous for both its animals—which include rhinos, leopards, and the world's largest population of Verreaux's eagles—and its unusual granite rock formations called kopjes. The best known of these is a set of precariously balancing boulders known as the Mother and Child Kopje.

Zimbabwe has 16 official languages, one of the highest numbers in the world.

FUNNY MONEY

Zimbabwe suffered terrible economic problems in the 2000s. Inflation grew out of control, going from 32 percent in 1998 to an estimated 11.2 million percent a decade later. Prices rose so fast that people didn't have enough money to buy goods. At one point, the government issued a 100 trillion dollar bill, before the whole currency was suspended in 2009. A new currency was introduced in 2019 that is now used alongside foreign currencies such as the US dollar and the South African rand.

MOZAMBIQUE

Mozambique has over 1,400 miles of coastline, much of it made up of picture-perfect tropical beaches. Its waters support an incredible array of marine species, while parks protect some of the continent's most iconic animals. The cities groove to beat of marrabenta, a traditional dance music.

KEY FACTS

Capital: **Maputo**
Official Language: **Portuguese**
Currency: **Mozambican Metical**
Population: **30.1 million**
Area (land): **303,623 sq. mi.**

MASKED DANCING

The mapiko is a traditional story dance performed by a man wearing a carved wooden mask-helmet (known as a *lipiko*) in the shape of a human head. Originally part of an initiation rite to help prepare children for the adult world, the dance is now often used as a way of commenting on current events or to remind people of their history. The dancer wears the mask to channel the spirit of dead ancestors.

Mozambique has a very young population, with around 45% of the people age 15 years or younger.

SEA COWS

Bazaruto Island, off the country's southern coast, is home to one of East Africa's last populations of dugongs. These large, slow-swimming mammals spend all their time in water, grazing on sea grass—from which they get their nickname, "sea cows." Although they look a bit like giant seals, they're actually more closely related to elephants. Dugongs use their large snouts to suck up huge amounts of vegetation each day.

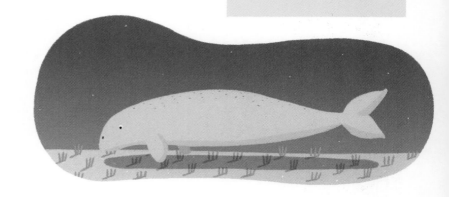

A FLAG WITH A DIFFERENCE

Mozambique has the world's only flag that features a modern weapon, a type of machine gun called an AK-47. It is shown on the flag crossed with a hoe, a symbol of farming, on top of a book, a symbol of education.

The Zambezi River flows from northwest to southeast through the middle of the country, finally reaching the Indian Ocean on Mozambique's coast.

ESWATINI

Known as Swaziland until 2018, this small nation tucked between South Africa and Mozambique is the last remaining absolute monarchy in Africa. Although it maintains many of its traditions, Eswatini is becoming more modernized thanks to its young population. Much of the land is preserved in parks, providing a home for many of Africa's famous big animals, including black rhinos.

KEY FACTS

Capital: **Mbabane, Lobamba**
Official Languages:
Swazi, English
Currency: **Swazi Lilangeni,**
South African Rand
Population: **1.1 million**
Area (land): **6,643 sq. mi.**

ROYAL POWER

Eswatini is an absolute monarchy, which means that the monarch rules the country directly, not through an elected leader. The tradition in Eswatini is for the monarch to be a king known as a *Ngwenyaman* ("Lion"), who rules alongside his mother, the *Ndlovukati* ("Great She Elephant").

Eswatini's traditional Reed Dance, or *Umhlanga*, involves hundreds of girls bringing tall reeds to the queen's residence to repair its fence, before dancing and feasting takes place.

LESOTHO

Set inside South Africa, Lesotho may not be that large, but it's by far the biggest enclave (country surrounded entirely by another country) in the world. It owes its state of isolation mainly to its altitude and the trickiness of its terrain. Much of Lesotho is covered in mountains, from which it gets its nickname, "The Kingdom of the Sky."

KEY FACTS

Capital: **Maseru**
Official Languages:
Sesotho, English
Currency: **Lesotho Loti,**
South African Rand
Population: **1.9 million**
Area (land): **11,720 sq. mi.**

STRAW HATS

The black shape at the center of the Lesotho flag depicts a type of conical straw hat known as a *mokorotlo*. A traditional garment of the Basotho people—the ethnic group that makes up over 99 percent of Lesotho's population—the hat is worn by chiefs to show their authority and has become a symbol of the nation.

The Matekana Airstrip is located high in the mountains and extends all the way to the edge of a 1,600-foot cliff. Pilots find it an extreme challenge to land here.

NAMIBIA

With the Kalahari Desert in its eastern half and the Namib Desert in its west, Namibia is the driest country in southern Africa. The people and animals that live here—including elephants, lions, ostriches, black rhinos, and scorpions—have to be hardy to thrive in these harsh conditions. Namibia is Africa's least densely populated country.

SKELETON COAST

The sand dunes of the Namib Desert roll right down to the Atlantic coast. Here a combination of dense fogs and sharp rocks just offshore has contributed to numerous shipwrecks over the years. Their rusting hulls have given this area the nickname the Skeleton Coast, because the frames of the ships look like giant metal bones slowly being consumed by the sand.

EXTREME SAND SPORTS

Many people like to experience Namibia's giant dunes through the sport of sandboarding. This involves hurtling down the side of a dune on a wooden board or, if you prefer the sand-skiing option, two boards. The world record speed for sandboarding was set in Namibia in 2010, when a German thrill seeker sped down the dunes at over 90 miles per hour.

The Namib Desert, believed to have formed around 55 million years ago, possesses some of the world's tallest dunes, formed by strong winds blowing sands in from the coast. The biggest are over 1,150 feet high.

NATURAL SUN PROTECTION

The Himba people of Northern Namibia protect themselves from the harsh desert sun (and insect bites) by covering their bodies and hair in a special paste called *ojitze*. This is made from a mixture of butterfat and ochre pigment (red-colored clay) and gives the people a distinctive, rust-colored appearance.

Namib means "area where there is nothing" in the local Nama language.

SPACE VISITOR

The largest known intact meteorite was discovered in 1920 on a farm in northeast Namibia. Known as the Hoba Meteorite, the giant rectangular lump of iron weighs around 60 tons and therefore has been left where it was found. It's believed that when this great chunk of space rock landed, around 80,000 years ago, Earth's atmosphere slowed it down. This meant it didn't disintegrate like most meteorites.

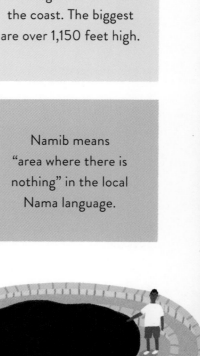
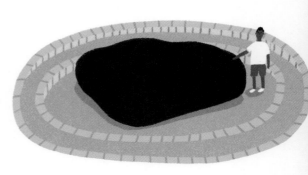

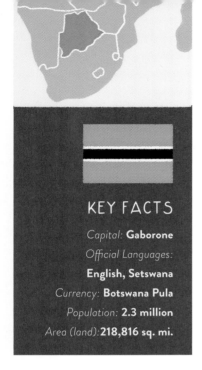

BOTSWANA

Botswana's fortunes changed dramatically in 1967, just a year after independence, when diamonds were discovered here. The wealth this brought to the nation has been spent on health care, education, and improving the infrastructure, as well as establishing a network of national parks and reserves to protect its plentiful wildlife.

KEY FACTS

Capital: **Gaborone**

Official Languages: **English, Setswana**

Currency: **Botswana Pula**

Population: **2.3 million**

Area (land): **218,816 sq. mi.**

Botswana's Orapa Mine is the world's largest diamond mine.

OKAVANGO DELTA

Although around 70 percent of Botswana is covered in desert, the country boasts one of the continent's lushest environments in the form of the Okavango Delta. Most rivers empty into the ocean, but the Okavango River comes to an end on land, spreading out into a depression to form a mass of swampy grasslands. This environment provides a home to an abundance of wildlife, including lions, leopards, elephants, rhinos, hippos, and crocodiles.

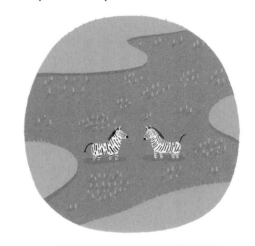

KEEPING A LOOKOUT

The country's most iconic animal is the meerkat. These cute members of the mongoose family live in large family groups in the Kalahari Desert. They spend most of the day foraging for food, such as insects, lizards, and deadly scorpions (thankfully, they're immune to their stings). In order to avoid becoming a meal for something else (such as an eagle), meerkats make sure there's always at least one member of the group on lookout duty—standing on its hind legs on the tallest available structure, ready to sound the alarm at the first sign of danger.

Botswana has the world's largest population of African elephants, estimated at around 130,000 individuals.

SAN PEOPLE

The San people have inhabited Botswana for thousands of years. Indeed, there are examples of San rock art in the Tsodilo Hills that are believed to be 24,000 years old. Although many San have moved to urban areas, there are thought to be around 10,000 still living in the wild, practicing a traditional hunter-gatherer lifestyle. They are hugely skilled at making the most out of scarce water resources, using ostrich shells as water stores, which they bury underground.

SOUTH AFRICA

South Africa is a land of rolling grasslands, high plateaus, and some of Africa's largest cities. Now truly democratic after the abolition of apartheid in the mid-1990s, it is a vibrant, cosmopolitan place. It's also absolutely packed with wildlife, ranging from elephants and lions to penguins and great white sharks.

KEY FACTS

Capital: **Pretoria, Cape Town, Bloemfontein**
Official Languages: **English, isi Zulu, Afrikaans, 8 others**
Currency: **South African Rand**
Population: **56.5 million**
Area (land): **468,909 sq. mi.**

FLAT TOPS

The country's best-known landmark is a flat-topped mountain overlooking the country's second-largest city, Cape Town. Table Mountain's main plateau stands over 3,500 feet high and is flanked by two peaks: Devil's Peak to the east and Lion's Head to the west. People can hike or, if they want to take it easy, ride a cable car to the top to enjoy the views over the city.

NELSON MANDELA

One of the towering figures of recent international politics, Nelson Mandela spent much of his early life protesting against the policy of apartheid then in force in South Africa. This discriminated against the majority black population who were kept apart from the white population (apartheid means "apartness") and given fewer rights. Nelson Mandela was sent to prison for 27 years for his protests. After his release, he helped oversee the ending of the apartheid system and, in 1994, he was elected president following the country's first free elections. His death in 2013 was mourned around the world.

South Africa is the only country to have hosted the men's soccer, rugby, and cricket World Cups.

South Africa's nickname is the "rainbow nation" because of its mixture of cultures and languages.

BIG HOLE

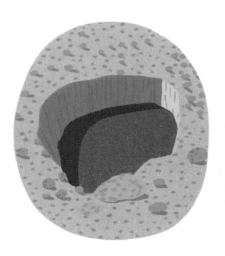

In 1871, diamonds were discovered in Kimberley, South Africa. This led to a diamond rush, with thousands of people arriving to try and make their fortune. Over the next 40 years, a giant pit was excavated using picks and shovels, from which diamonds were extracted. By the time the diamonds ran out, the pit extended 790 feet into the ground. Now appropriately known as the Big Hole, the abandoned pit is half filled with water and is a tourist attraction in its own right.

Although it takes up just 1% of Earth's land, South Africa has around 9% of Earth's plant species.

MADAGASCAR

The fourth-largest island in the world, Madagascar sits 250 miles off the east coast of Africa. It split away from the continent 13.5 million years ago, and its plants and animals evolved in isolation. This has created an incredible ecosystem unlike any other on Earth, where new species are still being discovered.

KEY FACTS

Capital: **Antananarivo**

Official Languages:
French, Malagasy

Currency: **Malagasy Ariary**

Population: **26.9 million**

Area (land): **224,534 sq. mi.**

In the west of the island is a stretch of road lined with baobabs —the national tree of Madagascar. Some of the trees along this road are thought to be a thousand years old.

A WORLD OF ITS OWN

The island's lush and varied landscape includes rainforests, grasslands, deserts, mangrove forests, and coral reefs. Almost 90 percent of the 250,000 wildlife species that live on Madagascar are completely unique to the island. They include:

- almost half of the 200 known species of chameleons
- satanic leaf-tailed gecko • tomato frog
- plowshare tortoise

SPIRITS OF THE NIGHT

There are over 100 species of lemurs, and all of them are native to Madagascar. Leaping from tree to tree and hopping sideways along the forest floor, these incredibly varied creatures range from the tiny mouse lemur to the long-fingered aye-aye. The Latin word *lemur* means "spirits of the night"; perhaps they were named for their eerie calls and large, reflective eyes.

MALAGASY PEOPLE

Humans have lived on Madagascar for around 1,300 years, and the population today is made up of around 20 different ethnic groups. Most of the people in Madagascar live in rural areas, farming crops such as rice and coffee. The island's culture reflects Southeast Asian traditions as well as those of East Africa.

FUSION FOOD

The food of Madagascar has French, Chinese, Indian, and African influences. Rice is such an important staple ingredient that the Malagasy verb meaning "to eat" (*mihinam-vary*) translates as "to eat rice." A typical Malagasy lunch consists of rice served with a meat or vegetable dish, usually coated in a spicy sauce. One of the island's most important culinary exports is vanilla—roughly 80 percent of the world's vanilla comes from Madagascar.

MAURITIUS

The island nation of Mauritius is located in the Indian Ocean, east of Madagascar. People have lived on the island only for a few hundred years. Before that, a rich and unique habitat developed undisturbed for millennia. Today visitors are drawn to Mauritius for its incredible wildlife, idyllic beaches, and welcoming culture.

WILD WONDERS

Mauritius is home to some amazing (and some amazingly rare) animals and plants. They include the Mauritian fruit bat, the ornate day gecko, and an endangered species of palm tree called the blue latanier. Since the arrival of people in the 1500s, however, the island's native wildlife has been threatened by human interference and the introduction of nonnative species, such as rats, cats, and dogs. The dodo, Mauritius's most famous animal, was hunted to extinction by European settlers in the 1600s.

KEY FACTS

Capital: **Port Louis**
Official Language: **English**
Currency: **Mauritian Rupee**
Population: **1.3 million**
Area (land): **788 sq. mi.**

At the southwestern tip of the island, the ocean's currents have created a spectacular optical illusion. From above, it looks like a giant "underwater waterfall"—in fact, it's a pattern created by sand and silt deposits.

MAURITIAN MENU

Mauritian people are descended from African, Indian, Chinese, Dutch, and French settlers, and the island's cuisine reflects this diverse heritage. Here are just a few of the dishes you might come across:

• Dholl puri—*a split-pea flatbread, served with curries and chutneys*
• Rougaille—*a rich tomato stew containing either meat or fish, plus onion, garlic, and thyme*
• Palm heart salad—*a Mauritian delicacy made from the center of a palm tree (it's also known as "millionaire's salad" because it's so expensive)*
• Boulet—*a Mauritian take on Chinese dim sum, made up of steamed dumplings stuffed with meat, fish, or vegetables and served in a broth.*

HINDU CELEBRATIONS

Almost half of the population of Mauritius is Hindu, and the religion's festivals are an important part of the Mauritian calendar. The Maha Shivaratri is a three-day festival in honor of the Hindu god Shiva. Around 500,000 Hindus take part in a pilgrimage to the island's holy lake, the Grand Bassin, to celebrate.

COMOROS

The recent history of these volcanic islands off the east coast of Africa has been somewhat unstable. There have been several coups since the country's independence from France in 1975, and there are ongoing arguments about the island of Mayotte, which Comoros wants to claim but which has voted to remain part of France.

KEY FACTS

Capital: **Moroni**

Official Languages: **Comorian, French, Arabic**

Currency: **Comorian Franc**

Population: **846,000**

Area (land): **863 sq. mi.**

PERFUME PROVIDER

Much of the islands are given over to the growing of spices, including vanilla, cinnamon, and cloves. Its main product is a yellow tropical flower called ylang ylang, the aromatic oil of which is used to make perfume. Comoros is responsible for 80 percent of the world's supply of this oil.

At 7,746 feet, Mount Karthala on the largest island, Grand Comore, is Comoros' highest point. It's erupted at least 20 times in the past 200 years.

SEYCHELLES

Africa's smallest country consists of 115 paradise-like islands in the Indian Ocean. Colonized by Europeans in 1500s, the Seychelles are a mix of French, British, African, Indian, and East Asian influences. They're a particularly popular tourist destination for people wanting to relax on beautiful beaches.

KEY FACTS

Capital: **Victoria**

Official Languages: **Seychellois Creole, English, French**

Currency: **Seychellois Rupee**

Population: **95,900**

Area (land): **176 sq. mi.**

GIANT SEEDS

Found only on two islands in the Seychelles, a palm tree known as the coco de mer (coconut of the sea) produces the world's largest seed, which can reach 20 inches in diameter and weigh 55 pounds. Unlike coconuts, coco de mer seeds are too heavy to float, and they sink if they fall in the sea. Once on the bottom, the insides rot away, and the outer shell may rise to the surface. The first sailors to see these seeds rising thought they must have grown on trees on the seabed.

The northernmost island, Bird Island, is home to around 700,000 pairs of sooty terns and also provides a nesting site for green and hawksbill turtles.

AFGHANISTAN

Often seen as the link between Central Asia and South Asia, Afghanistan is a land of vast snow-capped mountain ranges, rolling plains, and thousands of years of history. Although the country has been damaged by recent warfare, many of its ancient traditions survive. Nomads still heard yaks on the frozen peaks, and merchants fill the bustling city bazaars.

KEY FACTS

Capital: **Kabul**

Official Languages:
Dari, Pashto

Currency: **Afghan Afghani**

Population: **36.6 million**

Area (land): **251,827 sq. mi.**

BLUE MOSQUE

The turquoise domes of Afghanistan's Blue Mosque glitter under the baking sun in Mazar-i-Sharif, Afghanistan's fourth-largest city. Adorned with intricate Islamic tilework, the mosque is regarded as a symbol of tranquillity amid the city's busy market stalls. Fittingly, thousands of white doves—a traditional symbol of peace—flitter around the outside of the building.

Dating back to roughly 650 CE, the world's first oil paintings are believed to cover cave walls in Afghanistan's Bamiyan region.

KITE FIGHT

Kite fighting is a longstanding tradition in Afghanistan, with local tournaments taking place across the country. Unlike kite "flying," kite "fighting" is a highly competitive sport. Using strings coated in a sharp substance called *manja*, the kite flyer's aim is to cut the lines of all their opponents' kites, so they drop to the ground. The person with the last kite left flying is the winner. Teams of kite runners closely follow the battle, as it's the custom for the finder of a fallen kite to keep it.

Tsenga yee?
"How are you?"
in Pashto

Chutoor hasta?
"How are you?"
in Dari

HOUND DOGS

The elegant, long-haired Afghan hound is one of the world's oldest species of dogs, but don't be fooled by their flowing, glamorous locks. These dogs were first bred thousands of years ago to be hunters, traveling with nomadic tribes across mountainous plains, where their long hair helped keep them warm. The hounds were large enough to bring down antelopes and even fend off leopards.

KAZAKHSTAN

This sprawling Central Asian nation sees sweltering summers and freezing winters, where the land is divided between futuristic cities and huge, treeless plains. Indeed, people have been riding across this land for thousands of years. It was once an important stage on the Silk Road trading route linking Asia with Europe.

KEY FACTS

Capital: **Nur-Sultan**
Official Language: **Kazakh**
Currency: **Kazakhstani Tenge**
Population: **19 million**
Area (land): **1,042,360 sq. mi.**

Yuri Gagarin, the first person in space, took off from Baikonur in 1961.

SHOOTING INTO SPACE

If you want to head into space, then Kazakhstan is one of the best places to do it. It's home to the Baikonur Cosmodrome, the world's largest and busiest space-launch center. Founded in the mid 1950s when the country was part of the Soviet Union, it's still operated by Russia, which leases the land from Kazakhstan. It's hosted thousands of rocket launches, sending astronauts up to the International Space Station, satellites into orbit above Earth, and probes on missions across the solar system.

WILD HORSES

The people who ride their horses across the plains of the Kazakh Steppe are following an age-old tradition. It's believed that the animals were first domesticated here in Kazakhstan over 5,500 years ago. The ancient people used horses both for riding and for their milk—practices which have both continued to the modern day.

APPLE FATHER

Kazakhstan is the world's largest landlocked nation. Despite being miles away from the ocean, it maintains a small navy based in the Caspian Sea.

Now enjoyed around the world, the apple is thought to have its roots in the snowy foothills of Almaty, the country's largest city (and former capital). In fact, the city's name comes from the Kazakh term *Alma-Ata*, meaning "Father of Apples." Apple farming and production have since been transported around the world, initially through the Silk Road trade routes several thousand years ago.

KAZAKH DELICACIES

• Kumis—*fermented horse milk.*
• Beshbarmak—*boiled meat (horse or lamb) with noodles and onion sauce. It's considered the national dish.*

TAJIKISTAN

With mountains as far as the eye can see, this is one of the world's most high-altitude countries. Despite peaks taking up 90 percent of its area, Tajikistan was nonetheless once a major, if rather arduous, stage of the Silk Road. Visitors can still explore an elevated section of the route on the Pamir Highway.

KEY FACTS

Capital: **Dushanbe**
Official Language: **Tajik**
Currency: **Tajikistani Somoni**
Population: **8.8 million**
Area (land): **54,637 sq. mi.**

MEETING OF MOUNTAINS

Tajikistan marks the point where several mountain ranges meet, including the Himalayas, the Karakoram, and the Hindu Kush. Squashed between them is the Pamir Range, through which winds the Pamir Highway, one of the world's highest roads. It's been here since the days of the Silk Road, when it would have seen great caravans of traders laden with exotic goods, such as spices, teas, gold and silver, and medicine, trudging slowly westward.

Like a giant icy river, the 48 mi. long Fedchenko Glacier is always on the move and can shift up to 26 in. a day.

TURKMENISTAN

With the gigantic "black sand" Karakum Desert taking up three-fourths of the land, it's little surprise that this is one of Asia's most sparsely populated countries. Many people live in the capital, which was rebuilt in gleaming white marble when the country broke free of the Soviet Union in the early 1990s.

DINOSAUR TRAILS

Some of the world's longest and best-preserved dinosaur tracks can be seen in Turkmenistan's Köýtendag National Park in the Kugitang Mountains. In the 1950s, paleontologists discovered thousands of fossilized prints dating back to the late Jurassic period. They're scattered across a 1,300-foot-long slab of limestone, which has become known as the "Plateau of Dinosaurs." The tracks represent a range of prehistoric creatures—the largest are the tracks of a megalosaurus, a giant T. rex-like meat eater.

KEY FACTS

Capital: **Ashgabat**
Official Language: **Turkmen**
Currency: **Turkmenistan Manat**
Population: **5.5 million**
Area (land): **181,441 sq. mi.**

Nähilisiň?
"How are you?"

Owy, özüň nähili?
"I'm fine, and you?"

UZBEKISTAN

The most visited country in Central Asia, Uzbekistan sparkles with ancient treasures. Mountains, mosques, and minarets cover the landscape of a place where various different empires—Persian, Islamic, Mongol, Turkic, and Russian—have left their mark.

KEY FACTS

Capital: **Tashkent**

Official Language: **Uzbek**

Currency: **Uzbekistani So'm**

Population: **30.5 million**

Area (land): **164,248 sq. mi.**

The national drink of Uzbekistan is *kuk-choy*— green tea.

BLUE DOMES

The almost legendary city of Samarkand was once a major stop on the Silk Road and is Uzbekistan's biggest visitor attraction. It's centered on Registan Square, which is flanked by three massive madrasahs—Islamic educational buildings. Just to the north is the Bibi-Khanym Mosque. Adorned with deep-blue tiles, it was once the largest and most magnificent mosque in the Islamic world.

Uzbekistan is double-landlocked. This means that it's a whole two countries away from the nearest coast. The only other double-landlocked country is Liechtenstein.

KYRGYZSTAN

One of the smallest Central Asian nations, Kyrgyzstan has a rugged landscape scattered with lakes and hot springs. It's a traditional place. Outside the cities, roaming nomads still move across the country with livestock and portable tents known as yurts in tow.

KEY FACTS

Capital: **Bishkek**

Official Language: **Kyrgyz**

Currency: **Kyrgyzstani Som**

Population: **5.9 million**

Area (land): **74,055 sq. mi.**

HOT LAKE

Northeast Kyrgyzstan is dominated by Issyk-Kul, the second-largest mountain lake in the world, as well as one of the oldest, dating back 25 million years. Despite being surrounded by snow-capped mountains, the lake never freezes, even in the winter. This is owing to a combination of the lake's depth, its high salt content, and the surrounding hot springs. The lake's name translates as "Hot Lake."

The ancient tradition of hunting with eagles is still practiced in Kyrgyzstan by a few brave trainers who manage to train eagles with a 6-foot wingspan and giant talons to obey their commands.

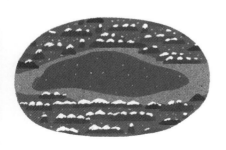

NORTH KOREA

Known today as the world's most isolated country, North Korea allows only a few thousand tourists each year. These visits are tightly monitored, so much of the country remains shrouded in secrecy. What is known is that it boasts a great ridge of mountains in its center, dotted with forests and lakes. The lives of the people, who mainly inhabit the coastal plains, are strictly controlled by the communist government.

KEY FACTS

Capital: **Pyongyang**
Official Language: **Korean**
Currency: **North Korean Won**
Population: **25.6 million**
Area (land): **46,490 sq. mi.**

UNFINISHED BUSINESS

The gigantic, pyramid-shaped Ryugyong Hotel in Pyongyang is by far North Korea's tallest building. It stands 1,080 feet high, towering above the surrounding capital. Although it was supposed to open in 1989, it remains unfinished. The exterior is complete, but various economic crises have seen work on the interior grind to a halt. The building remains eerily empty, making it the world's largest unoccupied building.

DMZ

Formerly one Korea, communist North Korea and democratic South Korea have been separate countries since just after World War II. Following the indecisive civil war of 1950–53, the two sides have been physically separated by a narrow strip of land 150 miles long and 2.5 miles wide. It's known as the Demilitarized Zone, or DMZ for short.

North Korea has the longest compulsory military service in the world: the minimum terms are 10 years for men and seven years for women.

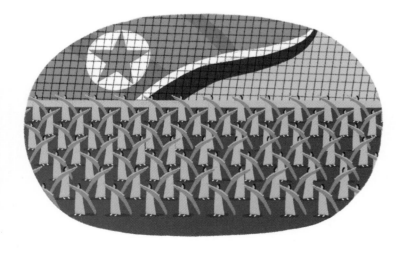

SUPER STADIUM

The award for the world's largest stadium goes to North Korea's Rungrado May Day Stadium, in Pyongyang. Offering 150,000 seats, it hosts various sports events as well as the annual Arirang Mass Games. These involve thousands of performers putting on tightly choreographed displays of gymnastics, acrobatics, and dance designed to demonstrate the togetherness of the country.

SOUTH KOREA

Located below North Korea, South Korea is a very different place: open, modern, and international. Much of its history remains intact, in the form of ancient palaces and traditions, but these now sit alongside buzzing high-tech industries and the futuristic skyscrapers of its megacity capital, Seoul.

KEY FACTS

Capital: **Seoul**
Official Language: **Korean**
Currency: **South Korean Won**
Population: **51.8 million**
Area (land): **37,421 sq. mi.**

KOREAN WAVE

In recent years, South Korea's K-pop (Korean pop) music has taken the world by storm. The most well-known K-pop group is BTS, an award-winning boy band that performs to screaming crowds all over the globe. K-pop songs can span a range of genres, and band members must both sing and dance. If it's catchy, it's K-pop!

CULINARY KOREA

Often warming and spicy, popular Korean dishes include:
• Bulgogi—*thin slices of grilled meat (beef or pork) in a sweet and savory marinade.*
• Bibimbap—*rice with meat and vegetables, usually topped with a fried egg.*
• Kimchi—*a tangy, bright orange-red pickle made with fermented vegetables.*

FEMALE FREEDIVERS

Try to imagine what it must be like to hold your breath for three minutes while diving dozens of feet down into the ocean. This is what life is like for the *haenyeo*—the diving women of South Korea's Jeju island. The female freediving tradition stretches back centuries, although today fewer than 5,000 divers remain. *Haenyeo* dive without breathing equipment every day to catch seafood, such as urchins, octopuses, and sea cucumbers, while men take care of the home and children. Divers have to spend years in training to be able to handle the extreme cold and water pressure.

South Korea has the fastest Internet speed in the world.

TECHNO FANS

South Korea is home to some of the world's best known technology firms, including:
• Samsung—manufacturer of electronics, including smartphones
• Hyundai—manufacturer of automobiles, including electric cars.

CHINA

Everything about China is big: it's population (the biggest of any country), its landscape—made up of endless rivers, mountains, and deserts—its giant cities, and its cultural influence on the world. China's civilization stretches back thousands of years, and today it's a global superpower with huge political and economic might.

KEY FACTS

Capital: **Beijing**
Official Language: **Mandarin**
Currency: **Renminbi (Yuan)**
Population: **1.3 billion**
Area (land): **3,600,947 sq. mi.**

CHINESE CREATIVITY

We can thank China for several technological innovations that have helped shape the world. The country's four classic inventions of ancient times are paper, printing, gunpowder, and the magnetic compass. We owe them for some fun creations too, such as kites and fireworks—the latter was one of the early uses of gunpowder.

THE GREATEST WALL

Snaking through northern China is one of the most astonishing feats of engineering of all time—the 13,170-mile-long Great Wall of China. Built and maintained over a two-thousand-year period, the "wall" is actually made up of a number of different structures that were originally joined together by the first Chinese emperor, Qin Shi Huang (259–210 BCE). Much of the early wall was made of packed earth.

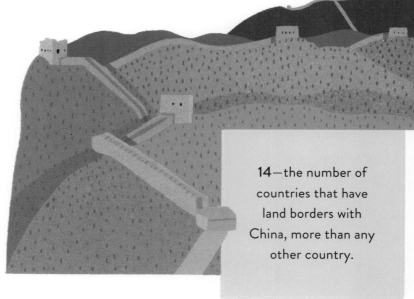

14—the number of countries that have land borders with China, more than any other country.

Beijing's spectacular complex of imperial palaces, the Forbidden City, contains around 9,000 rooms.

CLAY COMPANIONS

When the first Chinese emperor, Qin Shi Huang, died in 210 BCE, he didn't face the afterworld alone. Buried alongside him were 8,000 life-size clay soldiers and horses that formed a "Terracotta Army" to protect him in the next life. Amazingly, the tomb and its army were forgotten for over two thousand years until accidentally rediscovered by farmers digging a well in 1974. Today people can visit the army at a museum complex that has been built over the tomb just outside the city of Xi'an.

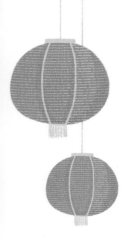

CHINESE NEW YEAR

Celebrated by millions of people every year, Chinese New Year is a 15-day festival filled with color, spectacle, and—above all—family time. Homes are cleaned, lanterns and decorations are hung in every town, parades fill the streets, and fireworks are lit to ward off evil spirits. Each year is represented by a different animal from the Chinese Zodiac.

China has more than 100 cities with over one million inhabitants. The largest of all is Shanghai, with a population of around 26 million people.

ZODIAC ANIMALS

There are 12 Chinese Zodiac animals, which repeat according to a fixed pattern:

Animal	Year
Rat	2020
Ox	2021
Tiger	2022
Rabbit	2023
Dragon	2024
Snake	2025
Horse	2026
Goat	2027
Monkey	2028
Rooster	2029
Dog	2030
Pig	2031

CHINESE CUISINE

From noodles to tea, dumplings to spring rolls, Chinese food is enjoyed all over the world. Many cities outside China have their own Chinatown areas, complete with Chinese restaurants, candy stores, and supermarkets. In China there is a huge range of options for eating out: traditional teahouses, fine-dining places, wok-to-plate fast food hatches, and all-you-can-eat buffets.

PANDA PROGRAM

One of the world's most beloved creatures, the black and white giant panda is found in the wild only in China. Once critically endangered, these pandas' numbers have been stabilized thanks to intense conservation efforts, which have involved both a captive breeding program and the restoration of their forest habitats. It's the only bear species to eat just plants—and it eats a lot of them. An adult panda can spend up to 16 hours a day chomping its way through 40 pounds of bamboo.

TAIWAN

Taiwan operates as an independent country with its own government and laws. However, China considers Taiwan part of China, even if it doesn't directly control it. Despite the constant tension between the two territories, Taiwan does its best to get on with things, enjoying dense green forests, tall mountain peaks, tea plantations, and the sizzling night markets of Taipei.

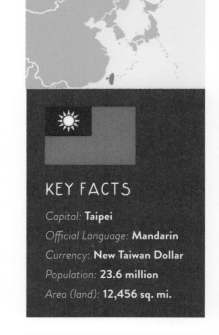

KEY FACTS

Capital: **Taipei**
Official Language: **Mandarin**
Currency: **New Taiwan Dollar**
Population: **23.6 million**
Area (land): **12,456 sq. mi.**

TEMPLES AND SHRINES

Tiny Taiwan is teeming with temples and shrines. There are around 4,000 of them in total, catering to the quarter of the population that practices Buddhism. Many enjoy idyllic locations, such as the Changchun ("Eternal Spring") Shrine, which has been built halfway up a mountain, directly over a waterfall.

The national animal of Taiwan is the Formosan rock macaque.

90% of the population lives in western Taiwan. Most of the eastern part of the country is forest-covered mountains.

HIGH-ALTITUDE TEA

Taiwan has a long history of producing tea, which grows well on its cool, damp mountain slopes. The country's plantations produce four main types of tea—oolong, black, green, and white—in countless varieties. The island is responsible for about 20 percent of the global sales of oolong tea.

RAINBOW VILLAGE

One of the country's most unusual attractions, Rainbow Family Village is a tiny settlement where all the houses have been painted in vibrant colors depicting a kaleidoscope of designs. It's all the work of one man, Huang Yung-Fu, a former soldier now known as "Grandpa Rainbow," who saved the village from the threat of redevelopment. Eleven of the houses, including Huang's own, were saved. The village now attracts hordes of visitors.

CIVIL WAR SPLIT

From 1927 to 1949, China was engaged in a civil war between nationalists and communists. Eventually, the communists won, taking over the mainland, while the nationalists fled to Taiwan, where they've been ever since. After decades as a military dictatorship, Taiwan is now a democracy. Both countries consider themselves to be the true ruler of the other.

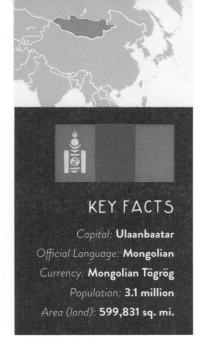

MONGOLIA

Mongolia's endless golden deserts are home to miles of rolling sand dunes, where nomads travel on horseback and rocky mountain ranges hide treasure troves of dinosaur fossils. This land once lay at the heart of Ghenghis Khan's empire, which would become the largest contiguous (made up of connected territory) empire in history.

KEY FACTS

Capital: **Ulaanbaatar**
Official Language: **Mongolian**
Currency: **Mongolian Tögrög**
Population: **3.1 million**
Area (land): **599,831 sq. mi.**

MONGOLIAN SPORTS

The three most popular sports in Mongolia are:
- Horse racing
- Archery
- Wrestling

DINO BONES

Huge numbers of dinosaur fossils have been uncovered in Mongolia's Gobi Desert, and there are no doubt countless more waiting to be found. Eighty million years ago, this was a lush, fertile place where tank-like ankylosaurs and long-necked sauropods thrived. The world's first dinosaur egg nest was discovered here, as was a fossil of a velociraptor and a protoceratops locked together, having died mid-fight—the velociraptor's arm was still trapped between the protoceratops' jaws.

COOL DESERT

You might think that all sandy deserts are scorching hot but, because much of the Gobi occupies high ground, it has a relatively cold climate. It endures four-month-long winters, when the sand dunes can be whited by frost (and sometimes even snow). These are followed by short bursts of summer, when temperatures can quickly shoot up to 90°F. Locals describe the country as often experiencing four seasons in one day.

GOT THE HUMP

Mongolia's most iconic animal is the Bactrian, or two-humped, camel. They're smaller and hairier than their single-humped dromedary counterparts from Arabia. Their humps don't store water (as is sometimes thought) but fat, which can be used as food when resources are scarce. They have a thick, woolly coat—to protect them against the harsh Gobi winters—which they shed when spring arrives.

JAPAN

Japan manages to be both one of the most traditional nations on Earth and one of the most modern. It's a place of ancient pagodas and video games, zen gardens and robots, cherry trees and bullet trains. Its cities, particularly the megalopolis Tokyo, are among the largest and most densely packed in the world.

BLOSSOMING NATION

Japan's springtime sees beautiful pink cherry trees blossoming across the country. It's a hugely anticipated event, with TV forecasters reporting on the predicted arrival of the flowers. Although the trees bloom for just two weeks, the full season can last five months. It begins when the first flowers appear on the southern island of Okinawa and finishes when the last blossoms are spotted on the northern island of Hokkaido, sometimes as late as May.

Now known affectionately as "Cat Island," Japan's Aoshima Island has over 150 wild cats roaming around—that's more than ten times the number of human residents.

CELEBRATING SUSHI

Though loved around the world, the Japanese delicacy of sushi is often misunderstood. Many people think it always contains raw fish, but that's not the case. The main part of the dish is actually vinegared rice served in rolls. This can be accompanied by a range of other ingredients, which can include raw fish, but could also be vegetables, pickles, and garnishes. Grab your chopsticks, soy sauce, and enjoy.

JAPANESE CRAFTS
- Origami—*the art of paper folding*
- Ikebana—*the art of flower arranging*
- Bonsai—*the art of growing miniature trees.*

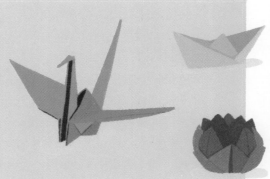

JAPANESE COMBAT SPORTS

- **Sumo**—*a form of wrestling featuring very large wrestlers*

- **Kendo**—*sword fighting with bamboo swords*

- **Jiujitsu**—*a form of unarmed close combat.*

SHINTO SHRINES

The majority of people in Japan follow a belief system called Shinto. This involves the worship of spirits—known as kami—who are believed to reside in all things. By providing offerings to kami at shrines, Shinto worshippers aim to bring harmony to the natural world. Many people have shrines in their homes, and there are also around 80,000 public Shinto shrines across the country.

While humans like to bathe in Japan's hot thermal baths called onsens, Japanese macaque monkeys take dips in the warm natural springs of Jigokudani Monkey Park. Also known as snow monkeys, these are the most northern-living primates on the planet.

COMIC CHARACTERS

Japanese comic books and cartoons, known as manga, are enjoyed by many people around the globe. Many manga works have been adapted into movies, television shows, and video games, known as anime. Well-known anime features include the popular TV series *Pokémon*, and *Spirited Away*, which was produced by the famous Japanese movie company Studio Ghibli.

Japan is home to some of the biggest video game companies in the world, including Nintendo, the manufacturer of the Switch console, and Sony, the maker of the Playstation.

LOOK TO THE FUTURE

As a leader in AI (artificial intelligence) technology, Japan is robot crazy. Whatever use you can think of, there's probably a Japanese robot for it. There are android priests teaching Buddhism, robot pets, and robot store assistants that are wired to read human emotions. One Japanese factory even has a factory line of robots that create other robots.

INDIA

One of the most diverse countries in the world, India is a colorful blend of people, cultures, languages, and religion. No fewer than four major belief systems have their origins here. A mixture of mountains, deserts, and jungles, the landscape is as filled with wildlife as the cities are with people.

KEY FACTS

Capital: **New Delhi**
Official Languages:
Hindi, English
Currency: **Indian Rupee**
Population: **1.3 billion**
Area (land): **1,147,956 sq. mi.**

SNOW-WHITE WONDER

Widely recognized as one of the world's most beautiful buildings, the Taj Mahal is a vision of bright white marble domes, minarets, and countless shimmering precious stones. Located in the northern Indian city of Agra, it was constructed between 1632 and 1653 for the Mughal (Islamic) Emperor Shah Jahan to house the tomb of his favorite wife, Mumtaz Mahal. The building would also go on to hold Jahan's own tomb.

TIGER TIGER

India's national animal is the majestic Bengal tiger. There are around 3,000 of these elusive hunters hiding in the country's jungles and grasslands. That's around 70 percent of the world's total tiger population. Their stripes help camouflage them in dense vegetation, allowing them to sneak up on prey undetected. No two tigers share the same pattern of stripes—they are as unique as fingerprints.

FOODIE NATION

Indian food is offered at (and ordered from) restaurants around the world as if it's a single type of a cuisine. But at its source in India, it varies greatly from one region to the next. Rice is a staple for every meal in the south, while coconut is the most-used ingredient in palm tree-fringed Goa, and flatbreads, known as *naans* or *parathas*, are common in the north. The term "curry" describes a broad range of different dishes, from spicy pork vindaloos to mild, almond-based kormas.

RELIGIOUS RANKINGS

If we judged how spiritual a nation is by counting how many religious buildings it has, then India would probably be a clear winner. It's bursting with temples, churches, and mosques, and the religions of Hinduism, Buddhism, Sikhism, and Jainism all emerged on Indian soil. Today the majority of people here are Hindus, who believe in reincarnation and consider the great Ganges River in northern India to be sacred. It is thought that if a person's ashes are scattered on this river, they will be transported to their next life.

YOGA ORIGINS

Today yoga is a mainstream form of exercise and relaxation and is practiced by people around the world. But the roots of this spiritual and physical discipline go way back to second-century BCE India. Although used by many people just as a way of staying in shape, the underlying philosophy of yoga is grounded in the pursuit of meditation and calm, along with a focus on breathing and concentration.

Indian festivals are full of color, family, and food. Two of the biggest festivals, celebrated both here and around the world, are Diwali, the Festival of Lights, and Holi, the Festival of Color.

WILDLIFE SPOTTING

With great stretches of forest, India is one of the world's most biodiverse places. Animals to spot include:

- elephants • flamingos
- king cobras • leopards • Asiatic lions
- peacocks • reticulated pythons • rhinos
- sloth bears • snow leopards • tigers.

PAKISTAN

The Indus civilization emerged here in the 2000s BCE, when great cities were erected on its plains before mysteriously disappearing. Today's Pakistan, which came into being in 1947, also boasts huge urban centers, as well as a diverse landscape that stretches from the Himalayas in the north, down through forests and deserts, to the Arabian Sea on the southern coast.

KEY FACTS

Capital: **Islamabad**
Official Languages: **Urdu, English**
Currency: **Pakistani Rupee**
Population: **233 million**
Area (land): **297,637 sq. mi.**

PEACE PRIZE

The Pakistani activist Malala Yousufzai is the youngest person to have won the Nobel Peace Prize. She was awarded the honor in 2014 when she was just 17 years old, for her work campaigning for the educational rights of children—particularly young girls. Two years earlier, she had been traveling on a bus in northern Pakistan when she was shot by a member of a terrorist group called the Taliban, which objects to female education. She made a full recovery and continues to fight for change around the globe.

28,251 ft.—the height of K2, the world's second-highest mountain, found in Pakistan's Karakoram Range.

BIG HORNS

The national animal of Pakistan is the markhor, a type of mountain goat. An expert climber, it's perfectly at home in the country's rocky, rugged terrain. The males are easy to spot, with their enormous twisty horns that curl upward like a corkscrew and long, shaggy beards. Also roaming the peaks of Pakistan are rare snow leopards and the endangered Himalayan brown bear.

FUTURISTIC ANCIENTS

Pakistan's long-lost city of Mohenjo-daro, once part of the Indus Valley Civilization, was only discovered by archaeologists in the 1920s. Dating back to between 2500 and 1900 BCE, it was one of the earliest and most advanced civilizations in the world. The city was designed in ways that many modern city planners still follow, with a grid-like street plan, buildings made out of bricks, a sewer system, household baths, and even indoor toilets. It was a city way ahead of its time.

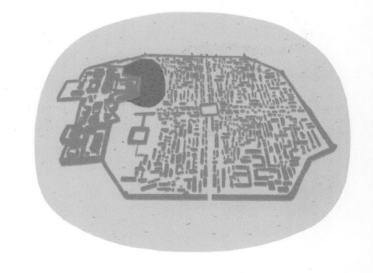

NEPAL

There's no ignoring the mountains in Nepal. But the great stretch of the Himalayas that covers the northern half of the country doesn't tell the whole story. There are also great cities, thick forests and, in the south, low-lying grasslands and swamps, not to mention a history that goes back thousands of years.

KEY FACTS

Capital: **Kathmandu**
Official Language: **Nepali**
Currency: **Nepalese Rupee**
Population: **30.2 million**
Area (land): **55,348 sq. mi.**

The flag of Nepal is the only national flag in the shape of a double triangle, rather than a square or rectangle.

BUDDHISM BEGINS

Lumbini, at the foot of the Himalayas, is one of the most important pilgrimage sites for Buddhists, as it's believed to mark the birthplace of the Lord Buddha. Buddha was originally known as Prince Siddharta Guatama, and he gave up his privileged life to become a wandering philosopher and spiritual teacher. Today many people follow his teachings, which have the overcoming of suffering to achieve a state of enlightenment (total peace and understanding) as their goal.

RHINO CONSERVATION

Nepal has made major efforts to preserve its population of rare greater one-horned rhinos. Chitwan National Park provides a protected space where these slow-moving giants can live peacefully. The rhinos have since staged a recovery, with their numbers having grown to more than 600 from under 100 when the park opened.

MIGHTY HIMALAYAS

Formed between 40 and 50 million years ago, the mighty Himalayas stretch for 1,550 miles across Asia. The Nepalese section contains the world's tallest peak. Known to the wider world as Mount Everest, and locally as Chomolungma (meaning "Goddess Mother of the World"), this great mountain sits on Nepal's border with China. After many failed attempts by other climbers, New Zealander Edmund Hillary and local Sherpa Tenzing Norgay became the first people to reach the summit in 1953.

Nepal is also the best place to try and spot the Himalayas' famous ape-like monster— the Abominable Snowman, or yeti.

HIMALAYAN TOP FIVE

The top five highest mountains the world:

	Name	Country	Height
1.	Everest	Nepal	29,032 ft.
2.	K2	Pakistan	28,251 ft.
3.	Kanchenjunga	Nepal	28,169 ft.
4.	Lhotse	Nepal	27,940 ft.
5.	Makālu	Nepal	27,765 ft.

BHUTAN

This mountain nation is a deeply traditional place, where almost everyone wears national dress, the roads don't have traffic lights, and monasteries cover the landscape. Bhutan is known for its environmental awareness as well as its government's novel program to measure the nation's wellbeing, called the Gross National Happiness Index.

KEY FACTS

Capital: **Thimphu**

Official Language: **Dzongkha**

Currency: **Bhutanese Ngultrum**

Population: **782,318**

Area (land): **14,824 sq. mi.**

TIGER'S NEST

One of Bhutan's most visited sites is the Paro Taktsang, or Tiger's Nest Monastery, which is perched precariously on a jagged cliff face. Both its name and location are explained by the legend of how the holy Buddhist figure Padmasambhava arrived in the country in the 700s on the back of a flying tigress that landed on the cliff face. Padmasambhava then headed out across the land to convert the population to Buddhism. The journey to the monastery for the modern visitor is almost as challenging, as it can only be reached by a steep hike across the clifftops.

Bhutan's Gross National Happiness Index came into existence in 1972. It's a way for the government to try and measure the collective wellbeing of the nation, rather than just its wealth.

CARBON NEGATIVE

Bhutan has an official dress and etiquette code, called *Driglam Namzha,* which states that men should wear a robe called a *gho* and women should wear a dress called a *kira.*

Many countries are currently striving to lower their carbon emissions and protect the environment, but Bhutan has gone a little bit further than most. Almost three-fourths of the country is covered in forest, which takes more carbon dioxide from the atmosphere than it emits. This means Bhutan isn't only carbon neutral, it's carbon negative. Sixty percent of the forests are protected from development, and the nation is also actively investing in renewable energy and electric cars.

TAKING AIM

Bhutan is the only country in the world where archery is the national sport. Competitions are held across the land, and there are dedicated archery fields in many villages. Traditionally, bows were made from bamboo, but today modern "compound" bows, which have a range of extra devices, including pulleys and cables to help with accuracy, are common.

BANGLADESH

A flat, low country spread out around the world's largest river delta, Bangladesh is dominated by water. Cities line rivers and coastlines, wildlife thrives in tropical mangroves, people work in rice paddies, and rain deluges the country during the monsoon season.

"Amar Sonar Bangla"
(My Golden Bengal)
—the national anthem
of Bangladesh.

STRIPES, SPOTS, AND SWAMPS

Bangladesh's lush landscape boasts over 700 rivers, including the mighty Ganges, as well as rolling paddy fields, mangroves, and swamps. The Sundarbans region on the southern coast is home to one of the world's biggest mangrove forests, as well as large tracts of fertile farming land. Rare species, including Bengal tigers and leopards, can sometimes be glimpsed amid the vegetation.

COLORFUL RICKSHAWS

Zooming through every city street in the country, the three-wheeled pedal rickshaw is one of the easiest and speediest ways to get around. There are hundreds of thousands of rickshaws in the nation's capital, Dhaka, alone. Many are painted with bright, colorful designs that can depict a range of different subjects—animals, flowers, movie stars—or whatever the owner requests of the local artists who paint them by hand.

MIXED-UP ANIMAL

It might sound like something you'd make up, but the sloth bear is a real animal found in Bangladesh's forests and grasslands. It was named by an 18th-century zoologist who thought, mistakenly, that its shaggy coat and long, curved claws meant that it was related to sloths. In fact, it's 100 percent bear. It uses its claws to break into tough termite mounds, which it then sucks up with its long snout.

SRI LANKA

Often referred to as the "Pearl of the Indian Ocean" (because of its beauty) and the "Teardrop of India" (because of its shape), colorful Sri Lanka lies off the southern coast of India. It's one of the world's best wildlife-watching destinations, with animal-filled forests and grasslands. There are plenty of other attractions too, including beautiful beaches, rolling tea plantations, and Buddhist and Hindu temples.

KEY FACTS

Capital: **Sri Jayawardenepura Kotte, Colombo**

Official Languages: **Sinhala, Tamil**

Currency: **Sri Lankan Rupee**

Population: **22.8 million**

Area (land): **24,954 sq. mi.**

PILGRIMAGE PEAK

Sri Lanka is not short of holy places, but perhaps its most famous is Adam's Peak, a 7,359-foot-high mountain in the center of the country. Every year, thousands of people trek up to the summit, which is a holy site for no fewer than four religions. The focus for every visitor is a small rock formation at the top which, depending on what religion you follow, is the footprint of either Buddha, the Hindu god Shiva, or the Christian-Islamic first man, Adam.

Sri Lanka's flag features a golden lion holding a traditional Sri Lankan sword called a *kastane*.

TREKKING TRUNKS

Elephants roam freely across Sri Lanka's national parks. One of the best places to see them is in Minneriya National Park during the dry season from July to October. At this time, large groups of up to 300 elephants come together in an event known as "The Gathering" and head to an ancient reservoir to drink, bathe, and feast on the grass still growing at the water's edge.

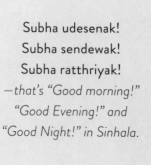

Subha udesenak!
Subha sendewak!
Subha ratthriyak!
—that's "Good morning!"
"Good Evening!" and
"Good Night!" in Sinhala.

STILT FISHERMEN

On Sri Lanka's southern coast, some locals have come up with a unique way of fishing. Known as stilt fishermen, they dig a narrow pole into the seabed just off the shoreline. Then they perch above the waves and try to land their catch. The most popular time to stilt fish is during the monsoon season, when the seas can often be too rough for fishing boats.

THE MALDIVES

For many people, the Maldives is paradise on Earth. This low-lying nation is made up of around 1,200 islands ringed with white-sand beaches and groups of thatched cottages perched on stilts over the ocean waves. Warm, crystal-clear waters lap the shore while, farther out, is a teeming undersea world of colorful coral reefs and clown fish.

KEY FACTS

Capital: **Malé**
Official Language: **Dhivehi**
Currency: **Maldivian Rufiyaa**
Population: **391,904**
Area (land): **115 sq. mi.**

The thatched roofs of the country's water bungalows are constructed from the country's national tree —the coconut palm.

GLOW IN THE DARK

The waters of the Maldives are the stage for one of nature's great magic tricks. On certain nights, the ocean appears to be lit up with a bright blue glow. It may look like magic, but it's an entirely natural phenomenon called bioluminescence, caused by tiny creatures called plankton. When the water around them is disturbed by the movement of a fish, or even a wave, they produce a chemical light, which it's believed they use to try and confuse potential predators.

The sparkling-white beaches of the Maldives are as rare as they are stunning. They're part of just 5% of the world's beaches that are formed from coral.

DISAPPEARING ACT

The future of these low-lying islands is under threat because of rising sea levels. The government has introduced a raft of environmental policies with the aim of protecting coral reefs and cutting carbon emissions. But without international action, there's a chance the islands may one day slip under the waves.

GIANT SWIMMERS

The Maldives is perfect for snorkeling and scuba diving. Its waters are clear, calm, and full of incredible marine creatures, even in shallow waters. Local residents include clown fish and parrotfish, who are occasionally joined by migrants such as hawksbill turtles and whale sharks, the biggest fish in the world. Growing up to 62 feet long, whale sharks are entirely harmless, feeding only on plankton and small fish. They love to roam warm seas and are easily recognized by their light-colored spots and big, round mouths (and because they're absolutely huge).

MYANMAR
(BURMA)

Myanmar is an ancient land and, in recent decades, a troubled one that has seen many internal conflicts. Thousands of Buddhist golden pagodas are scattered across its mountainous, tropical landscape. Elsewhere, the country is home to lakes, winding rivers, mud volcanoes, and an abundance of wildlife, including tigers, elephants, and monkeys.

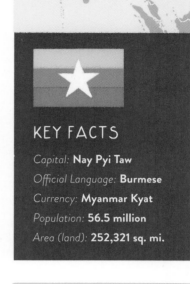

KEY FACTS

Capital: **Nay Pyi Taw**
Official Language: **Burmese**
Currency: **Myanmar Kyat**
Population: **56.5 million**
Area (land): **252,321 sq. mi.**

GOLDEN MONUMENTS

The country's shiny, gold-capped pagodas are among its most famous sights. Perhaps the most famous of all is the Kyaiktiyo Pagoda, which sits on a gold-colored boulder, which is itself perched precariously on a cliff edge. It looks as if it could be toppled over by a gust of wind but has remained there for hundreds of years, held in place, so it's said, by a strand of Buddha's hair.

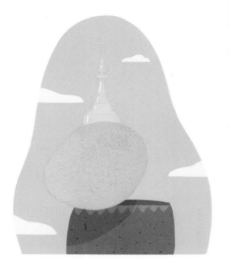

"Kaba Ma Kyei" (Till the End of the World)—the national anthem of Myanmar.

PADDLE POWER

The fishermen of Inle Lake in central Myanmar have devised a unique way of rowing their boats—by using their legs. They stand with one leg on the end of their boat to balance and the other wrapped around the paddle to row and steer. The method was adopted to allow the rowers to see over the thick reeds that blanket the lake, and also to free up their hands to use their fishing nets.

A paste made from the ground-up bark of Murraya trees is used as a natural sunscreen in Myanmar.

MUD VOLCANOES

Myanmar's Minbu region is specked with mud-filled craters that look like they belong on the surface of the Moon. These natural phenomena are known as "mud volcanoes" and are created when gases beneath the ground are forced to the surface, bringing with them oozing masses of earth.

LAOS

KEY FACTS

Capital: **Vientiane**
Official Language: **Lao**
Currency: **Lao Kip**
Population: **7.4 million**
Area (land): **89,112 sq. mi.**

The only country in Southeast Asia without a coastline, little Laos is a serene nation. Almost three-fourths of it is covered in sparsely populated mountains and forested hills. Most of the people inhabit low-lying areas near the Mekong River, living in colorful cities and towns surrounded by rice paddy fields.

The "s" in Laos is silent, so the word should rhyme with "how" and not "house."

LIGHTING UP THE SKIES

Every year in Laos, a mass of fireworks is launched into the sky as part of the *Bun Bang Fai* (Rocket Festival), which also involves float processions and performances of music and dancing. The ceremony happens just before the rainy season, and the rockets are fired as requests for rainfall from *Phaya Thaen*, the god of rain.

A human skull dating back 63,000 years was found in Laos's Tam Pa Ling cave in 2008, making it the oldest human fossil yet discovered in Southeast Asia.

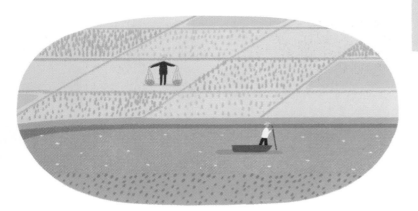

MIGHTY MEKONG

At 2,700 miles, the Mekong River is the longest river in Southeast Asia and a vital resource for many nations. It marks Laos's southern border with Thailand, and the capital city, Vientiane, sits on its banks. Fertile lands on the river's banks are used for cultivating rice. In 2019, a hydroelectric dam was completed on the river in northern Laos.

STICKY FINGERS

Sticky rice, or *khao tom*, is cultivated and eaten in many countries, but Laotians are the world's biggest consumers. The national dish is a staple of most people's diets and is usually eaten with the fingers. Because it takes a little longer to be digested than other varieties of rice, it's often eaten for lunch by Laotian monks who have to fast after midday.

THAILAND

Thailand is one of the world's most visited countries. Every year, millions of tourists head here to experience its mix of lively cities, wildlife-filled rainforests, tropical party islands, and of course its super-tasty food. The only country in Southeast Asia not to have been colonized, Thailand has an identity all of its own.

KEY FACTS

Capital: **Bangkok**
Official Language: **Thai**
Currency: **Thai Baht**
Population: **68.9 million**
Area (land): **197,256 sq. mi.**

FLOATING MARKETS

Bangkok is crisscrossed by waterways, including the country's major river, the Chao Phraya, as well as dozens of canals. Before the city was modernized, it was often easier to get around by boat than on land. Traders began setting up markets to cater to the constant throng of people sailing by. Many of these markets still operate and are filled with slender boats selling a range of colorful fruits and vegetables, as well as local crafts.

The country was formerly known as Siam. It officially changed its name to Thailand in 1939.

FOOD FOR ALL TASTES

Popular around the world, Thai cuisine aims to create food with the perfect balance of five basic tastes: sweet, salty, spicy, sour, and bitter. Try:
- Tom yam goong—*hot and sour soup with shrimp*
- Pad thai—*stir fry with meat, vegetables, scrambled egg, beansprouts, and rice noodles*
- Som tam—*salad with green beans, chilli, and shredded papaya*
- Massaman curry—*mild, spicy curry with meat, coconut milk, and potatoes*
- Green curry—*sweet curry made with green chillis and Thai basil.*

STRANGE STACKS

Tall, rugged limestone stacks known as karsts rise up out of the ocean off the coast of the southern island of Khao Phing Kan. These strange outcrops give the landscape an otherworldly look and have featured in several movies.

Bangkok is the short version of the capital city's name. See if you can pronounce the full version: *Krungthepmahanakhon Amonrattanakosin Mahintharayutthaya Mahadilokphop Noppharatratchathaniburirom Udomratchaniwetmahasathan Amonphimanawatansathit Sakkathattiyawitsanukamprasi.*

VIETNAM

Long, narrow Vietnam stretches down the eastern side of Southeast Asia. Its northern regions feature limestone islands and cool mountain villages, while its southern regions are packed with idyllic beaches. Throughout the country, delicious steaming bowls of Vietnamese food and piping-hot coffee are served up.

KEY FACTS

Capital: **Hanoi**
Official Language: **Vietnamese**
Currency: **Vietnamese Dong**
Population: **98.7 million**
Area (land): **119,719 sq. mi.**

Around 1,025 mi. long, Vietnam is just 30 mi. wide at its narrowest point.

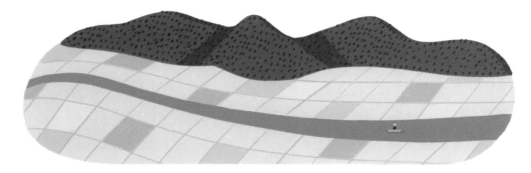

RIVER POWER

Vietnam is dominated by two large rivers: the Mekong in the south and the Red River (or Song Hong, as it's known locally) in the north. Most of the country's population lives around these great waterways, relying on them to irrigate the nation's vast network of rice paddies. The capital, Hanoi, is located on the Red River.

PHENOMENAL PHO

The Vietnamese national dish is called pho, pronounced "fuh," a hot, spicy noodle broth made with either meat or tofu. The dish is influenced by the cuisines of both China and France, which once ruled this nation, but given a dash of Vietnamese flair. There are dozens of different types of pho, and it's sold everywhere from street food stalls to high-end restaurants.

BIKING AROUND

The most common way to get around Vietnam is by motorcycle or scooter, and pretty much everyone does it. Motorbikes make up around 80 percent of the vehicles on the streets of Vietnam's cities, and there are around 50 million motorbikes darting across the nation in total.

Vietnam is the world's largest exporter of black pepper, producing about a third of the global supply.

CAMBODIA

Cambodia is best known for its sprawling medieval temple complex, Angkor Wat, which almost all tourists to the country make a point of visiting. But there are plenty of other sights to check out, including steamy jungles, winding rivers, and the cities' vibrant night markets.

KEY FACTS

Capital: **Phnom Penh**
Official Language: **Khmer**
Currency: **Cambodian Riel**
Population: **16.9 million**
Area (land): **68,153 sq. mi.**

ANGKOR WAT

The world's largest religious building, Angkor Wat covers an area of over 400 acres in the Cambodian jungle. Constructed in the early 1100s as a Hindu temple, it was later transformed into a Buddhist one. Gradually, as the centuries passed, it became less used, although it was never fully abandoned. The millions of tourists who visit Angkor Wat each year are often greeted by monkeys skipping along the walls. The grounds are so huge that many people choose to tour it using motorized rickshaws known as tuk-tuks.

Cambodia is the only country where the national flag features a picture of a specific and identifiable building—Angkor Wat, shown against a red and blue background.

MULTIUSE CLOTH

Many people in Cambodia wear a traditional head garment called a *krama*, which is made by folding a single piece of (usually checked) cloth. It can also be worn over the face or around the body or as a skirt or as a bag or as a baby carrier. In fact, some people say there are over 60 different uses for the *krama*. It's a very versatile cloth.

BUG MARKETS

Cambodia's cities are famous for their night markets, where stalls stay open late (sometimes till midnight) selling jewelry, clothes, local crafts, and street food. Here you have the chance to sample some unusual dishes, including bugs. Fried creepy-crawlies, such as crickets, cockroaches, and even tarantulas, are considered tasty, savory, nutritious snacks in Cambodia.

Cambodia's stretch of the Mekong is home to a small population of rare Irrawaddy dolphins.

MALAYSIA

Malaysia is split into two main parts. Peninsula Malaysia (or Western Malaysia), which sits just below Thailand, is home to the country's biggest cities and most of its people. Eastern Malaysia, which takes up a large section of the island of Borneo, is still covered in great areas of tropical forest that provide a refuge for many rare animals.

KEY FACTS

Capital: **Kuala Lumpur**
Official Language: **Malay**
Currency: **Malaysian Ringgit**
Population: **32.6 million**
Area (land): **126,895 sq. mi.**

Malaysia's rainforests hold a smelly secret: the rafflesia, the world's biggest flower. Growing up to 3 ft. wide, the flower has a pungent stench like rotting meat, which attracts flies that help spread the flower's pollen.

FOREST "PEOPLE"

East Malaysia's rainforest is one of the only places in the world where you can see orangutans in the wild. One of the "great apes," these fascinating, intelligent animals with their distinctive, shaggy orange coats are one of our closest relatives in nature. Indeed, orangutan means "person of the forest" in the Malay language. Sadly, these apes are now critically endangered because of hunting and habitat loss.

JUNGLE LIFE

Although much has been chopped down for agriculture, Malaysia's rainforests still take up around half of the country's land. There are several different types, including cloud forests on high ground, tidal swamp forests along the coast, and sparse heathland forests known locally as *kerangas* in lowland areas. In the densest parts of the forest, the canopy is so thick that very little sunlight reaches the forest floor. Numerous animals prowl the murky depths, including rhinos, monitor lizards, and tigers.

STREET SERVICE

Street food is a big deal in Malaysian cities, with street vendors seemingly serving an array of sizzling, spicy dishes on every corner. Malaysia's cuisine has been heavily influenced by other countries in the region, especially India and China. One of the most popular dishes is satay, which consists of meat or tofu skewered on bamboo sticks, grilled over a flame, and drizzled with a creamy peanut sauce.

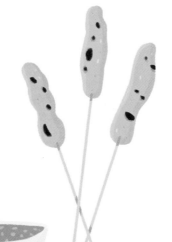

Selamat pagi/
Selamat tengah hari/
Selamat Petang/
Selamat Malam—
"Good morning"/
"Good afternoon"/
"Good Evening"/
"Good Night" in Malay.

SINGAPORE

Singaporeans live in a modern city-state known for its neatly planned streets, snazzy shopping malls, and sleek architecture—but there's more to it than designer buildings. Singapore is also trying to be a green city and has introduced numerous environmental policies that have won awards in Asia.

KEY FACTS

Capital: **Singapore**
Official Languages: **English, Mandarin, Malay, Tamil**
Currency: **Singapore Dollar**
Population: **6.2 million**
Area (land): **274 sq. mi.**

MEGA GARDEN

Singapore is small and cramped with not much room for nature, but the authorities are doing their best to add some anyway. There are now laws ensuring that all new buildings include sections of greenery in their structures, so many skyscrapers now have walls of climbing plants or roof gardens. Gardens by the Bay is a futuristic-looking collection of lawns, flower beds, ponds, greenhouses, and high-tech vertical gardens called "supertrees," which can be explored on suspended walkways.

Singapore is a busy place, both on land and at sea. Its port is one of the busiest in the world, with around 130,000 vessels calling here every year.

The Flower Dome in the Gardens by the Bay is the world's largest glass greenhouse, covering an area of 3 acres.

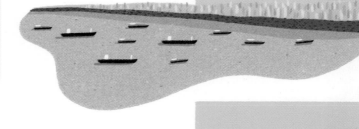

AIRPORT AWARDS

Singapore's airport, Changi, has won the "World's Best Airport" award eight years in a row. With a huge range of attractions on offer in the terminal, including a butterfly garden, a luxurious swimming pool, and a movie theater, people passing through here are rarely bored while waiting for their flight.

Littering is illegal in Singapore and punishable by fines. Repeat offenders have to pay a hefty charge and clean the streets wearing a brightly colored vest.

BRUNEI

On the northern edge of the island of Borneo sits Brunei, a tiny sliver of a nation. It's actually made up of two small, unconnected areas of land a few miles apart. In the mid-20th century, it discovered oil, which has turned it into one of the world's richest nations. Most of the people live in the western half, while the east is still wild and forested.

KEY FACTS

Capital: **Bandar Seri Begawan**

Official Language: **Malay**

Currency: **Brunei Dollar**

Population: **464,478**

Area (land): **2,033 sq. mi.**

NOSY NEIGHBORS

Brunei's mangrove forests are home to one of the world's most unusual-looking monkeys, the proboscis monkey. The nose of a male proboscis monkey (proboscis means "nose") can grow up to 7 inches long, hanging over its mouth like a giant potato.

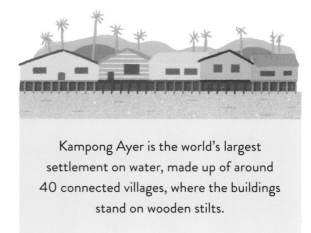

Kampong Ayer is the world's largest settlement on water, made up of around 40 connected villages, where the buildings stand on wooden stilts.

TIMOR-LESTE

Occupying the eastern half of the island of Timor, Timor Leste (East Timor) is one of the world's newest nations. For hundreds of years it was a colony of Portugal. Then, when the Europeans gave up control in 1975, neighboring Indonesia invaded. The country eventually gained independence in 2002.

KEY FACTS

Capital: **Dili**

Official Languages: **Tetum, Portuguese**

Currency: **US Dollar**

Population: **54,800**

Area (land): **101 sq. mi.**

CROCODILE CREEKS

Timor-Leste is known as the "land of the sleeping crocodile." According to myth, there was once a boy who became friends with a giant crocodile. When the croc died, its body became the land of Timor-Leste, and its people are the descendants of the boy. Today's population continues to have a great respect for these scaly predators that still lurk in the country's creeks, swamps, and rivers.

Tais is a traditional, colorful cloth that's become a major part of the country's cultural identity. The intricately patterned material is turned into a variety of garments, and each region has its own style.

INDONESIA

Welcome to the world's biggest island nation. Indonesia is made up of over 17,500 islands that form a great arc between the Indian and Pacific Oceans. It's a very diverse country, home to one of the biggest cities on Earth, over 300 ethnic groups, and a landscape spanning volcanoes, jungles, mangroves, and coral reefs.

KEY FACTS

Capital: **Jakarta**
Official Language: **Indonesian**
Currency: **Indonesian Rupiah**
Population: **267 million**
Area (land): **699,451 sq. mi.**

DRAGONS DO EXIST

It may technically be a giant lizard, but you can definitely see how the Komodo dragon got its name. Growing up to 10 feet long, this scaly beast is the largest lizard on the planet. It uses its large, sharp claws and venomous bite to bring down prey, which include pigs and deer. Today these dragons are found on just three Indonesian islands: Komodo, Rinca, and Flores, where they're a protected species.

Selamat siang
—*"Good afternoon"*
Sampai jumpa
—*"See you later"*
in Indonesian.

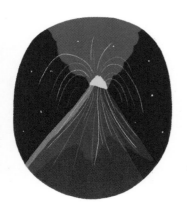

VOLCANO COUNTRY

Indonesia is a tectonic hotspot, with more active volcanoes—over 100—than any other country. It has witnessed some of the world's most devastating volcanic events, including Mount Tambora in 1815, which produced the largest eruption in recorded history, and Krakatoa in 1883, which exploded with a "boom" heard over 3,000 miles away. In more recent times, an undersea earthquake just off Indonesia's coast in 2004 caused a giant tsunami that spread across the Indian Ocean, devastating several countries and killing over 220,000 people.

Indonesia's national dish is *nasi goreng*—*spicy fried rice with meat, vegetables, sweet soy sauce, shrimp paste, and a fried egg.*

BIG BUDDHA

Borobudar Temple, located on the Indonesian island of Java, is the world's biggest Buddhist temple. At its peak is a central dome surrounded by 72 statues of Buddha. Its different levels represent the Buddhist notion of making one's way in life toward a state of nirvana, or contentment. Constructed in the 800s, Borobudar had been abandoned to the jungle by the 1300s. It was rediscovered in the 1800s and has since been restored to its former glory.

PHILIPPINES

Life in the Philippines can be super relaxed—on sun-kissed island beaches and in the warm, clear ocean; or super hectic—in busy, neon-lit cities full of karaoke bars and barbecue joints. With over 7,000 islands, there's plenty to see and explore. The country's culture is a mixture of local influences and those of the former colonial powers, Spain and the United States.

KEY FACTS

Capital: **Manila**
Official Languages:
Filipino, English
Currency: **Philippine Peso**
Population: **109.1 million**
Area (land): **115,124 sq. mi.**

With 107,500 people per square mile, Manila is the world's most densely populated city.

The island of Camiguin has seven volcanoes, which is more than the number of towns, although only one volcano is considered active.

BIG EYES

Found deep in the country's forests, the Philippine tarsier is one of the world's tiniest primates. It's just 6 inches tall, most of which seems to be taken up by its huge googly eyes—which are as big as its brain. In fact, its eyes are so large, the tarsier can't move them around in its eye sockets but must turn its head instead. They help the animal see at night, which is when it is mainly active, feeding on insects that it plucks from trees with its long fingers.

MYSTERIOUS MOUNDS

The center of the Philippines' Bohol Island is covered in over 12,000 conically shaped mounds called the Chocolate Hills. Most of the time, the mounds are green, but in the dry season the vegetation turns the cocoa-brown color that gives them their name. According to local legends, they were formed by giants throwing boulders at each other, while according to scientists, they were (less excitingly) formed by a rare type of limestone erosion.

BASKETBALL FEVER

Introduced to the country when it was ruled by the United States (1898–1946), basketball is hugely popular in the Philippines, with courts dotted across the country. Founded in 1975, the Philippines Basketball Association (PBA) is the world's second-oldest professional basketball league, after the NBA in the United States and Canada.

Manny Pacquiao, one of the Philippines' biggest stars, has a rather unusual career. He combines being a world champion professional boxer with his day job as a senator in the Filipino government.

GEORGIA

Often regarded as standing at the crossroads of Asia and Europe, Georgia has been ruled throughout the centuries by several other powers—including the Soviet Union—but is now independent. Its landscape is a mixture of mountains, vineyards, and wild forests that lead down to the sandy beaches of the Black Sea coast.

KEY FACTS

Capital: **Tbilisi**
Official Language: **Georgian**
Currency: **Georgian Lari**
Population: **3.9 million**
Area (land): **26,911 sq. mi.**

DEEP DOWN

Georgia's Veryovkina Cave is the deepest known cave on Earth. It was discovered in 1968 but not fully explored until 2019, when cavers managed to make it all the way down to a depth of 7,257 feet—or more than seven Eiffel Towers stacked one on top of the other.

CAUCASUS COUNTRY

In the northern part of the country, the dramatic Caucasus Mountains form a natural barrier, splitting Georgia from Russia. The highest peak is the 17,037-foot Mount Shkhara. The Caucasus is also the name given to the wider region, including the neighboring countries of Armenia and Azerbaijan.

The world's oldest evidence of wine making (and drinking) has been discovered in Georgia in the form of 8,000-year-old wine jars.

Georgia's ecology is hugely diverse, with 12 different climate zones. These range from humid subtropical areas to cool alpine regions and semidesert.

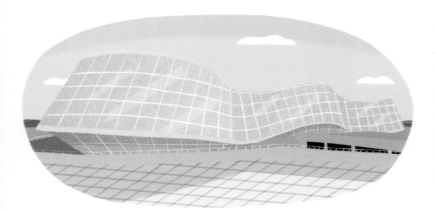

ARCHITECTURAL ADVENTURES

Since the country broke free of the Soviet Union in the early 1990s, Georgia's capital has seen a glut of new, experimental architecture. Tbilisi's House of Justice has a roof in the shape of a group of flying saucers; the Ministry of Internal Affairs looks like an ocean wave made of glass; and the Rhike Park Music Theater and Exhibition Hall resembles two huge periscopes laid on their sides (though it was never completed).

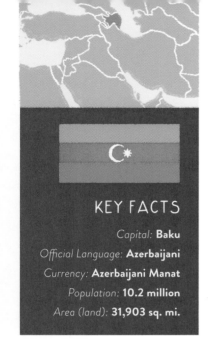

AZERBAIJAN

The country's name translates as the "Land of Fire," a fitting title for a country with vast reserves of oil and gas. The name probably dates back to a time when most of the people were Zoroastrians, followers of a religion who worshipped in "fire temples" where a flame was always kept burning. Today the majority of people here are Muslims.

KEY FACTS

Capital: **Baku**
Official Language: **Azerbaijani**
Currency: **Azerbaijani Manat**
Population: **10.2 million**
Area (land): **31,903 sq. mi.**

GRILL AND FLIP

The filled savory pancakes known locally as *kutabi* are one of Azerbaijanis' favorite foods, and the unofficial national dish. Stuffed full of cheese, meat, or vegetables (or all three if you're feeling hungry) and heaps of herbs, *kutabi* are toasted on a griddle pan and then served with a cooling yogurt dip.

Azerbaijan's national animal is the beloved yet endangered Karabakh horse, one of the most ancient breeds of horse on the planet.

ARMENIA

Known as the "land of churches," Armenia was the first nation in the world to adopt Christianity as its official religion. Unsurprisingly, the landscape is scattered with ancient churches and monasteries. Elsewhere this landlocked country boasts great stretches of mountains, lively cities, and fascinating architecture.

KEY FACTS

Capital: **Yerevan**
Official Language: **Armenian**
Currency: **Armenian Dram**
Population: **3 million**
Area (land): **10,889 sq. mi.**

CHURCH COUNTRY

In 301 CE, the kingdom of Armenia, the forerunner of the modern state, adopted Christianity as the national religion. The people then went about proving their faith by building churches across the land. There are now around 4,000 of them, occupying all sorts of different locations. These range from the fortress monastery of Haghpat, perched high on a hill overlooking a canyon, to Geghard, a holy grotto carved into the side of a mountain.

Chess is very popular in Armenia, and the country has produced several top players. It's also the only country in the world where the game is a compulsory subject in school.

TURKEY

Straddling Europe and Asia, Turkey has long enjoyed an amalgamation of cultures, religions, and cuisines. It's a vast nation where vistors can take in everything from the bazaars and coffee shops of its largest city, Istanbul, to the ruins of previous civilizations (Greek, Roman, and Ottoman) and long stretches of Mediterranean coast.

KEY FACTS

Capital: **Ankara**
Official Language: **Turkish**
Currency: **Turkish Lira**
Population: **82 million**
Area (land): **297,157 sq. mi.**

HANGING OUT AT THE HAMMAM

Public bathing has been popular in Turkey since Roman times. Often ornately decorated baths, known as *hammams*, are found in towns and cities across the country. A visit usually involves sweating in a very hot steam room before taking a very cold bath (or shower)—and then repeating the whole process several times. It's supposed to be very good for you.

TYPICAL TURKISH DISHES

Köfte—*small meatballs*
Dolma—*meat and rice wrapped in vine leaves*
Shish kebab—*skewers of meat grilled over a fire.*

COTTON CASTLE

At first glance, the bizarre landscape of Pamukkale ("Cotton Castle") in western Turkey looks like something from another planet. But these snow-white terraces dotted with metallic-blue pools are entirely natural. They're the result of a hot spring depositing a mineral called travertine as it bubbles out of the ground, which builds up to form icy-looking layers.

In the Turkish region of Cappadocia, much of the landscape has been eroded into a collection of strangely shaped peaks known as "fairy chimneys."

SWEET DELIGHTS

Turkish delight, known locally known as *lokum*, is a popular confection made of supersweet cubes of jelly. Dusted with icing sugar, they're traditionally flavored with rose water, although these days many different varieties are available, featuring pistachios, cherries, hazlenuts, and more.

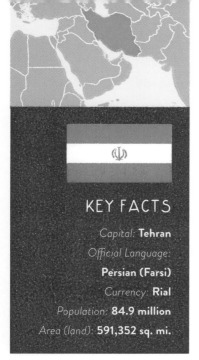

IRAN

Previously known as Persia, Iran provides a link between the Middle East and Central Asia. In ancient times, it controlled a huge empire that regularly battled with Rome. Many of its traditions date back to this time, including carpet making and poetry writing. Most people live in a fertile plateau running through the country's center.

KEY FACTS

Capital: **Tehran**

Official Language: **Persian (Farsi)**

Currency: **Rial**

Population: **84.9 million**

Area (land): **591,352 sq. mi.**

Originally a Zoroastrian tradition, the New Year festival of *Nowruz* has been celebrated here for thousands of years. It normally take place on or around March 20.

RUGS ARE ALL THE RAGE

Intricately woven, luxurious Persian carpets are sold around the world. Traditionally made from sheep's wool and colored with natural dyes made from grapes, pomegranates, cochineal (bright red bugs), and spices, a handmade carpet can take months to complete. The oldest known Persian carpet dates back to the 400s BCE.

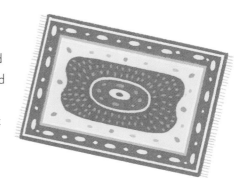

POETRY, PLEASE

Throughout the past 2,500 years, Iranians have often been found holding poetry recitals or effortlessly quoting their favorite verses. The country has produced numerous noted poets. Perhaps the most famous is Hafez, whose poems about love, known as *ghazals*, which were written in the 1300s and are still widely read today.

FELINE GOOD

The long-haired cat breed known as Persian originated here in the Middle Ages. From the 1600s onward, these cats began to be exported, and the breed is now one of the world's most popular. Iran is also home to some slightly larger felines: cheetahs. A small population of the world's fastest land animal lives in the Kavir National Park in northern Iran.

Khosh aamadid
— *"You're welcome"*
in Farsi

The Azadi Tower, one of the country's most famous monuments, was erected in 1971 to mark 2,500 years of Persian history.

IRAQ

Known as the "cradle of civilization," Iraq was one of the places where the planting of crops, rearing of animals, and building of cities first began. It's seen everything in its time, including the rise and fall of empires and several recent wars, but has managed to keep hold of its traditions throughout.

KEY FACTS

Capital: **Baghdad**
Official Languages:
Arabic, Kurdish
Currency: **Iraqi Dinar**
Population: **38.8 million**
Area (land): **168,868 sq. mi.**

BETWEEN THE RIVERS

The region's earliest civilizations were established in a region called Mesopotamia. This occupied an area of fertile ground between two rivers: the Tigris and the Euphrates (Mesopotamia means "between two rivers"), which still flow through Iraq. The states that emerged here from the 3000s BCE onward would dominate the region for thousands of years.

CITY OF WONDERS

In the 500s BCE, Iraq was home to Babylon, the largest city in the world at the time. Built on the banks of the Euphrates River, it boasted huge stepped temples called ziggurats, magnificent palaces and, according to legend, one of the Seven Wonders of the Ancient World, the Hanging Gardens of Babylon. The city eventually fell to conquerors and was abandoned. Its ruins have been excavated in recent times, although no evidence of the gardens has been found.

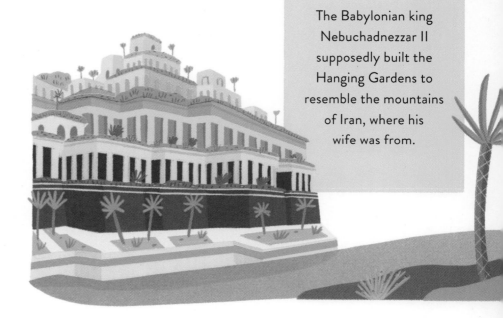

The Babylonian king Nebuchadnezzar II supposedly built the Hanging Gardens to resemble the mountains of Iran, where his wife was from.

ZIGZAGGING ZIGGURATS

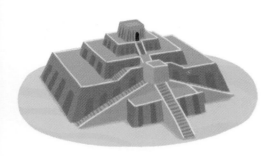

Ziggurats were enormous tiered buildings that dominated the skyline in ancient Mesopotamian cities. Acting as shrines to the region's gods, these great brick structures were believed to connect Heaven and Earth through a series of steps that wound around the ziggurat to the top.

Most people in Iraq still live in the fertile plains between the Tigris and Euphrates, just as they did thousands of years ago. The rest of the country is dominated by deserts and mountains.

KUWAIT

Kuwait is a tiny desert state. Although its history goes back hundreds of years, until recently it was a low-key place where most people made their living through trade and fishing. The discovery of oil in the mid-20th century changed all that, and today Kuwait is a wealthy land with towns and cities full of gleaming glass buildings.

KEY FACTS

Capital: **Kuwait City**
Official Language: **Arabic**
Currency: **Kuwaiti Dinar**
Population: **2.9 million**
Area (land): **6,880 sq. mi.**

In 2001, archaeologists unearthed the remains of a 7,000-year-old reed boat on the northern coast of Kuwait, one of the oldest boats ever discovered.

The name Kuwait comes from an Arabic term meaning "fortress built near water."

WATER IN THE DESERT

Kuwait is one of the only places on Earth without any permanent natural rivers, streams, or lakes. Instead, the country relies on the desalination (removing the salt) of seawater to make its water drinkable. Much of this water is stored in a network of strange-looking water towers. Some look like giant striped mushrooms, while others resemble futuristic skyscrapers with huge domes holding millions of gallons of liquid.

MUD, SKIP, AND JUMP

The land-leaping fish known as mudskippers are found along Kuwait's coastline. These bizarre creatures have special adaptations that allow them to both swim underwater and skip around on land. When in water, they breathe using their gills, while out of water they rely on air trapped in chambers in their gills.

ROBOTIC RIDERS

Kuwaitis have long loved camel racing. But this ancient sport took a futuristic turn in 2005 when robot jockeys began to be used instead of human ones. Smaller and cheaper than the real thing, these mini mechanical riders are given their instructions through remote control by trainers who follow behind the camels in vehicles. Some robots are even equipped with walkie-talkies so the trainer can talk directly to their camel.

BAHRAIN

The smallest nation in the Middle East by area, Bahrain is made up 33 natural islands, plus several artificial ones, in the Persian Gulf. Most of the people live on the largest one, Bahrain Island. With the majority of the country taken up by desert, Bahrain has traditionally made its living from its shores—particularly pearl fishing—and, in more recent years, through oil and banking.

KEY FACTS

Capital: **Manama**
Official Language: **Arabic**
Currency: **Bahraini Dinar**
Population: **1.5 million**
Area (land): **293 sq. mi.**

TREE OF LIFE

Bahrain is 92 percent desert, but even in these driest of conditions, life can sometimes find a way. In the middle of Bahrain Island stands Shajarat-al-Hayat, also known as the "Tree of Life," a 30-foot-tall mesquite tree alone in the sands with no other trees as far as the eye can see. No one is entirely sure where it gets its water and nutrients from, but it's been doing it for a long time. It's believed to be around 400 years old.

"Bahrain" means "two seas," which is believed to be a reference to the waters on the western and eastern sides of the main island.

DIVING FOR PEARLS

For over 4,000 years, until the 1930s, Bahrain's main industry was fishing for pearls—the shiny, semiprecious stones that form inside oysters. The men who collected the pearl oysters from the sea floor didn't use any special equipment, just a peg on the nose to help them hold their breath as they were lowered into the sea on weighted ropes.

Less than 3% of Bahrain's land is suitable for growing crops, so fish and seafood are widely eaten.

SPINNING SHAWARMA

One of Bahrain's most popular dishes is *shawarma*—thinly sliced pieces of meat (typically chicken or lamb) stacked into a tower and then roasted on a rotating skewer. It's usually served in a pita or flatbread with salad and sauces.

KEY FACTS

Capital: **Doha**
Official Language: **Arabic**
Currency: **Qatari Riyal**
Population: **2.4 million**
Area (land): **4,473 sq. mi.**

Qatar relies so much on foreign workers that Qatari citizens make up just a ninth of the country's overall population.

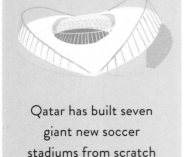

Qatar has built seven giant new soccer stadiums from scratch to host the 2022 FIFA World Cup.

QATAR

With enormous oil reserves, Qatar is per person the richest nation on Earth, although that wealth is not divided equally among the population. Much of the money has been spent modernizing the country, particularly its capital, Doha, which now has hundreds of shiny new buildings glittering under the desert sun. Despite all the new architecture, the country still tries to keep up many of its old traditions.

FALCON FANS

The sport of falconry—hunting using birds of prey—is very popular in Qatar. The best hunting birds are bought and sold at the aptly named Falcon Souq in Doha—basically a giant supermarket for birds. Any ill or injured birds can be treated at the nearby Falcon Hospital using state-of-the-art equipment.

SAND AND SURF

At the southeastern end of the country is an inlet of the Arabian Sea known as *Khor Al-Adaid* ("The Inland Sea"), one of the few places in the world where the desert meets the sea. Here waves lap the rolling sand dunes, creating a unique ecosystem where sea turtles rub shoulders with desert foxes.

WILD SUCCESS STORY

Qatar's national animal, the Arabian oryx, was considered extinct in the wild in the mid-20th century. But, thanks to some remarkable conservation efforts, oryx reared in captivity have gradually been reintroduced to the Qatar countryside and across the region. There are now over a thousand oryx roaming the wilds of the Arabian Peninsula.

OMAN

Oman occupies the eastern edge of the Arabian Peninsula. Although most of its interior is desert, much of its long coastline is humid and fertile. This is where the majority of people live and where the capital, Muscat, is located. A major port since medieval times, Muscat is known for its museums, markets, and shopping districts.

KEY FACTS

Capital: **Muscat**
Official Language: **Arabic**
Currency: **Omani Rial**
Population: **4.6 million**
Area (land): **119,499 sq. mi.**

TENDING TURTLES

Ras Al Hadd, Oman's easternmost village, is home to a reserve for endangered green sea turtles. Roughly 20,000 female turtles return to the beaches here every year, climbing clumsily up the shore to lay their eggs in the sand. Staff at the reserve help protect the nests from being disturbed and also take tourists on night tours of the beach—when they may be able to spot baby turtles hatching and then scuttling their way down to the sea.

SINBAD SETTING

Sohar, the former capital of Oman, was supposedly the birthplace of Sinbad the Sailor—the legendary hero of the collection of Middle Eastern folk tales known as the *One Thousand and One Nights*. The port serves as the backdrop to Sinbad's adventures, which see him sail around the world in search of treasure, encountering pirates, shipwrecks, and mythical beasts on his way.

"Dune bashing," which involves cruising over desert sand dunes in a 4x4 vehicle, is very popular in Oman.

OMANI OASES

Notably greener and more lush than many of its neighbors, Oman has a number of natural pools, oases, and wadis (seasonal rivers). These include the Bimmah Sinkhole, a natural limestone pool near the eastern coast, and Wadi Shab, a deep gorge where people can swim in cool blue-green waters.

UNITED ARAB EMIRATES

KEY FACTS

Capital: **Abu Dhabi**
Official Language: **Arabic**
Currency: **UAE Dirham**
Population: **9.9 million**
Area (land): **32,278 sq. mi.**

The UAE is a state made up of seven connected emirates (kingdoms). Once a sleepy, small-scale place, the UAE has transformed into a hyper-modern country. Its streets are lined with enormous skyscrapers, while offshore are several artificial vacation islands. Most of this development has been paid for with oil money, although the country is fast becoming a major destination for tourism and business.

THE SEVEN EMIRATES

- Abu Dhabi
(the capital)
- Ajman
- Dubai
(site of largest city, Dubai)
- Fujairah
- Ras Al Khaimah
- Sharjah
- Umm Al-Quwain

Dubai is known for its spectacular firework displays. The New Year's Eve celebration of 2014 saw 479,651 fireworks launched in just six minutes, or 1,332 per second— a world record.

BIGGEST BUILDING

Towering over the slickly modern Dubai skyline, the Burj Khalifa is the tallest building on the planet. Looking somewhat like a giant shiny talon, the 2,722-foot building holds several world records, including having the greatest number of floors of any building (163) and the longest elevator ride. It houses apartments, hotels, office spaces, shopping facilities, and viewing platforms open to the public.

PALM TREE ISLAND

Dubai is famous for its artificial vacation islands, many of which have unusual shapes. Perhaps the most famous is the Palm Jumeirah, which has been built in the shape of an enormous palm tree (when seen from above). The tree's "trunk" forms a bridge connecting to the mainland, along which runs a monorail, while the tree's "leaves" are home to apartments, hotels, and vacation villas.

WELCOME, WORKERS

Dubai is home to a lot of people, although the vast majority are from overseas. Around 88 percent, or almost nine million people, are immigrants who have come here to find work. Many are employed building the country's seemingly never-ending sequence of skyscrapers. Most of these foreign workers are from the South Asian countries of India, Bangladesh, and Pakistan.

YEMEN

Yemen's recent history has been tumultuous and anguished. Since the early 2010s, it's been involved in a civil war that has caused widespread misery. When peace hopefully returns, the people can go back to enjoying a beautiful land of eucalyptus and fig trees, deserts, and highlands, with a long, curving coastline taking in both the Red Sea and the Arabian Sea.

KEY FACTS

Capital: **Sanaa**

Official Language: **Arabic**

Currency: **Yemeni Rial**

Population: **29.8 million**

Area (land): **203,850 sq. mi.**

DRAGON'S BLOOD

A strange, unique land where the trees bleed and the spiders are blue, Yemen's largest island, Socotra, sits south of the mainland in the Arabian Sea. It's the only place in the world where you can see the blue baboon (which despite its name is not a monkey but a big, hairy, and very blue spider) and dragon's blood trees. The latter look like giant green mushrooms and get their slightly gruesome name from their ruby red sap.

COFFEE CONNOISSEURS

Coffee originated in northeast Africa. From the 1400s to the 1700s, the Yemeni port of Mocha was the world's largest coffee marketplace. Its name lives on in the popular chocolate-coffee drink. Coffee continues to be grown in Yemen today.

The national animal of Yemen is the extremely rare Arabian leopard. Arabian leopards are smaller and nimbler than their African and Asian cousins.

DIVIDED COUNTRY

From 1962 to 1990, the country was split into two nations: North Yemen and South Yemen. Eventually, the two were united, but the peace didn't last long. The country has been blighted by civil unrest and warfare in recent years, and many refugees from Yemen have fled to neighboring nations and beyond.

SAUDI ARABIA

KEY FACTS

Capital: **Riyadh**
Official Language: **Arabic**
Currency: **Saudi Riyal**
Population: **34.1 million**
Area (land): **830,000 sq. mi.**

The largest country in the Middle East, Saudi Arabia was the birthplace of Islam and is still the site of its holiest places. Ruled since 1932 by an absolute monarch, this huge, desert-covered country is also the region's richest. It has huge oil wealth—much of which has been spent creating giant, modern cityscapes.

HOLIEST PLACE

Saudi Arabia is home to Mecca, the holiest city in Islam, where the prophet Muhammad, the founder of Islam, was born. Within the courtyard of the Great Mosque of Mecca, Al-Masjid al-Ḥarām, sits an ancient, black, cube-shaped building known as the Kabaa or "House of God," which is the most sacred site in the Islamic world. Every Muslim is supposed to make a pilgrimage, or Hajj, to Mecca at least once in their lifetime. Once there, they perform the ritual of circling the Kabaa seven times in a counterclockwise direction.

Every day Muslims pray toward Mecca, making sure they are facing in the direction of the city from wherever they are in the world.

OIL OPPORTUNITIES

The country is greatly reliant on fossil fuels. It has the world's second-largest supply of oil and fifth-largest gas reserves, both of which it extracts from deep beneath the desert. With just under half the country's wealth coming from sales of oil, Saudi Arabia needs to find new sources of income before all its oil has been extracted in around 100 years.

Around 100 camels are bought and sold every day at the Camel market in Riyadh.

ANCIENT ART

Just outside Jubbah, in the northwest region of Saudi Arabia, there is a collection of ancient rock carvings. Created by some of the country's earliest peoples, the carvings—known as petroglyphs—depict camels, goats, and warriors in chariots. They were created by etching away the top dark layer of the rocks to reveal a lighter layer below.

In 2018, Saudi Arabia became the last country in the world to pass a law allowing women to drive.

JORDAN

Jordan's rocky desert landscape might appear inhospitable, but people have been living here for thousands of years. Today it's one of the region's most peaceful nations, having largely avoided the conflicts of its neighbors. It's a welcoming place, with thousands of tourists arriving each year to explore the ancient city of Petra, the seemingly endless deserts of Wadi Rum, and its Red Sea coast.

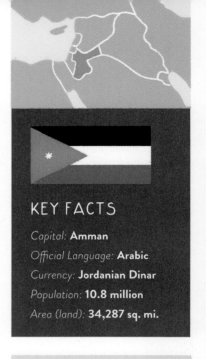

KEY FACTS

Capital: **Amman**
Official Language: **Arabic**
Currency: **Jordanian Dinar**
Population: **10.8 million**
Area (land): **34,287 sq. mi.**

LOCAL DISHES

Jordanians are passionate about food. Some of the country's favorite dishes include:

• Mansaf—*sharing platter of meat, rice, toasted pine nuts, and yogurt sauce, served with thin bread called shrak for dipping (the national dish).*

• Kunafa—*sweet pastry pie with a cheese filling.*

• Zaarb—*Bedouin barbecue of meat and vegetables cooked in a hole in the sand.*

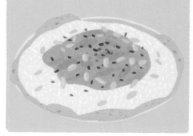

MISTAKEN FOR MARS

The deep red rocks of the sandstone valley Wadi Rum look so otherworldly that they've provided the backdrop for several movies set on Mars. Full of sand dunes, canyons, and mountains, the Wadi attracts lots of visitors, some of whom stay overnight in special desert camps, although they need to make sure they're properly equipped. It can be blisteringly hot on summer days and absolutely freezing at night. Tens of thousands of prehistoric rock carvings have been discovered here, some dating back 12,000 years.

Jordan's deserts are protected by a special police force called the Desert Patrol.

Jordan is almost— but not quite— landlocked, with a short 16 mi. coastline along the Red Sea.

THE ROSE CITY

Only accessible via a narrow 0.75-mile-long gorge, the ancient city of Petra is the country's main tourist attraction. Its ornate buildings were carved directly into the towering sandstone cliffs around 2,000 years ago by the people of the Nabataean Kingdom, a great trading empire. Eventually, the empire fell and the city was abandoned. It lay undiscovered by the outside world until the early 1800s. It's known as the "Rose City" because of the light red color of its rocks.

ISRAEL AND THE PALESTINIAN TERRITORIES

KEY FACTS

Capital: **Jerusalem**
Official Language: **Hebrew**
Currencies: **Israeli New Shekel,**
Jordanian Dinar,
Egyptian Pound
Population: **8.6 million Israel,**
2.9 million Palestinian
Territories
Area (land): **10,478 sq. mi.**

The spiritual homeland of several faiths, this rugged, beautiful land is a deeply contested place. There is a longstanding conflict between Israelis and Palestinians over ownership of the territory. Currently, it's divided between the country of Israel, which takes up most of the land and where the majority of the people are Jewish; and the Palestinian Territories, which is split into two unconnected areas—the Gaza Strip and the West Bank—where the majority of people are Arabic.

More than a million prayer notes are stuffed into the cracks of the Western Wall each year.

SACRED SITES

This ancient land is covered with sacred sites. These include Bethlehem, where Christians believe Jesus was born, and the Western Wall, the remains of a temple destroyed in 70 CE, where Jews still come to pray. Temple Mount is regarded by Jewish people as the place where God first made man and by Muslims as the place where the prophet Muhammad ascended to heaven.

STAYING AFLOAT

Marking the lowest place on land on the face of the Earth (1,300 feet below sea level), the Dead Sea is a lake on the borders of Jordan, Israel, and the West Bank. Its water is so salty (ten times more salty than seawater) that nothing, except for some very hardy microorganisms, can live in it. All that salt also makes the water super buoyant—visitors flock here to swim, or just float on the surface, as it's almost impossible to sink.

GROVES GALORE

So many olive groves cover the landscape around the Palestinian village of Battir in the West Bank that UNESCO gave it the nickname the "land of olives and vines." Some of these vines have been around a long time—the oldest are believed to be around 4,000 years old. The olive harvest is a major annual event for Palestinians.

LEBANON

Stretched out along the Mediterranean Sea, Lebanon has a history that goes back at least 5,000 years. It's been shaped by many different peoples, including Phoenicians, Greeks, Romans, and Arabs. Today followers of several different faiths—including Muslims, Christians, Buddhists, and Druze—live alongside one another, particularly in the multicultural capital, Beirut.

KEY FACTS

Capital: **Beirut**
Official Language: **Arabic**
Currency: **Lebanese Pound**
Population: **5.4 million**
Area (land): **3,950 sq. mi.**

PHOENICIAN PURPLE

The Phoenicians were an ancient people that emerged in Lebanon in the 1000s BCE. Skilled shipbuilders and sailors, they forged an empire that stretched across the Mediterranean and out of which would later emerge the even more powerful state of Carthage (see page 95). With the wealth they built up from trade, the Phoenicians created several large cities in Lebanon, such as Tyre, which is still inhabited today. Perhaps their best-selling product was a rich purple dye made from a rare type of sea snail.

Only the Roman emperor was allowed to wear a toga dyed in Phoenician purple.

HUNGRY FOR HUMMUS

The much-loved Middle Eastern side dish or dip known as hummus has been perfected in Lebanon. A creamy blend of chickpeas, tahini, garlic, olive oil, and lemon, it's often served with grilled pita bread, halloumi, meat, or falafel. Lebanon holds the record for the largest portion of hummus ever cooked, weighing a whopping 23,043 pounds.

HARDY CITY

Lebanon's capital, Beirut, is a resilient place. Over the course of its history, the city has suffered greatly due to conflicts and warfare. But, like the phoenix, it's always risen again, having rebuilt itself no fewer than seven times. The most recent damage occurred in August 2020, when a warehouse full of a dangerous chemical called ammonium nitrate exploded, sending out a huge shockwave that killed over 200 people, caused over $15 billion worth of damage, and left more than 300,000 people homeless.

Lebanon has just one river that flows all year round, the Litani.

Lebanon has a multitude of ancient ruins, including Iron Age tombs, Roman baths, and Crusader fortresses.

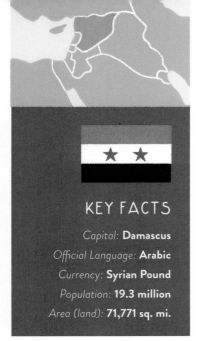

SYRIA

History lovers are always entranced by Syria, which is littered with artifacts left behind by the people of past civilizations. The capital, Damascus, is one of the oldest continuously occupied cities in the world and is full of relics, temples, and mosques. Sadly, the country is currently in the midst of a traumatic civil war which has resulted in many Syrians losing their lives or taking refuge in other countries.

KEY FACTS

Capital: **Damascus**
Official Language: **Arabic**
Currency: **Syrian Pound**
Population: **19.3 million**
Area (land): **71,771 sq. mi.**

Liquorice is widely grown and consumed in Syria, often in the form of a drink used as an herbal remedy.

WATER WHEELS

In medieval times, Syrian farmers constructed huge wooden waterwheels known as *norias*. These were used for raising water up out of rivers and into channels where it could be transported to fields to irrigate crops. Several surviving wheels are on display in the city of Hama.

POPULAR PETS

Syrian hamsters, which live in dry regions in the northern part of the country, have become popular pets around the world—mainly because they're easy to tame (and very cute). In the wild, hamsters spend their days in underground burrows away from the searing sun, coming out at night to feed on plants, grains, and insects. They can store excess food in their large cheek pouches.

Syrian hamsters are pregnant for just 16 days before giving birth. They can produce litters of up to 20 babies. That's a lot of hamsters!

SANDY STORMS

Strong winds are common in Syria's coastal areas throughout the year. Sometimes they can whip up huge sandstorms known as khamsin that darken the skies and force everyone indoors. Some khamsin are over 3,000 feet high.

OCE

ANIA

AUSTRALIA

The land "Down Under" is as diverse as it is large. Because Australia shifted away from the rest of the world's continents millions of years ago, its wildlife is unique, too. Home to one of the world's most ancient cultures, the country is famous for its sunny climate and surf-perfect beaches.

ONE OF A KINDS

Because of the country's remote location in the southern Pacific Ocean, Australia's animals have developed in their own special ways. They certainly have their own take on child rearing. This is where you'll find both the world's only egg-laying mammals (the spiny echidna and duck-billed platypus) and the majority of its marsupials, which carry their young in the mothers' special furry pouches.

KEY FACTS

Capital: **Canberra**
Official Language: **English**
Currency: **Australian dollar**
Population: **25.4 million**
Area (land): **2,966,153 sq. mi.**

Australia's Fraser Island is the largest sand island on the planet. Its golden shores stretch for over 75 mi.

MARVELOUS MARSUPIALS

Kangaroos and koalas may be the best known, but Australia is home to over 300 species of marsupials. See how many of these you recognize:
• bettong • bilby • dunnart • quokka • quoll • sugar glider • Tasmanian devil • wallaby • wombat

Australia has so many beaches—over 10,000—that if you were to visit one a day, it would take you around 27 years to relax on them all.

DEADLY ANIMALS

Some of the scariest and most venomous creatures on Earth lurk here. Swimmers need to watch out for sharks, as well as deadly aquatic stingers such as the blue-ringed octopus and box jellyfish. On land, people need to watch out for funnel-web spiders and various snakes, including the inland taipan. Though rather ordinary-looking, the taipan carries enough venom to kill 100 people. Thankfully bites are rare, and there's a medicine people can take (known as antivenin) to counteract the poison.

RED ROCK

The Outback, a scorching area of desert (and semidesert), stretches across the middle of the country. It's so flat that you can see for miles in places, although there's not much to look at because it's too hot for many plants to survive. But rising above the barren landscape is perhaps Australia's most famous landmark and an icon of the country, the great red rock of Uluru. The sandstone monolith is considered sacred to many indigenous Australians—it has been a place of ceremony for local tribes for generations.

ABORIGINAL ART

The country's indigenous inhabitants, known as Aboriginal Australians, are believed to have arrived here over 60,000 years ago. Today they continue to practice one of the oldest cultures in the world, which has been passed down the generations in the form of songs, stories, dance, and art. There are examples of Aboriginal rock art—many depicting animals—dating back tens of thousands of years.

WORLD'S GREATEST REEF

Stretching for an incredible 1,400 miles, the world's largest coral reef system, the Great Barrier Reef, lies off Australia's northwest coast. Half a million years in the making, it's been slowly built up by countless generations of coral. Much of it is teeming with brightly colored tropical fish, spiky crustaceans, and inquisitive turtles. Sadly, recent years have seen areas of coral die back and lose their color—a process known as bleaching—as a result of climate change.

BIG BLOW OUT

Every year, the country's largest city, Sydney, puts on a stunning New Year's Eve display, with fireworks lighting up the night sky above some of the country's most famous landmarks, including the Sydney Harbour Bridge and Sydney Opera House.

Most of Australia's population—and its largest cities, including Sydney and Melbourne— are located in the southeast, where the majority of the country's fertile land is found.

PAPUA NEW GUINEA

Papua New Guinea occupies the eastern half of the island of New Guinea (Indonesia occupies the west) as well as 600 smaller islands. Much of the land is rainforest-covered mountains where some of the world's spectacular animals live. The people here form hundreds of ethnic groups and speak an equally diverse range of languages.

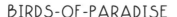

WILDLIFE WATCHING

Mountainous and isolated, many of the country's landscapes remain largely untouched by humans, making them a wildlife-watching haven. Species to look out for include the cassowary (a giant dinosaur-like bird), the big-beaked Papuan hornbill, fruit bats, and the tree kangaroo.

More than 700 different tribes live in Papua New Guinea, and together they speak more languages than anywhere else on earth —over 800.

BIRDS-OF-PARADISE

Largely free of predators, Papua New Guinea's forests are home to many species of the worlds' most glamorous birds—birds-of-paradise—one of which features on the country's flag. The males sport dazzling plumage, with long tails and spectacular crests, and perform elaborate dances to try to impress the females. Some have unusual names, including:
• black-billed sicklebill • Jobi manucode • Magnificent Riflebird • Obi paradise-crow • Splendid Astrapia • Superb Bird-of-Paradise • Twelve-wired Bird-of-Paradise.

Papua New Guinea makes up less than 1% of Earth's land but boasts around 5% of its biodiversity.

The Tolai people of the island of East New Britain still trade shells as currency. Called *tabu*, the sea snail shells are grouped together in a long chain before they are traded.

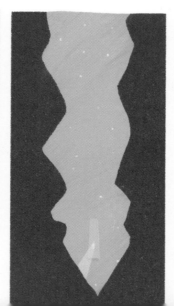

DEEPEST DEPTHS

Just under 1,200 miles north of Papua New Guinea lies the lowest point of the Earth's surface, the Mariana Trench. The canyon plunges down to a depth of 36,037 feet below sea level—that's deeper than Mt. Everest is tall. The creatures that live here are adapted to the crushing water pressure and total darkness. Only a handful of people have descended to the bottom of the trench, protected within super-strong submersibles, including the movie director James Cameron in 2012.

FIJI

Fiji is made up of 333 large islands and about 500 smaller ones. Most are uninhabited, with the majority of the population crammed onto just two: Viti Levu and Vanua Levu. The country's popular image is of a sun-drenched paradise—tropical reefs, endless beaches, and picturesque volcanoes—and that's not too far from the truth.

KEY FACTS

Capital: **Suva**

Official Languages: **Fijian, English, Fiji Hindi**

Currency: **Fijian Dollar**

Population: **935,974**

Area (land): **7,056 sq. mi.**

The country's national drink is a peppery concoction made from a local root called *kava*.

There are over 2,000 species of orchids in Fiji's Garden of the Sleeping Giant.

FIJIAN FIRES

Fire-walking ceremonies have been performed on the Fijian island of Beqa for generations. Traditionally, men walk across burning-hot stones barefoot—without getting burned. Legend has it that the ceremonies began long ago when a fisherman caught a small god disguised as an eel. In exchange for his life, the god granted the man the ability to tame fire, which gave him and his descendants the ability to walk on hot, fiery stones. (Boringly, scientists say that the fire walkers' success is owing to the speed with which they walk across the stones.)

ONE SWELL WAVE

Surfers flock to Fiji to take on its waves, particularly those at a place called Cloudbreak near the island of Tavarua. Here the waves regularly exceed 20 feet and have the reputation for providing one of the best—and most challenging—surfs on the planet. The reefs where the waves form is owned by a local surf resort, so if you want to try riding the surf, you need to get in line: the resort restricts the number of surfers here in order to protect the environment.

ANCIENT SANDS

Fiji is known across the world for its golden sands, and nowhere is there more to be found than at the towering dunes of Sigatoka National Park. Here thousands of years worth of sediment have washed down the Sigatoka River and onto the coast, covering an area of 1,600 acres and creating rolling dunes up to 200 feet in height.

Rugby is Fiji's most popular sport, and the locals are pretty good at it. The national team won the World Rugby Sevens Tournament in 2019 and also took gold at the 2016 Olympics.

SOLOMON ISLANDS

Six main islands and over a thousand tiny isles make up this South Pacific country. Together they offer a wealth of different ecosystems and natural attractions. There are deep lagoons, shipwrecks, swamps, reefs, beaches, rainforests, and active volcanoes —the latter erupt both on land and out at sea, spewing lava directly into the water.

KEY FACTS

Capital: **Honiara**
Official Language: **English**
Currency:
Solomon Islands Dollar
Population: **685,097**
Area (land): **10,805 sq. mi.**

BAMBOO BEATS

The 'Are'are people from the island of Malaita are famous for their panpipe music. The instruments are hand-sculpted by the locals from bamboo plants. Each set of pipes consists of about three to nine tubes, carefully shaped to sound different pitches. The pipe music isn't written down but has been passed down from player to player through the generations.

The Melanesian megapodes, or scrub fowl, don't sit on their eggs. Instead they use the heat from underground volcanic activity to keep them warm.

VANUATU

Prone to storms, earthquakes, and volcanic eruptions, this string of islands has been declared by the United Nations to be among the most naturally dangerous places in the world. But it's also one of the most naturally beautiful places, with dozens of tropical islands. No wonder its name means "Our Land Forever" in the local language.

KEY FACTS

Capital: **Port-Vila**
Official Languages: **Bislama, English, French**
Currency: **Vatu**
Population: **298,333**
Area (land): **4,706 sq. mi.**

ORIGINAL BUNGEE

The men of Pentecost Island perform an ancient daredevil ritual every year. Known as *nagol*, or land-diving, it involves the men climbing a tall wooden platform and then leaping off, head first. Vines strapped to their feet and tied to the top of the tower pull taut to stop them from smacking into the ground. This activity is believed to have been the inspiration for the modern extreme sport of bungee jumping.

Vanuatu has the world's only underwater post office that receives and delivers waterproof postcards, written with nonsmudging ink and embossed with special stamps.

KIRIBATI

KEY FACTS

Capital: **Tarawa**

Official Languages:
English, Gilbertese

Currency: **Australian Dollar**

Population: **111,796**

Area (land): **313 sq. mi.**

Pronounced "Kiri-bass," Kiribati is a tiny country of 33 low-lying tropical islands. Once ruled by the UK, when it was known as the Gilbert Islands, the country gained its independence in 1979. Its inhabitants, who are known as *I-Kiribati*, are spread out among the islands, so boats are one of the main ways of getting around.

LOCAL WARRIORS

Though they now form one nation, in the 1600s and 1700s, there were frequent battles between the islands. At that time, warriors defended themselves using locally sourced equipment—spears tipped with sharks' teeth, armor made from thick coconut fibers, and helmets formed from the spiky skin of puffer fish.

The Phoenix Islands Protected Area covers an area of over 150,000 sq. mi. and provides a haven for wildlife.

NAURU

KEY FACTS

Capital: **Yaren**

Official Languages:
Nauruan, English

Currency: **Australian Dollar**

Population: **11,000**

Area (land): **8 sq. mi.**

A tiny speck of land surrounded by endless ocean, Nauru is the world's smallest island country. Throughout its history, it's been controlled by various foreign powers, including Germany, Japan, Britain, Australia, and New Zealand, but finally achieved independence in 1958.

GUANO ISLAND

For centuries, the people here lived by fishing and farming. But in the early 20th century, the island began to be extensively mined for phosphate—an important ingredient in fertilizer—found in the guano (bird poop) blanketing the island's rocks. For a brief period, profits from mining made Nauru's population among the richest in the world. However, guano supplies are now almost completely exhausted, leaving behind severe economic and environmental problems.

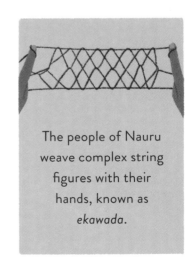

The people of Nauru weave complex string figures with their hands, known as *ekawada*.

MARSHALL ISLANDS

With thousands of islands spanning 750,000 square miles of Pacific Ocean, it's little wonder that the people of the Marshall Islands are highly skilled sailors and fishers. The country's population is spread out over the 29 main islands, all of them atolls—ring-shaped areas of coral.

BIKINI BOOM

Though independent since 1979, the islands were formerly controlled by the United States. From 1946 onward, the US military conducted numerous nuclear tests here, blowing up several large bombs on one of the country's islands—Bikini Atoll. Coincidentally, the two-piece bathing suite was invented around the same time and was named after the atoll because it seemed like a tropical-sounding name.

KEY FACTS

Capital: **Majuro**

Official Languages: **Marshallese, English**

Currency: **United States Dollar**

Population: **77,917**

Area (land): **70 sq. mi.**

The breadfruit grown here can be boiled, fried, roasted, and ground into flour, while the bark can be turned into clothes and used to build canoes. You can even get a sticky glue-like material from the fruit's juice.

FEDERATED STATES OF MICRONESIA

With 600 islands across one million square miles in the Pacific, Micronesia consists of a city's worth of land spread out over a country's worth of ocean. The picturesque islands have been ruled by various nations over the centuries, but many of its indigenous traditions remain.

MONEY STONES

The state's westernmost island of Yap is famous for having developed perhaps the world's most cumbersome form of currency: gigantic stone disks, known as *rai*. Although the dollar is now the day-to-day currency, the stones are still sometimes used for traditional transactions. However, as many of the stones are too heavy to move, the islanders keep a record of who is supposed to own what.

Chuuk Lagoon is one of the world's largest ship graveyards. Scuba divers come to explore the many World War II planes and ships scattered across this seabed.

KEY FACTS

Capital: **Palikir**

Official Language: **English**

Currency: **United States Dollar**

Population: **102,436**

Area (land): **271 sq. mi.**

PALAU

With waters home to sharks, jellyfish, colorful corals, and giant clams, Palau is as celebrated for its offshore attractions as it is for what's on land. That territory consists of hundreds of small islands, many blanketed with dense vegetation.

KEY FACTS

Capital: **Ngerulmud**
Official Languages:
Palauan, English
Currency: **United States Dollar**
Population: **21,685**
Area (land): **177 sq. mi.**

FRIENDLY JELLIES

Jellyfish Lake on Eil Malk Island has become a popular destination with snorkelers. As the lake's name suggests, they come to swim with the thousands of gently pulsing golden jellyfish that inhabit the water—and which follow the same route through the lake every day, tracking the path of the Sun.

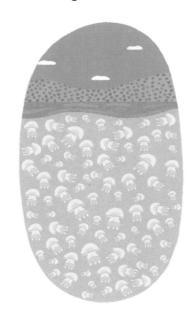

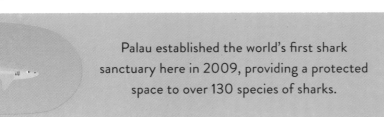

Palau established the world's first shark sanctuary here in 2009, providing a protected space to over 130 species of sharks.

TUVALU

The world's fourth-smallest country, Tuvalu is a peaceful land of nine low-lying coral islands in the Pacific Ocean, far from any major settlements. In this idyllic, tranquil world, the palm trees vastly outnumber the people.

KEY FACTS

Capital: **Funafuti**
Official Languages:
Tuvaluan, English
Currencies: **Tuvaluan Dollar,**
Australian Dollar
Population: **11,342**
Area (land): **10 sq. mi.**

COCO NUTS

The main crop in Tuvalu is the coconut. The flesh and milk of this hairy nut show up in many of the nation's dishes, often accompanied by some of the various species of fish and other seafood found in local waters. Nothing goes to waste—over the years, the Tuvaluans have devised ways of putting all parts of the coconut plant to use, from weaving baskets out of palm leaves to creating ropes with coconut husks.

Tuvalu's airstrip is more often used as a playground and meeting place than it is for planes. The locals use it to play sports, go for walks, and gather with their families.

SAMOA

Made up of two main islands, plus several smaller ones, Samoa lies right next to the International Date Line. In fact, American Samoa, which forms part of the same group of islands but which belongs to the US, lies on the other side. So if you make the half-hour flight from Samoa to American Samoa, you'll be going 24 hours back in time.

KEY FACTS

Capital: **Apia**
Official Languages: **Samoan, English**
Currency: **Tālā**
Population: **203,774**
Area (land): **1,089 sq. mi.**

BLOWHOLES

On the island of Savai'i, the Alofaaga blowholes are a collection of natural volcanic tubes running between the ocean and a cliff top. When waves hit the shore, water is forced up into tubes and explodes out of the top of the holes on the cliff with great force—fountains can be 65 feet in height. Locals often throw coconuts onto the water as it erupts and watch them get tossed high into the sky.

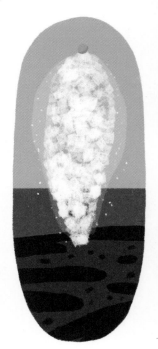

The phrase *fa'a Samoa,* or "The Samoan Way," has become a national motto used to sum up Samoa's culture and approach to life.

BODY ART

Tattoos have long been an important part of Samoan culture. Called pe'a, traditional Samoan tattoos are inked onto young men as a rite of passage, covering them from the knees to the waist with black geometric shapes. These types of tattoos take a long time (and are extremely painful) and should only be created by a tattoo master, known as a *tufuga ta tatau,* using traditional implements made of bone and shell.

SKIPPING AHEAD

Samoa skipped forward a whole day in 2011 so as to move across the International Date Line and align with Australia and New Zealand. They jumped from December 29 to December 31.

COLORFUL DANCES

Dance, known as *siva,* is an important part of Samoa's identity. There are several different forms, including:
- *Fa'ataupati*—the Samoan "slap" dance; men clap, stomp their feet, and slap their bodies to provide the beat.
- *Ma'ulu'ulu*—traditional dance performed by groups of women, some sitting, some kneeling, and some standing.
- *Siva Afi*—The "Fire Knife" dance; performers dance while twirling a ceremonial knife.

TONGA

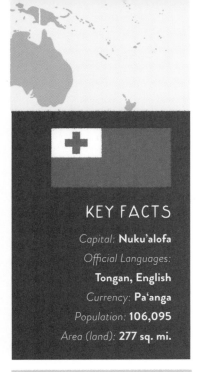

Tonga is a chain of more than 170 islands stretching north to south for about 500 miles across the Pacific Ocean, with most people living on the largest one, Tongatapu. This idyllic tropical nation is proud of its status as the only Pacific nation not to have been colonized by a foreign power.

KEY FACTS

Capital: **Nuku'alofa**
Official Languages: **Tongan, English**
Currency: **Pa'anga**
Population: **106,095**
Area (land): **277 sq. mi.**

Tonga is very spread out, with its islands divided into five groups. The northernmost group, the Niuas, is actually closer to Samoa than the rest of Tonga.

NOW YOU SEE IT, NOW YOU DON'T

Fonuafo'ou, or "New Island," is the top of a submarine volcano which alternately appears and disappears due to an ongoing combination of eruptions and erosion. In the 1800s, it grew to a height of 1,050 feet above sea level before submerging in 1896. By 1930, it had risen again, only to drop back below the waves 20 years later. The island is currently hidden, planning its next move.

WHALE MIGRATION

Pods of humpback whales turn up in Tonga's waters between June and October every year. They arrive having undertaken the longest migration of any mammal in the world. Females swim over 3,000 miles between their feeding grounds in the freezing Antarctic to the warm Tongan waters where they give birth to their young. Once the calves are strong enough, they'll make the long journey back again with their parents.

JUST THE FOX, PLEASE

Tonga's only native land mammal is a large fruit bat known as the flying fox. The bats' numbers are flourishing, not just because of the island's abundant fruits, but because they are considered the personal property of the Tongan king and therefore are strictly protected.

NOT SO FRIENDLY

In the West, Tonga was once known as the Friendly Islands. The name was given to the country by the British explorer Captain Cook after a banquet was held in his honor when he visited in 1773. Little did he know that the locals had planned the meal as a distraction so they could ambush his ship. In the event, the plan was called off at the last minute.

NEW ZEALAND

Out on its own, surrounded by ocean, over 1,200 miles from Australia, New Zealand was the last major territory to be inhabited by humans. It's made up of two main islands, named North and South, plus 600 smaller ones. The country is home to vibrant cities and a collection of incredible natural wonders.

KEY FACTS

Capital: **Wellington**

Official Languages: **English, Māori, NZ Sign Language**

Currency: **New Zealand dollar**

Population: **4.9 million**

Area (land): **102,138 sq. mi.**

A traditional Māori greeting called the *hongi* involves two people pressing their noses together.

MĀORI CULTURE

New Zealand's first inhabitants, the Māori, arrived on the islands around 1,000 years ago from eastern Polynesia. They formed a distinct culture that remains strong to this day, despite the many problems caused by the arrival of Europeans from the 1600s onward. Today around 16 percent of the population has Māori heritage. Their name for the country is *Aotearoa*, which means "The Land of the Long White Cloud."

Sheep outnumber people in New Zealand by about five to one.

ADVENTURE CAPITAL

Known as the "Adventure Capital of the World," Queenstown on South Island is a thrill-seeker's paradise. Every year, visitors flock here to take part in a range of extreme activities, from skiing, rock-climbing, and rappelling to bungee-jumping, skydiving, and paragliding. In fact, the first commercial bungee jump company was established here in 1988, offering daring volunteers the chance to leap off Shotover River's Kawarau Bridge.

GLOW IN THE DARK

There's no need to bring a flashlight when visiting Waitomo Caves on North Island, as the walls are illuminated by thousands of glowworms that make them shine like a starry night sky. The caves were discovered in the 1800s and have been a popular tourist attraction ever since, with tourists taking boat rides through the glowing caverns.

The mysterious Moeraki Boulders are a collection of almost perfectly spherical rocks on Koekohe Beach in South Island. Nobody knows how the stones formed, but geologists believe they may be 60 million years old.

RUGBY ROUTINE

New Zealanders love one sport above all others—rugby union. Seemingly the whole country comes together to cheer for the national men's team, known as the All Blacks. The team is the most successful in the world, having won the Rugby World Cup three times (most recently in 2015). It's known for performing a traditional ceremonial Māori challenge called the *haka* before each game. This sees players undertake a sequence of warrior-like stances and movements, accompanied by chants, bulging eyes, and sticking-out tongues.

SPECIAL CREATURES

Left isolated and alone for millions of years, New Zealand's animals were able to evolve in their own unique ways. There are no native mammals here other than bats, and very few predators. As such, many of New Zealand's birds are flightless, including the takahe, the kakapo (a very rare, ground-living parrot), and the national bird, the kiwi. Insects have also grown larger to take on roles usually occupied in other ecosystems by mammals—and none are as large as the giant weta, a rat-sized grasshopper that's one of the planet's heaviest insects.

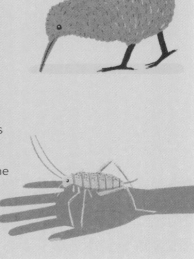

At 85 letters long, a hill near the town of Pōrangahau on North Island has the longest place name on the planet. See if you can say it: Taumatawhakatangihangakoauauotamateaturipukakapikimaungahoronukupokaiwhenuakitanatahu!

DEPENDENCIES AND OVERSEAS TERRITORIES

With entries on every country, this book has the whole world covered, right? Well, not quite. Across the planet, there are areas of land that look like they should be countries but aren't—usually because they belong to another place. There are several different types, and they are known by various names. Here is a list of some of the world's main noncountry territories, and who they belong to.

OVERSEAS TERRITORIES

Overseas Territories come in many forms. Some are regarded simply as part of another country. For instance, French Guiana in South America is legally part of France despite being located on a different continent. Other territories have a looser relationship with their country, and some are largely (but not entirely) independent.

There used to be more overseas territories, many of which formed parts of larger empires. As these empires came to an end, so the countries became independent. Some current overseas territories will probably become independent countries in the future.

DISPUTED TERRITORIES

Some areas are claimed by more than one country. One of the largest disputed territories is the Western Sahara in Africa, which is claimed both by neighboring Morocco and by a group known as the Polisario Front. There is no international agreement on who has the rightful claim.

CHINA
Hong Kong
Macau

DENMARK
Faroe Islands
Greenland

FRANCE
French Guiana
French Polynesia
Guadeloupe
Martinique
Mayotte
New Caledonia
Réunion
Saint Barthélemy
Saint Martin
Saint Pierre & Miquelon
Wallis & Futuna

NETHERLANDS
Aruba
Caribbean Netherlands
Curaçao
Sint Maarten

NEW ZEALAND
Cook Islands
Niue
Tokelau

UNITED KINGDOM/ BRITAIN
Anguilla
Bermuda
British Virgin Islands
Cayman Islands
Channel Islands
Falkland Islands
Gibraltar
Isle of Man
Montserrat
Saint Helena
Turks & Caicos

UNITED STATES
American Samoa
Guam
Northern Mariana Islands
Puerto Rico
US Virgin Islands

KEY FACTS

Area (land): **5.5 million sq. mi.**

Ice: **Covers 98% of land**

Fresh Water:
Holds 70% of world's supply

Rainfall:
Less than 0.4 in. per year—
*meaning that Antarctica
is officially classified as a desert*

Temperature:
**Average from 14°F on the
coast to −76°F inland**

One of Earth's seven continents doesn't have any countries at all, mainly because it doesn't have a permanent human population. Mostly made up of a great mass of ice and snow encircling the South Pole, Antarctica is the world's coldest, driest, and windiest continent. But that hasn't stopped several countries from making claims to its territory.

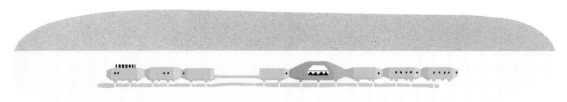

JUST VISITING

It is the incredible harshness of Antarctica's climate and terrain that has prevented it from being settled. Nobody lives here permanently, although several countries maintain research stations that are regularly visited by scientists. So the continent's human population may be as high as 5,000 in the summer, dropping to around 1,000 in the winter.

LATE DISCOVERY

Antarctica was the last continent reached by humankind. As far as we know, it was seen for the very first time in 1820 by the Russian naval officer Fabian Gottlieb von Bellinghausen. It wouldn't be until 1911 that a group of explorers led by the Norwegian Roald Amundsen was able to travel across the land to the South Pole itself.

PENGUINS NOT PEOPLE

People may be thin on the ground, but there is an incredible abundance of wildlife in Antarctica. This is mainly located in the surrounding Southern Ocean, where marine mammals include blue whales, orcas, and leopard seals, and on the coast where enormous penguin colonies form in the breeding season.

DIVIDED BY SEVEN

Seven countries claim a portion of Antarctic territory: New Zealand, Chile, Argentina, Australia, France, the United Kingdom, and Norway. However, there is no agreement among the international community about who owns what. What is agreed is that the 260,000 sq. mi. Marie Byrd Land isn't claimed by anyone at all. It's the largest territory on Earth that doesn't belong to a country.

KEY WORLD STATS

LARGEST COUNTRY:

Russia

COUNTRY WITH THE TALLEST POPULATION:

Netherlands

COUNTRY WITH THE YOUNGEST POPULATION:

Niger

SMALLEST COUNTRY:

Vatican City

COUNTRY WITH THE SHORTEST POPULATION:

Indonesia

COUNTRY WITH THE OLDEST POPULATION:

Japan

COUNTRY WITH THE MOST ACTIVE VOLCANOES:

Indonesia (129)

COUNTRY WITH THE MOST OFFICIAL LANGUAGES:

Bolivia (37)

WORLD'S NEWEST COUNTRY:

South Sudan (2011)

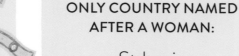

WORLD'S RICHEST COUNTRY:

USA

ONLY COUNTRY NAMED AFTER A WOMAN:

St Lucia

MOST BIODIVERSE COUNTRY:

Brazil

COUNTRY WITH THE MOST PYRAMIDS:

Sudan (255)

COUNTRY WITH THE HIGHEST WATERFALL:

Venezuela (Angel Falls)

CLOSEST COUNTRY TO OUTER SPACE:

Ecuador

COUNTRY WITH THE DRIEST DESERT:

Chile (Atacama)

MOST POPULATED COUNTRY:

China (1.3 billion)

COUNTRY WITH THE MOST FOREST:

Suriname (97.6%)